The Library of World Biography

Also by Harold Z. Schiffrin

SUN YAT-SEN AND THE ORIGINS OF THE CHINESE REVOLUTION

MILITARY AND STATE IN MODERN ASIA *(editor)*

1997

Sun Yat-sen,
Reluctant Revolutionary

by Harold Z. Schiffrin

THE LIBRARY OF WORLD BIOGRAPHY

J. H. PLUMB, GENERAL EDITOR

Little, Brown, and Company — Boston — Toronto

FIRST EDITION

LIBRARY OF CONGRESS CATALOGING IN PUBLICATION DATA

Schiffrin, Harold Z
    Sun Yat-sen, reluctant revolutionary.

    (The Library of world biography)
    Includes bibliographical references and index.
    1. Sun, Yat-sen, 1866–1925. 2. China — Presidents — Biography. I. Title.
    DS777.S33   951.04′1′0924   [B]   80–16100
    ISBN 0–316–77339–5

BC

Published simultaneously in Canada
by Little, Brown & Company (Canada) Limited

PRINTED IN THE UNITED STATES OF AMERICA

Contents

Foreword

OF THE CIVILIZATIONS DISCOVERED by Western Europeans, only China's was as intellectually and technologically sophisticated as those of the West — in some ways it was even more so. To some Western philosophers in the eighteenth century, its social principles and customs seemed far more intellectually justifiable than their European counterparts. The Chinese mandarins, content with both their philosophy and their social structure, found the Westerners as irritating and unpleasant as a plague of wasps. But alas, the wasps could not be brushed off. Imperial China, which had still seemed eternal in 1780, was declining by 1840 and facing total collapse and destruction by 1910. The conflicts this rapid decay entailed for the Chinese intellectuals were complex and confusing. Loyalty permeated the Chinese mind far more thoroughly than it did the European, but ever increasingly the question became louder and more insistent: loyalty to what? To the Chinese way of life, to the imperial throne, to the moral principles of Confucius, or to the vague sense of the superiority of China? Dare the Chinese hope that if once freed from European aggression all that was best in European science, techniques and social teaching would be fused with the principles of Confucius and so create a renewed China? Or was it necessary to destroy all the attitudes and beliefs of imperial China? The result of such conflicts was a seesawlike ambivalence to things Western — thoughts as well as techniques.

No one's life is more symbolic of this confusion than Sun Yat-sen's, a life of dramatic events and intellectual groping toward a political program that would unite the

Chinese masses (they consisted, in one of Sun's bitter, telling and thoughtful phrases, "of the poor and the poorer"). Deeply attracted by things Western, Sun became a Christian, and most of his early ideas were derived from Western sociology and politics; yet, as his experience developed, he reacted against the rapacity of Western imperialism. This generated a further conflict in his program for action. Would it not be better to strengthen the throne in order to throw out Western and Japanese predators? On the other hand, with the support of the West, it might even be possible to overcome the rigid and corrupt imperial system. Could it be that a strong China might only evolve by succumbing totally to the West?

Hence, there is a drama of ideas, fascinating and full of suspense, in this biography of Sun Yat-sen, as well as the spectacular drama of his personal life. Indeed, few lives have been more dramatic. Take, for example, his incarceration in the Chinese embassy in London, from which he was rescued in the nick of time.

The greatness of Sun lies as much in what he symbolized as in what he achieved, since for much of his life failure followed failure, policy collapsed on top of policy. Even so, the clear goals of his struggle, whatever the tactics (and they could be devious), always shone through his writings and his actions — not only freedom for China but its renewal through the liberation of the masses. In Sun's vision liberation would lead not to one more Western-style, industrialized country but to a country that was still deeply Chinese, a true union of one of the most sophisticated cultures the world had known and all that was valuable from the West. That aim still remains to be accomplished, and the survival of Sun Yat-sen's reputation lies in this fact — that his vision was far greater than his political ideology. Because of that vision, whatever the leadership of China he has been and will be revered.

— J. H. PLUMB

Sun Yat-sen
Reluctant Revolutionary

Prologue

THERE ARE NATIONAL IDOLS who seem to shrink in significance when viewed dispassionately. Yet they are never really debunked or demolished because the people who celebrate them do not view them dispassionately; they identify with them almost instinctively as personifications of salient national moods and aspirations. But because the sentiments they represent are so widely diffused, these idols can serve many faiths.

Sun Yat-sen belongs to this elusive category of national heroes. As the symbol of China's quest for resurgence, he was retroactively co-opted by almost every possible political persuasion. The scramble for his mandate, which began with his death in 1925, attracted — among others — the right, left and center factions of his own party, the Kuomintang; their Communist rivals; and pan-Asian Japanese expansionists and their Chinese collaborators during World War II.

Today, Sun's memory is exalted in Taiwan, where it provides legitimacy for the Nationalist regime. But his reputation also remains inviolable in the People's Republic, where even that of Confucius has been smeared. Moscow, too, purveys a separate version of the legend, and includes "betrayal" of Sun among Peking's purported heresies.

However confusing, none of the polemical interpretations of Sun's role can be dismissed out of hand as sheer propaganda. For what adds to his fascination as an object of study is that in life as well as death, Sun Yat-sen could often be many things to many men. Contradictory postures — not only at different times, but at one and the same time — were part of his political style.

Furthermore, it is not merely when partisan accounts plead their own cases but when they agree that they may exaggerate: all share a predilection for magnifying Sun's talents and achievements.

Emphasizing Sun's symbolic role rather than his tangible accomplishments, however, does not necessarily demean him or belittle his long struggle for recognition. To be one of the few historical personalities still honored on both shores of the Taiwan Strait is, after all, no small achievement. Nor does one have to overlook Sun's limitations and handicaps in order to substantiate his importance.

As a man, Sun was without doubt extraordinary, but personal inadequacies, no less than objective constraints, hampered his pursuit of heroic ambitions. Most people fail to realize the full potential of their endowed ability; Sun tried to go way beyond his. He chose revolution as his vocation — he was China's first professional in the field, and never left it — but persistence rather than brilliance distinguished his performance. He was neither a great strategist nor a profound ideologist. His thirty-year career was dogged by failure and frustration, and what he often found most frustrating was the failure of others to take him seriously. Though improvisation and dissimulation carried him far, they cast a cloud over his credibility.

For a long time few Chinese intellectuals accepted his leadership unconditionally. Accustomed to measure political capacity by intellectual achievements, heirs to the Confucian tradition were skeptical about Sun. Even his reputation as a shrewd conspirator, which to some extent compensated for the lack of intellectual prestige, did not hold up. Sun chose allies indiscriminately, and his plots, though imaginative, too often ended in fiasco. He was essentially a poor organizer and a naive judge of men.

Yet, he was rarely without some followers and patrons who risked their lives and fortunes at his bidding. What attracted these true believers — who usually included a few adventurous or idealistic foreigners — were the qualities of personality that had distinguished him since adolescence: audacity and optimism, resilience, and above all, monumental self-confidence.

It was these qualities that sustained his extravagant ambition — and what an extravagant ambition, especially for a lower-class protégé of foreign missionaries in elitist, culturally exclusive China! — to personally mastermind the transformation of his country and lead it into the front rank of world powers.

Sun never realized his goal; others, more resourceful and astute, and also tougher and more ruthless, have had greater, though not unqualified, success. Yet Sun's single-minded pursuit of revolution had a cumulative effect. During the year or so before he died, when most foreigners either ridiculed or feared him, his countrymen, especially students and intellectuals, admired him more than any other public figure. Nationalism had become the presiding passion of their lives, and Sun embodied its militant spirit. Humiliated by imperialism and disgusted by warlord politics, nationalists tended to channel their hopes into the one man who had consistently expounded the notion of a sudden great leap toward modernization and international equality; and who, despite the amazing convolutions of his improvisatory style, projected a rare image of probity and selflessness.

This was the source of Sun's appeal. His biography, it is hoped, will show that his personality and style were uniquely geared to the crisis-mood that has characterized modern Chinese nationalism.

ONE

The Making of a Professional Revolutionary

SUN YAT-SEN WAS BORN on November 12, 1866, in the village of Ts'ui-heng (Hsiang-shan district) in the Pearl River delta of Kwangtung province, on China's southeastern coast. This was an appropriate birthplace for a man whose life and ambitions were to be so closely tied to the West. The densely populated delta, radiating from Canton, the provincial capital, is the oldest link between China and the maritime nations of Europe. After the arrival of the Portuguese in 1517, Canton became the major port for Western trade, and for almost one hundred years — from the middle of the eighteenth century until the Opium War — it remained the only legal point of entry on the China coast.

While the Mandarin Empire maintained its exclusiveness, the diverse and unstable societies of Western Europe were being dynamically transformed. A phenomenal growth of knowledge in the sixteenth century had touched off a cumulative process of sweeping innovation. Europe entered its modern age and began outstripping China in science and technology.

Though hardly stagnating, China changed qualitatively at a much slower pace than the post-Renaissance West. Confucian institutions, having evolved over centuries in a relatively uniform cultural setting, were the most resilient the world had ever known. More efficient than other premodern societies in organizing production and in controlling the forces of nature, China's agrarian-based bureaucratic system survived rebellions, political disunity, and conquest by Inner Asian tribesmen. Until well past the sixteenth century, systemic troubles never reached the critical level required for generating revolutionary change.

During this long interval — and while the modern European nation-state was taking shape — China rejected Western modes of trade and diplomacy. Treating "sea-barbarians" like traditional Asian tributaries, she insisted upon conditions for contact that catered to her sense of superiority and to her preference for autarky. Western traders, as far as China was concerned, could have accepted these terms or stayed at home. And since they still hankered after her silk and tea, China considered it more than generous to allow them limited access to Canton and Macao — a tiny peninsula on the southern edge of the delta — where they could exchange silver for the precious products of the Central Kingdom.

However, by the early decades of the nineteenth century an industrializing Europe had sufficient muscle to match its voracity. British traders, advance agents of the world's most rapidly expanding economy, were making fortunes — and also helping balance the books of the British East India Company — by smuggling Indian opium into the Canton delta. When the Chinese government tried to enforce its anti-opium laws, Britain went to war on behalf of free commerce. Though the First Opium War (1840–42) left the opium issue to be settled by a second conflict, it freed Europe from the illusion of Chinese power. The Celestial Empire, once likened to a forbidding giant, now seemed but a "wretched burlesque."

The war, however, created new illusions for both sides. Though Canton and four additional ports were opened under conditions favoring the West, trade, which was what the conflict had been all about, moved slowly. Where Chinese arms had failed, her traditional economy stood firm. It was decades before foreign goods made an appreciable dent in the self-sufficient Chinese market, and even then, Europe's dream of fabulous profits failed to materialize.

At the same time China was slow to appreciate the deadly power-potential and motives of her new enemy. Past masters of the art of taming recalcitrant tribes from Inner Asia, China's scholar-statesmen depended upon the same strategy of appeasement to control the new barbarians, whose strange order of values gave primacy to commercial profits. Postponing fundamental requirements for defense, they responded to Western pressure with wholesale concessions. In order to demonstrate the emperor's impartial benevolence — and to encourage competition among their enemies, another time-honored gambit — they willingly signed treaties that included the most-favored-nation clause: whatever each power gained at China's expense was automatically shared by the others.

In the words of a twentieth-century Chinese student of international law this turned out to be the "Magna Carta of alien rights in China." It enabled even second- and third-rate powers to benefit from such concessions as the surrender of Chinese control over tariff schedules and extraterritoriality, which gave foreigners and their protégés the protection of foreign laws and consular courts on Chinese soil. Years passed before Chinese statesmen began thinking about reciprocal or compensatory rights. But while clinging to the illusion of superiority, how could China have demanded equality?

Then, after imperialism took a vicious turn near the end of the century, the issue became one of survival rather than superiority. Nationalism replaced the traditional one-world concept. And in the 1920s Sun Yat-sen would speak for the new breed of nationalists when he charged that the unequal treaties had converted China into a "hypo-colony" — victim of all the powers and the responsibility of none.

Yet the case for victimization was not all that clear in the immediate aftermath of the Opium War. When first applied, and indeed, for several decades, traditional policies of appeasement and containment seemed to work. Confined to a few designated ports, the foreign presence was only slowly felt. However, among Chinese who did come into contact with Europeans and their way of life, Cantonese continued to be conspicuous.

Experience in doing business with Europeans — which among other skills included command of Pidgin English — enabled many of them to serve as intermediaries in Shanghai and other newly opened ports. In addition, Hong Kong, ceded to the British in 1842, was only ninety miles from Canton and even closer to the lower delta. The colony, populated mostly by Cantonese, offered modern educational opportunities and a close-up view of Western institutional practices. Finally, massive emigration after 1850 extended the ties of Kwangtung province to the outer world. Most of the overseas Chinese (*huach'iao*) communities that dot the globe today are filled with natives of Kwangtung and the neighboring province of Fukien.

Even so, it would be misleading to suggest that the southern Kwangtung Sun Yat-sen first knew had changed appreciably because of long exposure to foreign influences. If "the significant *non*-event in nineteenth century Chinese society was its unresponsiveness to the modern West," Kwangtung was no exception. "On the eve of the Sino-Japanese War (1894–95), [it] was still basically a 'traditional' society." It was thus a society in which classical learning, as tested by the examination system, was the main key to power and prestige. Merchants, emigrants and products of missionary schools — generally of lower-class, nonliterati origin — were viewed with scorn and suspicion by the dominant Confucian elite. Even when they served useful functions in the treaty ports, the influence of Cantonese experts in foreign matters was circumscribed. They were peripheral to the main channels of power, just as the treaty ports themselves had only limited effect upon the life and economy of the Chinese heartland.

Hsiang-shan, Sun Yat-sen's home district, produced a large share of these peripheral elements. Macao, which was part of Hsiang-shan, had served as the steppingstone for Jesuit missionaries in the sixteenth and seventeenth centuries, and in 1650 a Hsiang-shan native accompanied an Italian Jesuit to Rome. He was probably the first overseas Chinese student. Though marked by more mutual tolerance and understanding than later missionary efforts, the Jesuit interlude was short-lived. Two hundred years later, one Yung Wing, a student who had been born a few miles from Macao and had attended a Protestant missionary school there, went to America with the help of foreign patrons. Graduating from Yale in 1854, he was the first Chinese to receive a degree from an American university. Two other Hsiang-shan youngsters, also products of the school run by the Morrison Education Society (named after the pioneer Protestant missionary to China), accompanied Yung abroad for higher education. One, who became the first Chinese physician trained in Europe, eventually worked with missionary physicians in Canton and Hong Kong. The other became superintendent of the London Mission press in Hong Kong and also had the distinction of being the first Chinese to sit on a jury with Englishmen.

Hsiang-shan's real specialty, though, was its compradors, agents of foreign firms whose bicultural competence smoothed the way for Western enterprise all along the China coast, and who in some instances became successful entrepreneurs in their own right. So many came from this district that "Hsiang-shan man" was synonymous with "comprador." Here, too, missionary schooling was advantageous, and Tong King-sing, one of the leading compradors, had been Yung Wing's classmate at the Morrison Society school in Hong Kong.

Though compradors contributed to the development of modern business and industry, they never really broke the pattern of traditional bureaucratic restraints. Nor did other would-be innovators from Hsiang-shan, like some of those mentioned above, have much of an impact upon Chinese society. Often they ended up where they had started, working within the framework of missionary or other foreign institutions. Those who tried to influence official policy directly were usually frustrated. Yung Wing, for example, had with great difficulty secured approval of his plan to send 120 youngsters to the United States for ten to fifteen years of schooling and technological training. But fearing that Yung's charges had become too Americanized, conservative officials abolished the project in 1881, nine years after it had been launched, while most of the students were still in college or high school. The project did produce two university graduates (one of whom became China's foremost railroad builder), and a baseball team that won a celebrated victory against American boys in Oakland, California. Yung himself spent his final years in Hartford, Connecticut, pondering over lost opportunities to accelerate China's modernization.

Until he was close to thirty, Sun Yat-sen would appear destined to be a similarly frustrated product of modern education — another Hsiang-shan boy who had done well in foreign schools but whose talents were unappreciated at home.

When he was born the prospect of a decent education, modern or traditional, or of any chance of social advance-

ment, was remote. The Suns were a typical peasant family
in that like millions of others in rural China they had to
combine hard work with versatility merely to survive. If
anything, their clan was one of the weakest of the five in
Ts'ui-heng. Land hunger, always a problem in Kwangtung, was particularly acute in the village area, which was
enclosed by mountains and the sea. Agriculture in this
rocky and sandy terrain was limited, and many of the
hundred or so families of Ts'ui-heng engaged in fishing
and other occupations. Some breadwinners found em-
ployment in the nearby towns.

Sun's father, Ta-ch'eng, had worked in Macao, some
twenty-five miles to the south, for a few dollars a week.
He apparently saved enough to resume farming in Ts'ui-
heng, where he got married at the relatively late age of
thirty-two. Difficult circumstances may also account for
the lapse of ten years before the couple had their first
child, a son, born in 1854. There were five other children, including two who died young.

Ta-ch'eng's meager holdings — no more than half an
acre — were not enough to support his family, and after
the fifth child, Wen (Sun Yat-sen's original given name),
was born he took on extra work as the village watchman.
He also engaged in petty trading and in various odd jobs.
The rest of the family helped; and it was only when Wen
was eight that his father could let him go to the village
school. This was a sign that the family had risen to what
in recent years would be called "middle peasant" status.

The household also included the widows of two
younger brothers of Ta-ch'eng who had not been heard
from after setting out to join the California Gold Rush.
One, it later turned out, had drowned in the sea off
Shanghai, while the other apparently met an early death
in California. This was a common Cantonese tragedy.
Though the only alternative to an impoverished existence at home, emigration was extremely risky.

During this period — the latter half of the nineteenth

century — about 120,000 Cantonese, mostly from the delta region, left each year to work as coolies in Southeast Asia and the Americas. Sun Yat-sen would later recall with bitterness the illegal "pig" trade, for which Macao was one of the more notorious centers. Young Chinese, lured by promises of wealth or forcibly entrapped, were locked into "pigpens" and smuggled out in boats. If they survived the trip — one ship arrived in San Francisco in 1854 with one hundred out of five hundred Chinese passengers dead — they were auctioned off for work in the sugarcane plantations of Louisiana and Cuba, the guano islands of Peru, or wherever cheap indentured labor was sought as an alternative to the African slave trade, which was hardly more vicious or inhuman.

Sun, who came to know the *hua-ch'iao* of several continents intimately, would speak admiringly of their capacity to endure hardships. "Temporary" work abroad in order to get established at home could often mean long years of drudgery in a hostile, humiliating environment. According to Sun, an average emigrant, arriving in America at the age of twenty-five, could save enough after ten years to return to his village for marriage; he would labor overseas another ten years before being able to build a house in his native village; and it was only after a final ten years that he would have sufficient savings to buy some land at home and rejoin his family for the remaining few years of his life.

Not all *hua-ch'iao* remained laborers. Their aptitude for trade and long experience in a money economy could stand them in good stead, especially in the newly opened European colonies of Southeast Asia where indigenous populations lacked commercial orientations. Many *hua-ch'iao* became small shopkeepers, peddlers and middlemen, and some developed on a grand scale entrepreneurial talents that could never have been realized in traditional China. Nor could they expect much help from their home government as they struggled against discrimination. Even when it overcame its Confucian bias against emigration — the official ban on emigration was abolished in 1893 — the Chinese government was too weak to intervene effectively on behalf of its nationals overseas. *Hua-ch'iao*, therefore, were a likely target for nationalist agitation. Yet kinship loyalties took precedence over political interests. In most cases the prime concern was to improve the family's economic status. Even the moderate success of one emigrant relative could catapult a family into the upper echelons of village or district society.

It was in this way that the fortunes of the Sun family eventually improved. At the age of seventeen (1871) Sun Mei, the eldest child, accompanied a maternal uncle returning to Hawaii after a brief visit. Ever since the 1850s, when sugar had become a major crop, Chinese labor had been sought in the Islands. Chinese-style rice cultivation also offered opportunities, and with the help of his uncle Sun Mei made rapid progress. Soon he was part owner of a farm and the proprietor of a store in Honolulu. In 1876 he returned to Ts'ui-heng for a lavish wedding and earned a commission by bringing laborers back to Hawaii. A year later his younger brother joined him, having made the trip with their mother, who had gone to Honolulu for a visit. Sun Wen was thirteen years old when he was left in his brother's charge and directed toward the foreign learning that was expected to complement Sun Mei's natural talent for business and pave the way for further commercial success.

Until then Sun's schooling had been strictly traditional, but too short to give him a solid basis in classical Chinese learning. Yet as a formative influence the pre-Hawaii period was important. Sun lived in Ts'ui-heng long enough to be permanently impressed with the hardships of peasant life, and his earliest efforts to get into public service would focus on agricultural improvement. This was a theme to which he would frequently revert. In the crystallization of his political interests, however, childhood contact with the Cantonese antidynastic tradition had a more dramatic effect.

Until the beginning of the nineteenth century, the Manchus, who had founded the Ch'ing dynasty in 1644, had presided over the empire in exemplary fashion. Though alien conquerors, their earlier adoption of the Chinese bureaucratic system in southern Manchuria had facilitated their march through the Great Wall and into Peking. It also enabled them to co-opt the majority of the Chinese literati, who in turn granted them title to the "Mandate of Heaven." In legitimizing Manchu rule and in protecting its own interests, the Chinese elite was also conforming to the Confucian tradition: the ethnic origins of imperial incumbents were of less importance than their ability to ensure cultural and institutional continuity. The Manchus met this test; as converts to the Chinese philosophy of government they were impeccably orthodox. For the first 150 years of their rule the Confucian bureaucratic system, working smoothly and effectively, provided peace, stability and relative prosperity to China proper, while imperial armies earned awesome respect in the borderlands.

The ethnic issue, though muted, did not disappear entirely. Not all Chinese were easily reconciled to the fact that a few million former steppe warriors had conquered the country. The Manchus, though showing consideration for Chinese feelings and respect for Chinese culture, still emphasized their own social distinctiveness and status as conquerors. They held a disproportionately large share of high civil offices and a virtual monopoly of military leadership. And what probably annoyed ordinary Chinese even more was the quasi-parasitic existence of the bannermen — a hereditary, privileged group that included all Manchus and some Chinese and Mongols who were the descendants of early adherents to the Manchu cause.

This undercurrent of anti-Manchu racial animosity was more noticeable in the south, the last region to be conquered. Canton was only taken in 1650, six years after the fall of Peking, and hundreds of thousands of Cantonese paid with their lives for their stubborn loyalty to the fallen Ming dynasty. But all dynasties, including those founded by ethnic Chinese, had been born in bloodbaths, and it was only when more immediate causes of disaffection appeared that memories of earlier cruelties as well as the ethnic issue could be effectively revived and used against the Manchus. As China entered the nineteenth century such an opportunity arose.

The Ch'ing at that time was a weakening dynasty. In part, its troubles can be explained in terms of the cyclic pattern often used to describe the life span of Chinese dynasties. According to this pattern, the ruling house, like any hereditary institution, eventually loses some of its initial vigor. And with less vigilant control from the center, there is more likelihood of moral slackness among the Confucian gentry — literati serving either as bureaucrats or unofficial local leaders. This elite stratum, charged with administering the empire, is then able to augment its private economic interests at the expense of its public responsibilities. As administrators, tax collectors, landowners and usurers, gentry families and their adherents squeeze the peasants, and at the same time deprive the imperial treasury of revenue, which in turn leads to neglect of public works and defense. Thus the empire becomes more vulnerable to natural disasters — which can easily be interpreted as omens of Heaven's displeasure — and to border threats, both of which add to peasant misery and turbulence. In the end the dynasty falls victim to popular uprisings or foreign invasions, or a combination of the two. The cycle starts all over again when a new dynastic founder restores a viable balance between imperial needs, gentry affluence and peasant subsistence.

But in addition to cyclic imbalance, the downward phase of Manchu rule was symptomatic of a deadlier crisis. An unprecedented rise in population was straining the capabilities of the whole agrarian system, and not merely the administrative efficiency of the dynasty. Partly a result of good Confucian government under the Manchus, population had doubled during the eighteenth century and had passed the 300 million mark; by 1850 it was over 400 million, and the gap between productive capacity and population narrowed dangerously. This kind of crisis, which was systemic and not merely administrative, could not be managed by refurbishing the old order under new leadership. What China required was industrialization and modern science, for "input-output relationships of the late traditional economy had assumed a pattern that was almost incapable of change through internally generated forces." And in order to apply the benefits of modern industry and science China had to accommodate ideas and social relations that clashed with the Sino-centric, Confucian outlook. In short, even before she first heard the sound of foreign cannon China was reaching the point where modernization would be the only rational alternative to prolonged distress. The intrusion of the West merely compounded her difficulties, though it also demonstrated a possible solution.

Intensity of secret-society activity was always a good gauge of dynastic health, and as early as 1775 the White Lotus Society, the oldest of China's secret orders, broke out in rebellion in the north. This was the first attempt to challenge the Ch'ing in nearly a century. Serving as rural China's response to the pervasiveness of bureaucratic control, secret societies provided protection and mutual help, often cloaking illegal activities such as salt smuggling. Some also cultivated heterodox religious practices inspired by Buddhism, Taoism or Manichaeism, whose esoteric formulas for salvation appealed more to hard-pressed peasants than the sterile moral preachings of Confucianism. However, functioning on the local level as separate bands, they lacked cohesiveness and a common political purpose. Furthermore, the anti-Manchuism to which some of them subscribed during the Ch'ing period was more of an obligatory ritual than an incentive to action. But the existence of these blood brotherhoods, with their passwords, secret signals and hidden meeting places, meant that a potential rebel had at his disposal a ready-made vehicle for subversion.

When driven to desperation by hunger and oppression peasants were prepared to answer the call for a *ch'i-i* (uprising in the name of justice) issued by a secret-society notable. One society's transition from proscribed but innocuous sect to rebel movement was described in an early-nineteenth-century official report: "In normal times the society was engaged in daily worship of the sun and reciting scripture, claiming thereby to make its members invulnerable to weapons, fire or drowning; in times of famine and disorder, they might plot for the 'great enterprise,' " that is, try to establish a new dynasty. When they did rise up against the reigning dynasty, however, it was as rebels, not revolutionaries. Secret societies, dreaming of an idealized version of Confucian society, did not offer viable alternatives to the imperial bureaucratic system. Even when they contributed to the downfall of a ruling house they did not effect any basic political changes. Invariably the new imperial regime and its tightened bureaucracy would place the secret orders back on the proscribed list.

Yet the potential for fanatic fighting was there, and banded together under a strong leader they could control large stretches of the countryside and terrorize officials and gentry, and anyone else who defied their authority. The ordinary peasant, habitually cautious and obedient, would have to make a choice: whom did he fear more, the mandarin and his troops or the blood brotherhood which protected its members with magic incantations and threatened its enemies with eternal vengeance?

In 1796 White Lotus groups went on a rampage again, this time in the mountains of west-central China. Three provinces were ravaged. It took ten years and a heavy drain of government resources to quell the uprisings. "It was the officials," a captured leader declared at his trial, "who forced the people to revolt." Though weakened by government suppression, the White Lotus Society, often in different guises, as well as other secret orders, continued to exploit peasant dissidence. The circumstances that forced villagers to "tread the dangerous path" leading to hunger and tax riots and on to brigandage and open rebellion became more severe and widespread. In 1835 one observer reported that in the fourteen years since the accession of a new emperor "there had not been one prosperous year; inundations, drought, famine, risings, insurrections and other calamities were constantly occurring in one province or another."

Dynastic prestige plunged sharply five years later, when the Opium War exposed the Manchus to ridicule. Villagers in the Canton delta saw "foreign devils" stampede the vaunted banner troops, and Karl Marx, in an article for the New York *Daily Tribune,* subsequently concluded that "before the British arms the authority of the Manchu dynasty fell to pieces; the superstitious faith in the eternity of the Celestial Empire broke down."

Marx was writing in the summer of 1853, when insurgency had engulfed much of southern China and was still unchecked. The Taiping Rebellion (1850–64), which was to claim twenty to forty million lives, was probably the most destructive civil war in history. Though the Opium War, as Marx indicated, helped precipitate it, the uprising was essentially a product of China's internal crisis.

Starting among Hakka — a sublinguistic community that had migrated to Kwangtung province from the

north centuries earlier — the movement spread from the
southeastern provinces that had been affected by the foreign impact. Its founder, Hung Hsiu-ch'üan, was a frustrated candidate for a literary degree from Kwangtung. A
fanatic who showed signs of mental illness, Hung believed that he was God's youngest son. Blending Judeo-
Christian with ancient Chinese themes, and emphasizing
anti-Manchuism, he and his lieutenants fashioned a
counterideology that struck at the heart of Confucianism.
This was a departure from usual rebellions. It also foreshadowed the shape of things to come. What the Taipings
preached but failed to practice completely was a combination of primitive communism and a modern type of
totalitarian rule.

Their blueprint for establishing the Kingdom of God
was anathema to Chinese gentry no less than to Manchu
rulers. When the central government and its regular armies faltered, regional administrators took the initiative
in defense of tradition. Providing the best in the way of
Confucian leadership and benefiting from foreign assistance, these scholar-officials outmaneuvered and gradually
wore down the rebels. The Taiping leaders, predominantly nonliterati, had been brilliant guerrilla fighters,
but they were hopelessly inept in political administration. Their internal feuding proved costly. The exclusiveness of Taiping religious beliefs, which blocked full
cooperation with traditional secret societies, also weakened their cause. And finally, not all Chinese peasants were enamored of the Taipings' "share-the-wealth"
program.

Thus, the Confucian administration, which revealed
surprising recuperative powers within a less centralized
format, temporarily managed to restore order. But systemic causes of disorder persisted: land hunger could
only be briefly alleviated by the depopulating effects of
the Taiping and other nineteenth-century uprisings. Nor
was it possible for a weak China to achieve long-term

stability in foreign relations. Even while battling the Taipings — and the more traditionally motivated Nien rebels in the north — Peking had had to contend with Anglo-French invaders (1856–60). Peace, and limited assistance against the insurgents, had been purchased at the price of further concessions, while the Russians, who had not bothered to invade, received the largest territorial prize — the north bank of the Amur River and the Pacific coast of Manchuria.

Though for a while it seemed as if minimal sacrifices had sated foreign appetites, by the 1870s foreign relations took a turn for the worse. Soon the powers pressed new claims that by the closing decades of the century were to deprive China of its traditional predominance in East Asia. But even if foreigners had been reasonable in their attitude toward China — which they were not — the post-Taiping "self-strengthening" strategy of allowing limited modernization while trying to preserve tradition, would have had little chance of success. As it was, the escalating demands of rival imperialist powers did not give China time to concentrate on internal recovery.

In the meantime, the Taiping legacy endured. The specter of another mass uprising continued to haunt the establishment, while romantic legends about the rebels flourished in the lower reaches of society, especially in the southern stronghold of antidynasticism. It was here that Sun Yat-sen, while still an impressionable youngster, learned at first hand how peasant armies had rocked the empire in search of a better life and a restoration of national pride.

Sun's mentor was a Taiping veteran who returned to Ts'ui-heng and taught in the village school after escaping capture at the battle of Chia-ying, in eastern Kwangtung. (This battle, which took place in the beginning of 1866 — almost two years after Hung's death and the defeat of the main rebel force — marked the end of Taiping resistance south of the Yangtze River. Over ten thousand rebels were killed and more than fifty thousand were captured.) After waiting a few years until the rebel hunt had subsided, the teacher began to speak freely, and enthralled friends and pupils with accounts of Taiping exploits. For Sun, this was the beginning of a lifelong admiration of Hung Hsiu-ch'üan, and when he grew older and first became seriously interested in political affairs, he liked to think of himself as Hung's successor in the popular struggle against the Manchus. In some respects, too, Sun's early life would reveal interesting parallels with that of Hung.

But Sun's practice and theory of revolution were, of course, attuned to different times, and in addition, bore the imprint of his own personality and experiences. The first, and most glaring, contrast between the two was that while Hung, with a few months' instruction by an American missionary in Canton, had gained only a smattering of foreign knowledge, in Honolulu the teenage Sun began acquiring the systematic Western education and the self-assurance in dealing with foreigners that were to distinguish him from all other Chinese political leaders.

In September 1879, two weeks after classes started, Sun entered Iolani, a Church of England elementary school whose staff, except for one Hawaiian, was entirely British. Intended chiefly for Hawaiian and part-Hawaiian youngsters, the Bishop's School, as it was usually called — after its principal, Bishop Alfred Willis, head of the Honolulu diocese — also accepted a limited number of Chinese. There was no Chinese school in the Islands, and many Chinese children did not receive any formal education. Elder brother Sun Mei, however, was doing too well to relinquish the traditional hope of producing at least one scholar in the family. Furthermore, a short stay at the store before starting school showed that his brother had no enthusiasm for the abacus and account books. As a student he did much better, and for a time at least, Sun

Mei had no reason to regret spending $100 to $150 a year for his tuition and board.

While Hawaii at this time was being drawn closer to the American orbit — the Reciprocity Treaty of 1875 had marked the latest step toward mainland political and economic dominance — Iolani remained staunchly British and conservative in outlook. In the face of growing republican and American annexationist sentiment, the bishop preached loyalty to the Hawaiian monarchy. No one, therefore, was more shocked when in 1896 a former protégé achieved worldwide notoriety as the foremost enemy of the Manchu dynasty. At that time, Bishop Willis felt constrained to assure his flock that Iolani had not endowed Sun Yat-sen with the disposition for "hatching plots against magisterial authority."

But Iolani did provide Western learning, which, whatever its source, did not necessarily breed respect for "magisterial authority" in the China of the late Ch'ing period. On the contrary, as long as they were the main purveyors of Western ideas, missionary schools in the treaty ports and overseas would also unwittingly be the main incubators for subversive ideas. And though Iolani was only the first of the church establishments that educated him, it was there that Sun, fresh out of a tradition-bound Cantonese village, became addicted to Western learning.

English was the only language permitted on the school premises. While at first this posed some difficulty for the seven Chinese boarding students — most of whom, like Sun, did not know a word of the language — it made for rapid adjustment. When he graduated three years later, in 1882, Sun was awarded second prize in English grammar. Sun Mei, of course, was pleased. What did not please him was his brother's attraction to Christianity. Like most of his fellow immigrants, Sun Mei had come to the Islands to relieve family poverty, not to repudiate cherished ancestral beliefs and social customs. In their overseas communities, Chinese were no less resistant to Christianity than they were at home. Missionaries gained relatively few converts.

Yet Iolani's regimen, which included daily prayers, classes in Christian doctrine and compulsory attendance at Sunday services in Saint Andrew's Cathedral, pulled his younger brother in another direction. According to Bishop Willis, Sun, who sang in the school choir, would have been baptized had it not been for the objections of "heathen relatives." Two of Sun's classmates who shared his Christian sympathies were similarly frustrated by family opposition.

Still the obedient younger brother, he spent the next few months on Maui, where Sun Mei was making even more money as a planter, cattle raiser and merchant. By the fall of 1882, having once more found business boring, Sun persuaded his brother to allow him to resume his studies, this time at Oahu College (Punahou School), a high school that was the highest institution of learning in the Islands. Located a few miles from Honolulu, it was run by American Congregationalist and Presbyterian missionaries, whose own children, the future rulers of Hawaii, studied there. Sun was now thinking of a professional career. But he managed to spend only one year at Oahu. Learning that he was about to be baptized, his brother sent him back to Ts'ui-heng in the summer of 1883.

At home the seventeen-year-old Sun flaunted the fruits of his overseas labor. While still devoted to the memory of Hung Hsiu-ch'üan, he also spoke glowingly of Napoleon and George Washington — whom he had presumably learned to admire at American-oriented Oahu rather than at Iolani. His presumption of superior knowledge irritated the village elders. They dubbed him the "little foreign devil." But Sun, who as a child had already showed signs of self-assertiveness, was now completely uninhibited in pillorying village beliefs. In order to discredit idol worship, he mutilated the wooden figure of the Northern God, the patron deity of Ts'ui-heng and the surrounding villages. This was too much for the country folk to bear, and like Hung Hsiu-ch'üan, who had also made a mockery of local gods, Sun had to leave home while his family paid for the repair and propitiation of the damaged deity. Though he had not broken with his family — indeed, his father probably gave him financial help — Sun was now determined to follow his own mind regardless of his elders' preferences.

He resumed his education in Hong Kong. He first studied at the Diocesan School, a Church of England institution, and in the following year, 1884, transferred to Government Central School (later called Queen's College), a respected secondary school that offered instruction in Chinese and in English. Earlier, he had begun studying Chinese classics with Ch'ü Feng-ch'ih, a Christian minister connected with the London Missionary Society.

Although there are conflicting opinions concerning Sun's Chinese education — one report has it that he received tutoring in Chinese throughout his stay in Hawaii — it seems fairly certain that he did not undertake serious classical studies until this later period. And while subsequent rumors of his illiteracy in Chinese were unfounded, there is little doubt that no other Chinese political leader of his generation was as meagerly equipped with traditional learning. Yet because of his growing interest in politics it is not surprising that he wanted to become better acquainted with classical Chinese thought and history.

Later, Sun was to declare that the Sino-French War (1883–85), which took place while he was studying in Hong Kong, convinced him to work for the overthrow of the dynasty. This is questionable: his behavior during the next decade was not that of a confirmed revolutionary. Yet one can well imagine that the war and its repercussions in Hong Kong stimulated his political awareness. The failure to protect Annam (Vietnam) — a longtime Chinese tributary and a strategic buffer state — was another mark against the Manchu dynasty and the Confucian establishment, especially in the eyes of Cantonese who were sensitive about the security of China's southern border.

In September 1884, Sun caught a glimpse of lower-class patriotism in action. Responding to a proclamation of the Canton governor-general to "attack French ships and men," Chinese dockers refused to service a French war vessel that had arrived in Hong Kong for repairs after having participated in the attack on Foochow on the southern coast. The striking dockers were soon joined by coaling coolies and hotel employees. Hong Kong harbor was shut down for ten days, and eventually the French ship had to sail to Japan for repairs. This was Sun Yat-sen's first wartime experience, and it enabled him to contrast the fighting mood of the people with the government's inability to protect Chinese interests.

Personal matters also occupied his attention. In 1884 he was baptized by Dr. Charles Hager, an American Congregationalist missionary. Sun's baptismal name, chosen by his friend and tutor, Pastor Ch'ü, was Yat-sen, the name by which the world would come to know him. This same year his parents called him back to Ts'ui-heng. They had arranged a marriage for him. After the nuptial ceremonies Sun stayed in the village long enough to desecrate another local deity, "Madame Golden Flower," and then returned to Hong Kong, leaving his parents to pay another fine and to take charge of his young bride.

Toward the end of the year he also answered a summons from his brother in Hawaii. Infuriated by the news of Sun's iconoclasm, Sun Mei canceled a property transfer he had previously made in his favor, and ordered him to work for a living in the elder brother's flourishing business. Instead, Sun enlisted the help of an American missionary in Honolulu. The $300 raised among American businessmen enabled him to return to his studies in Hong Kong in the spring of 1885.

The following year, after having considered the ministry, the legal profession and a military career, Sun decided to study medicine. With the help of Dr. Hager, he was admitted to the Canton Hospital Medical School, an Anglo-American missionary institution headed by Dr. John Kerr, an energetic American who was dedicating his life to the promotion of modern medical facilities in China. In the meantime Sun Mei had forgiven his brother's maverick behavior and had resumed financial support. Sun, though, was fairly independent since his work in the hospital as an interpreter paid for tuition and board.

In Canton, he continued to receive private tutoring in Chinese and became more involved in political discussions. A fellow student, Cheng Shih-liang, revealed his connections with the Triads, the largest of the southern secret societies, and one whose lodges proliferated among the overseas Cantonese and Fukienese communities. Cheng, a Christian Hakka from Kwangtung and a graduate of a German missionary school, promised Sun that should he plan an antidynastic uprising, the Triads, who were ostensibly dedicated to overthrowing the Manchus, would be at his disposal. The two became fast friends, and Cheng was to figure prominently in Sun's early conspiracies.

In 1887 Sun transferred to the College of Medicine for Chinese in Hong Kong, which had just been established (it would become part of the future University of Hong Kong). Here there was less reason for restraint and Sun made no secret of his anti-Manchu views. He and a few friends spent hours discussing politics and were jokingly called the Four Great Bandits. Sun himself had the satisfaction of being identified with his hero, Hung Hsiuch'üan. He is also said to have experimented with bombs in the chemistry laboratory. Nevertheless, playing the revolutionary firebrand was still just a pastime. His immediate concern was to study medicine, for which he showed an excellent aptitude. He also came to believe that a bright student who, like himself, was digging deeply into the storehouse of knowledge that gave the West its superiority need not necessarily become a rebel in order to contribute to the modernization of China.

Sun's interest in reform, and some of his ideas, were probably inspired by Dr. Ho Kai, a British-trained barrister and a prominent civic leader in Hong Kong. The son of a Hong Kong businessman of Cantonese origin who had once preached the gospel for the London Missionary Society, Ho was a graduate of Aberdeen University, and had qualified both in medicine — for which he found little scope in Hong Kong — and law. After the death of his British wife, he established in her memory a free hospital for Chinese. When the Alice Memorial Hospital, which was administered by the London Missionary Society, was completed in 1887, Ho led the move to attach a modern medical school for Chinese. Supporting him, and volunteering their teaching services, were two Scottish physicians, likewise graduates of Aberdeen — Dr. Patrick Manson and Dr. James Cantlie. Manson, world-famous for his research on mosquito-borne diseases in Amoy, was the school's first dean, and after his departure in 1889 was succeeded by Cantlie, whose personal interest in Sun Yat-sen developed into a close and valuable friendship. Ho Kai, the school's honorary secretary, taught medical jurisprudence and physiology. He also showed Sun that a Chinese with a modern education was competent to comment on public affairs and need not restrict his expertise to a particular professional field.

When Ho made his debut as a pundit in a Hong Kong English-language newspaper in 1887 he charged that China's troubles were of her own making. The root cause was not Western maliciousness but Chinese backwardness. Nor was backwardness simply a matter of military weakness. The government's exclusive concern with tightening defenses, Ho argued, missed the mark, and in any case there was no sense in getting modern weapons without the trained manpower to use them. The real reason for China's low status in the world was "loose morality and evil habits, both social and political." Foreigners, to cite one example, demanded extraterritoriality because they distrusted China's legal system and the officials who administered it. And his basic criticism focused on the quality of the nation's leaders. The examination system, which emphasized literary talent, produced officials who were incapable of changing Chinese institutions along Western lines. At the same time, it excluded those who were best equipped for this role — the Chinese who had been trained abroad.

Yet gentry reform, despite its limitations, had its own impetus, and the mandarins against whose monopoly Ho was protesting were gradually feeling the need for expert assistance in dealing with foreigners and in managing modern enterprises. Ho himself never agreed to become a functionary under traditional leaders, but a few others, like his brother-in-law, Wu T'ing-fang, did. Wu, who had studied law in London and had become the first Chinese barrister in England, and the first Chinese lawyer in Hong Kong, had in 1882 joined the secretariat of Li Hung-chang, at that time China's most powerful official.

Near the end of his studies a similar possibility of finding a friendly niche in the establishment appealed to Sun Yat-sen. Academic success had strengthened his self-confidence, and the contrast between Hong Kong and Kwangtung, which he visited during vacations, reinforced his determination to work for change. That the same Cantonese whose lack of civic virtue at home exasperated him could become exemplars of good citizenship under a handful of British officials convinced him that poor leadership rather than inherent characteristics of the people was responsible for China's backwardness.

Sun's favorite author at this time, Charles Darwin, whose influence upon him was to be lasting, taught that adaptation was the condition for survival, and had not Ho Kai argued that Western-trained students knew better than Confucian classicists how to adapt to the modern world? Though the chances of earning recognition in high places were slim, Sun was too imaginative and optimistic to forgo a try. He also assumed that regional ties, always so important in China, would give him leverage in approaching prominent people.

In 1890 he wrote to Cheng Tsao-ju, a Hsiang-shan scholar and prominent bureaucrat. "Raising his head in the hope of being of some use in the world," Sun suggested that Western ways be studied in order to improve the nation's well-being. He mentioned the need for modernizing agriculture and sericulture, and emphasized the benefits of education and literacy. The strength of the nation, he said, depended upon the full use of human talent and upon "good customs." These were sound, if not particularly original, reformist notions, and Cheng, a former minister to the United States, probably found no reason to disagree. He also found no reason to take a personal interest in Sun Yat-sen.

Sun also approached Cheng Kuan-ying, the influential Hsiang-shan comprador who had been writing reformist essays since 1880. Cheng's arguments, which reflected the nationalist aspirations of the new merchant class in the treaty ports, had a strong effect upon Sun's thinking, and twenty years later would still be avidly read by the teenage Mao Tse-tung. Cheng was also a patron of *The Review of the Times* (*Wan-kuo kung-pao*). Sponsored by missionaries, this Chinese-language monthly was important for spreading knowledge of the West and its intellectual currents. It was also another likely stimulant of Sun's enthusiasm for reform.

While Cheng was impressed with Sun's ideas about agricultural innovation, apart from mentioning them in his own writings he apparently had nothing specific to offer. Still, Sun did not yet discard the hope of finding an official patron. And in a manner that was to become so characteristic of his mature political style, he simultaneously entertained other and even conflicting options. Besides Darwin on evolution, he enjoyed reading about the French Revolution. He therefore knew that a ruling apparatus sometimes becomes so atrophied that it has to be swept aside by violence in order to permit the march of progress. Revolution was an option that could never be completely discounted, especially by a professed disciple of Hung Hsiu-ch'üan. And no matter what path he chose in politics, the practice of medicine seemed to offer a way of escaping obscurity and of building a reputation. This, too, turned out to be more difficult than he anticipated.

Sun graduated in 1892. Only he and one other of the twelve students who had begun the course completed it successfully. Sun, who had been a favorite of Cantlie's, received the highest grades and the most prizes. Troubles began when the school's curriculum did not meet the standards of the Hong Kong General Medical Council, and Sun's degree did not enable him to practice modern medicine in the colony. In addition, Chinese who could afford to pay for medical treatment generally preferred traditional practitioners; only the poor went to Western missionary physicians, whose services were free.

Sun's solution was to combine herbalism with modern medicine. He set up a "Chinese-Western Apothecary" in Macao, conveniently close both to home and to Hong Kong, so that Dr. Cantlie could join him in difficult operations. Then the Portuguese authorities stepped in, and like the British in Hong Kong, showed that a Chinese modernizer was not necessarily welcome in a European colony. Either out of retaliation for Hong Kong's refusal to recognize Portuguese medical degrees, or — as Sun suspected — out of resentment of a Chinese who competed with their own physicians, they barred him from treating Portuguese. A further restriction forbade pharmacies from filling foreign doctors' prescriptions. Having been reduced to the status of an herbalist, in 1893 Sun decided to move to Canton. There he established an "East-West Apothecary" and several herbal shops. While associates prescribed herbs, Sun concentrated on surgery and seemed to be doing well until the overexpansion of his enterprise brought on financial troubles. But this can only partially explain the drastic step he took the following year.

Now nearing the age of thirty, Sun realized that a local medical practice was not an easy springboard to fame. He felt that his education, and knowledge of the outside world, so rare for a Chinese of his generation and yet so sorely needed by the country, could be used for bigger things. Thus, while struggling to establish his credentials in Macao, he had resumed experiments with explosives in his nearby village home. In Canton he renewed seditious discussions with a group that included Cheng Shih-liang; Yu Lieh, another Triad enthusiast; Ch'en Shao-pai, a former classmate in Dr. Kerr's medical school; and Lu Hao-tung, a boyhood friend from his native village. He also found time to spread antidynastic propaganda in the Chinese supplement he edited anonymously for a Portuguese weekly published in Macao.

However, when he finally left medicine, and with an abruptness that surprised his friends, it was in favor of another attempt to move official levers of power. This time he turned to no less a personage than Li Hung-chang, the empire's leading statesman since 1870.

The beginning of 1894 found Sun on his way north, bearing what he hoped would be his passport to recognition. This was his proposal for Li which Ch'en Shao-pai, who was better versed in the classical literary style, had read and corrected. Accompanied by Lu Hao-tung, Sun first stopped in Shanghai to discuss his plans with the comprador-scholar Cheng Kuan-ying. Through Cheng he met Wang T'ao, an unconventional literatus, who in addition to suggesting changes in Sun's manuscript gave him an introduction to a friend in Li's secretariat.

Sun's arguments followed closely those of Ho Kai and Cheng Kuan-ying, both ardent advocates of economic nationalism. He recommended the rational exploitation of manpower and resources needed for economic development, and criticized the one-sided emphasis upon military preparedness that characterized official-gentry responses to the foreign threat. Echoing Cheng in particular, Sun claimed that the "sources of foreign wealth and power do not altogether lie in solid ships and effective guns." Foreigners were stronger, he contended, because they made better use of human potential, because they were more efficient in utilizing their agricultural and natural resources, and because they gave free rein to commercial activities. In brief, Sun found that foreign superiority flowed from the application of science and knowledge that marks the modern industrial age.

Diagnoses of this type came easier to people like Sun and his mentors who were either outside the Chinese establishment or on its fringe. Self-made men whose main asset was their knowledge of Western ways, they were less bound by the cultural loyalties and the vested interests that diluted the usual gentry prescriptions for change.

Sun also followed Cheng in taking notice of Japan's transformation since the Meiji Restoration of 1868. Again, this reflected a broader and less culture-bound outlook than that of the literati, who until the Sino-Japanese War — which was brewing even while Sun was on his way to Tientsin — generally ignored the accomplishments of a traditionally despised neighbor. In trying to prove that the innate ability of the Chinese people, if properly nurtured, would enable them to surpass the West within twenty years, Sun pointed to the example of Japan. Despite having begun trading with the West and imitating Western methods *after* China, Japan was more successful, he said, because she had taken reform more seriously.

Probably because of his early childhood experience, Sun showed special concern for agricultural modernization. That the government should take an active interest in peasant welfare was an old and established principle of Chinese statecraft. Sun now urged that Western science and techniques be applied to improve agricultural productivity. He also made frequent reference to the "people's welfare" (*min-sheng*), an ancient expression that was cropping up in the reformist tracts of Ho Kai, Cheng Kuang-ying and other modernizers. Later, Sun was to use it to denote his version of socialism, the third of his famous Three Principles.

But Sun's main object was to sell himself, not his program. Moreover, his approach was unconventional: he frankly admitted that he lacked traditional elite attributes and could not pass an examination for a literary degree. Instead, he claimed accomplishments that he was sure were more essential for China's survival in the modern world:

> When I was young, I tasted the experience of overseas study. Western languages, literature, politics, customs, mathematics, geography, physics, and chemistry — these I have had an opportunity to study in a general sort of way. But I paid particular attention to their [the West's] methods of achieving a prosperous country and a powerful army, and to their laws for reforming the people and perfecting their customs.

Sun closed his presentation with a modest request. Praising Li as a statesman who appreciated men of talent, he asked that the Grand Secretary take him under his wing and enable him to study sericulture and other Western agricultural methods abroad, so that he could contribute to the improvement of Chinese agriculture.

In normal times Li, who enjoyed a reputation as a progressive, might at least have given him an audience. However, in June 1894, when Sun reached Tientsin, Li's attention was riveted on Korea, where Japanese intervention was forcing a reluctant China to respond. In July the

Japanese sank a British ship carrying Chinese reinforcements to the Hermit Kingdom, and on August 1 China and Japan declared war. Thus Li did not see Sun and it is doubtful whether he ever read his manuscript.

A more patient aspirant might have waited for another opportunity. But not Sun Yat-sen. He left Tientsin, finally convinced of the futility of pursuing official patronage. Ignored by the establishment, he resolved to overthrow it.

Although in October and November his reform plan was published in *The Review of the Times* — probably through Cheng Kuan-ying's influence — Sun could not be satisfied with advertising ideas from the sidelines. He saw himself as a man of action whose mission was to convert ideas into deeds. He had hoped that even a minor post in Li's entourage would have given him some authority to act and a chance to display his skills for an official audience. Now he assumed the posture of a Hung Hsiuch'üan. After Tientsin Sun was determined to create his own authority for the renovation of China.

At the end of the summer of 1894 he was on his way to Hawaii. Why Hawaii? Despite their distant location, Sun chose the Islands as his first target for revolutionary agitation because he considered money a prime requirement and his brother the most likely source. In addition to Sun Mei there was the Hawaiian overseas Chinese community as a whole. Though numbering only about twenty thousand, the *hua-ch'iao* population was almost exclusively Cantonese with a large representation from his home district of Hsiang-shan. These were the people whom he knew best. He shared their social origins and understood their aspirations and frustrations. Like himself, some were educated, and a few had become successful entrepreneurs like Sun Mei, with whose help he hoped to tap the resources of the wealthier of them.

Hung Hsiu-ch'üan had also built his movement around a core of relatives, friends and neighbors. Sun, however, was not following the Taiping or any traditional model for rebellion. The emphasis upon finances, which was to last through his career, was a result of his own revolutionary strategy, now beginning to take shape. He did not plan on building rebel power in mountain caves or on waging a long, drawn-out civil war. Sun believed that China had to modernize and get strong quickly if she were to withstand foreign pressure of the kind that Japan was already exerting. He saw the need for — and the feasibility of — a swift revolution, one that depended more upon money and manipulation than organized power.

Sun's first stop in the Islands was Maui, where his elder brother was nicknamed King. Sun Mei, who had been so upset over Sun's religious heresy, had no qualms at all about endorsing his political heresy. He promised money and provided introductions to key people in Honolulu. Yet after months of labor Sun discovered that though the *hua-ch'iao* had good reason to dislike the Manchu regime, few were willing to work for its subversion. Fear of jeopardizing their families at home and plain indifference to politics hampered his activities.

On November 24, 1894, Sun was finally able to convince some twenty young Cantonese to form an antidynastic organization. Its subversive purpose was cloaked under the innocuous name of the Society to Restore China's Prosperity (Hsing Chung Hui). This Hawaiian branch of what subsequently became a wider-based movement was not so much a political organization as a fundraising apparatus for support of Sun's conspiracies. Members paid a fee of five (Hawaiian) dollars and were urged to make further contributions. Among the early converts were the assistant manager of an American bank, a storekeeper, an interpreter for the Hawaiian government, a merchant-planter, and a former classmate at Iolani who had become a wealthy lumber dealer. Later, members were drawn from the laboring class that formed the bulk of the Hawaiian *hua-ch'iao*.

Because of the successful Hawaiian revolution of the previous year the idea of republicanism had gained some currency. Yet it was probably only the more educated members who shared Sun's antimonarchical views. Traditional anti-Manchuism motivated most of the rank and file, and some were hoping to realize their own ambitions by hanging on to the coattails of a "man of destiny."

In January 1895, when the Japanese were routing dynastic forces, Sun saw a chance for an early coup. Cutting short his campaign in the Islands and postponing plans to canvass the American *hua-ch'iao,* he embarked for Hong Kong to set up a base of operations. Left to themselves, his comrades in Hawaii enlisted more members, though financial contributions were disappointing. By October, when Sun made his first attempt at revolution, there were over one hundred members, mostly small businessmen and laborers. Remittances amounted to only HK$23,000 (HK$1 = US$0.50, approximately). Two supporters, his brother Sun Mei and the sugarcane planter Teng Yin-nan, who sold all his property, contributed more than half. Sun's Hawaiian campaign nevertheless set a precedent for *hua-ch'iao* involvement in home politics. Though results never measured up to expectations his subsequent effort to politicize overseas communities throughout the world would enable him to keep going when he lacked a solid constituency within China proper.

Activities in Hong Kong were of a different type, though here too money matters were important, given the "capital-intensive" type of revolution that Sun envisaged. For Sun, Hong Kong was to be a center of conspiracy, a launching pad for what he hoped would be a paralyzing thrust at the soft underbelly of the Manchu regime. It was also well suited to a foreign-oriented propaganda campaign.

In Hong Kong Sun's close friends who used to listen to him romanticize about the Taipings and speculate about a new anti-Manchu insurrection were now ready to follow him into action. Joining them was a similar circle of Westernized young men of nonliterati origins who were also convinced that the Manchus and mandarins were leading China to disaster. The leader of this group, Yang Ch'ü-yün, a Hong Kong–born Fukienese who was employed by the comprador to E. D. Sassoon and Company, was no less ambitious and confident than Sun. Moreover, he was five years older, and by all accounts a man of formidable personality and imagination. Thus on February 18, when the two groups formed the Hong Kong branch of the Society to Restore China's Prosperity — the head office was to be established in China at an undetermined date — the leadership post was kept vacant in order to postpone a clash between the contenders.

Members of the Hong Kong branch swore to "Expel the Manchus, to Restore China, and to Establish a Republic." This secret oath was probably an innovation; in other respects they generally followed Sun's Honolulu formula. The society did not present a specific political program, but its constitution revealed vigorous nationalist convictions and hinted at a revolutionary solution. It drew a frightening picture of a China threatened with partition by the foreign powers — "Our descendants may become the slaves of other races!" — and charged the government with moral bankruptcy and neglect of the "people's welfare." It called upon "men of determination" to save the "national entity" by unifying and educating the people, and by applying modern science to create national wealth and power. In short, these products of missionary schooling, some of whom were more at home in English than in Chinese, faulted traditional leaders and questioned the usefulness of traditional learning: preservation of the "national entity" required modern leaders and modern ideas.

Moreover, the modernization of China and its preservation were not posed as exclusively Chinese concerns.

Anyone, regardless of his nationality, was eligible for membership provided he was properly recommended and willing to work for the country's benefit. This invitation to foreigners, which may seem to have been strange for an organization whose avowed purpose was to prevent the foreign powers from raping China, reflected both pragmatic and ideological considerations. Sun and Yang and their followers saw no sense in alarming foreigners at a time when they were preparing to challenge the Manchu dynasty. Instead, they considered foreign support, or at least neutrality, a necessary condition for a successful revolution. They also assumed that a modern China would not only be strong enough to deter potential aggressors, but that by virtue of her modernity would remove the chief reason for aggression. They were convinced that if China carried out the institutional changes that Western missionaries, merchants and diplomats had been clamoring for, the threat of dismemberment would disappear. Just how much the society's "men of determination" were willing to accommodate foreign interests in order to isolate the Manchu regime was to be revealed during the following months.

The society's pragmatic approach was also seen in its fund-raising strategy, which appealed to the profit motive no less than to Chinese patriotism. Bonds or shares purchased for ten dollars (HK) each were to be redeemed for one hundred dollars "when the country was established." This euphemism was the closest mention of revolution in the constitution.

The society was never meant to be a self-contained, mass organization. Less than a dozen members were sworn in at the inaugural meeting. Yet a month later they were planning the capture of Canton. The Manchu government, humiliated by the Japanese, was in disarray, and the plotters saw a golden opportunity to set in motion and manipulate traditional vehicles for subversion. Their home province, Kwangtung, was to be the first target.

Afterward, responsive uprisings elsewhere and perhaps a push from the outside could be expected to overthrow the dynasty. In any event, various options were in the offing, and Sun Yat-sen, in this first test of his improvisatory talent, was ready to pursue them all.

TWO

The Search for "Benevolent Neutrality"

CHINA'S DEFEAT at the hands of Japan in 1895 had a potent, catalytic effect upon the pace and direction of her modern history. With a few stunning blows the Japanese nullified thirty years of Chinese "self-strengthening." They made a shambles of the only modern fleet that China has ever had, and broke up the international order that had prevailed in East Asia for over half a century.

What European statesmen called the Far Eastern Question arose soon after Japan imposed peace terms upon a hapless Li Hung-chang at Shimonoseki on April 17, 1895. Besides indemnifying the victors for the cost of the war — this amounted to about 160 million (US) dollars — China had to cede Taiwan and the south Manchurian peninsula of Liaotung. Less than a week later Russia, Germany and France forced Japan to disgorge Liaotung. But within six months Russia's own designs on Manchuria alarmed the British, who much preferred competing for China's trade than for her territory. Earlier in the year their vice-consul in Canton had still seen hope for the status quo: "It appears indeed that the Chinese

Government, though practically unarmed and helpless against a serious foreign foe, is strong enough to keep peace at home — to keep the great Chinese cow steady while foreigners extract the milk of which it is to be hoped that the Japanese will only be allowed their fair share."

The old order, however, was irretrievable. Instead of sharing commercial privileges, the powers, including Britain, were soon competing for exclusive preserves. While maintaining the fiction of Chinese sovereignty they followed the advice attributed to Count Cassini, the Russian minister to Peking: "If one wants anything in China, one must demand and take it without further ado." Within a few years the scramble for concessions and leaseholds would threaten China with partition and national extinction. It would also make it impossible to "keep the great Chinese cow steady." A rare sense of crisis was in fact brewing even before the country felt the full force of unbridled imperialist rivalries.

Japan's victory shocked the Chinese as they had never been shocked by disastrous wars with Europeans. That they could be so pitifully beaten by fellow East Asians, former beneficiaries of China's own great tradition, had not been imaginable. Humiliation, alarm, and an accelerated erosion of the government's prestige followed the full revelation of the nation's vulnerability. The war also stimulated serious rethinking about the strategy of China's response to the challenge of industrialized civilization. Was it only Japan's more effective use of modern arms, or was it also innovations in nonmilitary institutions that explained her success? This was a question that now became more pertinent for Confucian scholars. While the majority still recoiled from a sharp break with tradition, in the immediate aftermath of the war some took the unprecedented step of organizing and agitating for radical reform. Japan, the agent of their disillusionment, became the favorite object of emulation.

Westernized Chinese who had unsparingly belittled pre-1895 reform now had less reason than ever to trust in Peking's remedies. Even outright foreign domination and the chance for benevolent tutelage could seem preferable. In July a British official heard a particularly despairing confession from Wu T'ing-fang, Ho Kai's brother-in-law: "I would rather see China a second India than that she should go on as she is, disgraced, powerless, and with no hope of amendment."

The crisis mood also infected business circles, where there was growing resentment of foreign competition. Merchants began organizing and pressing for change, and in general, men of substance, who had been heavily taxed during the war, were increasingly skeptical of the government's willingness and ability to make effective use of revenue for national defense. Solid citizens were also worried about the authorities' ability to cope with the disorder that was spreading in the lower levels of society. Demoralized and unpaid, discharged soldiers flocked in droves to bandit gangs and secret societies throughout the country.

The disbanded Chinese army was especially menacing in Kwangtung, where there were additional factors aggravating the postwar trauma. Here, as in other southern coastal provinces, the loss of Taiwan was taken more seriously than in the north. Furthermore, for five years the province had been ruled by a governor-general whose corrupt practices had so antagonized the public that his dismissal in April may have been prompted by fear of impending rebellion. And since this official happened to be the elder brother of Li Hung-chang, who was in charge of the war effort, he had had an extra incentive for supporting the campaign in the north. He had raised a huge provincial army, and at the end of the war most of the soldiers were discharged and stranded in Kwangtung ports. As early as May, uprisings attributed to Triads and roaming bandits broke out in eastern Kwangtung and lasted for several months. There were fresh disturbances in September and October. In the meantime Sun Yat-sen and his fellow plotters were recruiting these same Triad and bandit elements for their projected coup in Canton, the provincial capital.

The Hong Kong conspirators had made their decision in March, before the shock of Shimonoseki. During the following months, while the prognosis for rebellion was becoming even more favorable than anticipated, they worked out their plans meticulously.

They planned to strike on October 26, the day of the "double-nine" festival (according to the lunar calendar), when crowds of holiday-makers would provide convenient cover. The attack was to proceed from several directions. A shock force of Triad members and other roughnecks recruited from the Kwangtung coast was to assemble in Hong Kong and reach Canton by ferry with arms and ammunition packed in barrels labeled Portland cement. Their mission would be to storm government offices and the military headquarters, kill or seize officials and officers, and thereby paralyze provincial leadership. Simultaneously Triads and bandits were to converge upon the capital from surrounding districts and neutralize loyalist troops. With Canton safely secured, the conspirators could hope for responsive risings throughout the province and beyond. Potential fighters were available. What was needed was audacity and money.

Finances were chiefly the responsibility of Yang Ch'ü-yün, who with his better connections in Hong Kong took charge of all activities there. One of Yang's recruits to the Society to Restore China's Prosperity, whose father had been with the first missionary protégés sent to America for study fifty years earlier, sold a house and contributed HK$8,000. And over HK$10,000 came from a secretive merchant who delivered the money to Yang in a cemetery. These funds, together with those remitted from Hawaii and an unspecified amount from Sun Yat-sen —

he contributed all he had saved from his medical practice — were sufficient to set the operation in motion.

Helped by his old friends Lu Hao-tung, who designed the revolutionary flag — a white sun against a blue background — and Cheng Shih-liang, the Triad expert, Sun himself took charge at Canton. There, within plain sight of the highest provincial authorities he set about weaving a subversive network that would reach into every stratum of Cantonese society. He showed himself to be a highly imaginative, courageous, but reckless conspirator.

Working closely with him in the Canton area were about thirty local members of the Society. These activists included several naval officers from Sun's home district of Hsiang-shan who were expected to subvert part of the Kwangtung fleet. A Chinese Christian pastor was another key member. Strategically located in one of the best-known streets of Canton, the religious bookstore he managed served as a secret meeting place and arms cache. Two members who came from Hawaii to join the action were expected to lead a contingent of fighters from their home district of Hsiang-shan. (Another member of the Hawaiian branch, the planter Teng Yin-nan, who had contributed generously to the war fund, was active in Hong Kong.) Sun is also said to have brought several Western sympathizers — "military experts" — from Hawaii, and one, an American (or British?) chemistry teacher, improvised a secret arsenal in a Canton suburb.

To help mask his real purpose Sun posed as an enthusiastic reformer. While he and his emissaries were secretly wooing Triad and bandit leaders with cash and the promise of loot, in public he promoted scientific agriculture, universal education and other reformist causes with which his name was already associated. In early October he announced the formation of the "agricultural study society" and attracted favorable notice in respectable circles. It also appears that Sun was angling for more serious cooperation from Cantonese gentry. At least one ambitious degree-holder knew what he was up to and was awaiting the outcome.

Liu Hsüeh-hsün, a prominent Hsiang-shan native who had amassed a fortune managing a popular lottery, saw in those troubled times a chance to realize his dream of founding a new dynasty. While avoiding personal risk he encouraged Sun's plotting, which he hoped to turn to his own advantage. Sun apparently fed this hope. Certainly he and his comrades were not intending to risk their lives to satisfy Liu's ambitions. That Sun nevertheless saw fit to cultivate him was typical of the fluid political style that was to become his trademark. Only someone as self-confident and optimistic as Sun could have bet so heavily on his ability to manipulate others.

This penchant for broad maneuvering, which carried with it the risk of ideological compromise, can also be explained by his eagerness to cut short the revolutionary process. As already mentioned, Sun felt that China's international position was too precarious to permit a prolonged, bloodletting upheaval. And with less than fifty hard-core conspirators in the Hong Kong–Canton area, recourse to extra-organizational elements was essential. In addition to the hungry fighters who were expected to swarm into the provincial capital, disaffected gentry could also be useful. Their wealth and prestige could lend an aura of solidity and respectability to an uprising led by foreign-educated Christian converts of lower-class origins. Yet it was their foreign backgrounds that the conspirators emphasized in Hong Kong when they were trying to win British approval there. The effort to solicit outside support required a marked softening of the nationalist, republican goals that the Society to Restore China's Prosperity had originally set forth.

Dr. Ho Kai, Sun's former teacher, acted as their shadow "foreign minister." Though he never joined the society he attended the initial meetings in Hong Kong. He was also instrumental in getting the British editors of the *China Mail* and the Hongkong *Telegraph* to act as press agents for the impending rebellion. In March, the *Mail*, which had previously printed Ho's anonymous articles on reform, disclosed that the "reform party" was planning to overthrow the Manchu dynasty and establish constitutional rule. The paper urged foreigners not to repeat the mistake of supporting the dynasty as they had done during the Taiping Rebellion. This new breed of revolutionaries, the editor announced, held views so enlightened that he found it difficult to attribute them to Chinese. Aiming to achieve power through "peaceful means if possible," they were determined to "rid their country of the iniquitous system of misrule which has shut out China from Western influences, Western trade, and Western civilization." The new regime, he went on, would make liberal use of foreign advisers in order to make its reforms effective. It would recognize all of China's obligations, would continue to offer the imperial customs as security for loans, and would temporarily place foreigners in charge of inland revenue as well. Above all, it would provide a "fresh outlet . . . for British enterprises and capital." And rounding out the image of a sober and restrained revolution was the declaration that it aimed to establish a new dynasty: "It is not proposed to set up a republic."

This statement of intentions was of course deliberately attuned to treaty-port aspirations and prejudices. Nevertheless, its spirit was consistent with the accommodative nationalism that was long to remain an integral ingredient of Sun Yat-sen's formula for achieving power and bringing about the regeneration of China. As already pointed out, he and his associates did not believe that significant change in China was possible without foreign consent, especially if attempted by people like themselves who lacked a powerful social base at home. (They had not forgotten the fate of the Taipings.) They also saw no inconsistency between satisfying foreign ambitions and fully restoring Chinese sovereignty and dignity. They saw themselves as representatives of Western civilization, and assumed that the Western powers, especially Britain, would perceive mutual advantages in having them bring the benefits of that civilization to China. Though again, in attributing any particular political attitude to Sun one must always consider his readiness to dissimulate, and his unlimited confidence in his ability to use other people and forces for his own ends.

Thus, aware that most foreigners were skeptical of the prospects for republicanism in China, the conspirators found it expedient to display a preference for a Chinese dynasty under foreign tutelage. This would sound more reasonable to old China hands, who, despite their exasperation with the Manchus, feared the disruptive effect of a more serious revolution. Actually, though the plotters were uncertain how far a coup in Canton would take them, in their secret deliberations they were still hoping that it would pave the way for a republic.

Two weeks before the intended uprising Yang, not Sun, was chosen for the "presidency" of the future provisional government. Though they deferred to Yang because of the importance of the Hong Kong base which he and followers controlled, Sun and his close comrades did not consider the issue closed. They assumed that Sun's key role in Canton would make him the natural leader if the coup succeeded. But on October 26, instead of storming government offices, the Canton conspirators were fleeing for their lives without having fired a shot.

Earlier, the police had become suspicious of Sun. But it was hard to convince the governor-general that he was more than a harmless eccentric spouting reformist platitudes. Moreover, until they had firm proof of criminal behavior the authorities were reluctant to risk involving foreign missionaries by detaining one of their protégés. By October 26, however, evidence of conspiracy was forthcoming from Hong Kong, where Yang's recruiting activities had attracted notice. Yang had in any case been unable to keep to the original schedule, and though the Canton group wanted to postpone the action, the police were already on their heels. Sun escaped, but his friend Lu Hao-tung and several other leaders were arrested. Then, on the twenty-eighth, Yang's assault force — some four hundred coolies who later claimed that they had been promised HK$10 a month to serve as "government soldiers" — was greeted by the police when it landed in Canton. Two of the passengers on the ferry, identified as recruiters, were held, while most of the others either escaped or were subsequently dismissed. The authorities were mainly concerned with the ringleaders. Lu and the others whom they had caught were executed. And more than anyone else they wanted to get their hands on Sun Yat-sen. They offered the highest reward for his capture.

According to the British consul, the Canton government felt fortunate in having forestalled a serious uprising. But he doubted whether the officials would make a searching inquiry. There was the feeling that it would reveal "inconvenient information," which would "compel them to follow up with such drastic measures . . . as would precipitate the rebellion which has not yet been averted." Instead, the government blamed a few agitators for "deluding" the masses. Yet Peking did not consider Sun and his companions ordinary agitators. Their Christian backgrounds evoked unpleasant memories of Hung Hsiu-ch'üan and other Taiping leaders.

Sun arrived in Hong Kong on October 29, and a solicitor to whom Dr. Cantlie referred him advised him and his friends to leave as soon as possible. Even if the British refused to extradite them it was considered prudent to get out of the reach of unofficial Manchu agents. Since the first available space was on a Japanese freighter, Sun, Ch'en Shao-pai and Cheng Shih-liang sailed for Kobe, where they landed on November 12. Sun now discovered that he was important enough to attract the attention of the Japanese press. The newspapers announced that "the leader of the Chinese revolutionary party" had arrived.

But after the failure of the Canton plot there was hardly any party worth mentioning. Both China and Hong Kong were out of bounds, and those of the original conspirators who were still at large became wandering refugees among the *hua-ch'iao* communities in various parts of the world. Yang Ch'ü-yün, after a brief stay in Southeast Asia, ended up in Johannesburg. There, only a few of the Cantonese merchants and laborers were willing to form a branch of the Society to Restore China's Prosperity.

Sun, too, found it difficult to whip up enthusiasm for further attempts at revolution. Of the several thousand Cantonese in Yokohama only fifteen appeared at the inaugural meeting of the branch over which Sun presided. Still, he was able to borrow enough money from two of his more devoted followers to pay for the trip to his next station, Hawaii. He was also more confident that he could hide his tracks. Having cut off his queue, grown a mustache, and put on a Western suit, he could easily be taken for a Japanese. Sun was darker in complexion than most Chinese. As described by the *China Mail* (December 3, 1896), he was of "average height, thin and wiry, and with a keenness of expression and frankness of feature seldom seen in Chinese."

Arriving in January 1896, he spent six months in the Islands with his family. His wife and their two children — a son born in 1891 and a daughter born in 1895 — and his widowed mother had left China in order to escape possible retaliation by the Manchu authorities. Another daughter would be born in November, and as long as Sun remained a fugitive his affluent and generous brother would take care of the entire family on Maui.

Though he failed to invigorate the moribund Hawaiian branch, Sun was once more able to raise travel expenses. Before leaving for the United States he unex-

pectedly ran into Dr. and Mrs. Cantlie, who were returning to England. Sun's plans for the future were indefinite
and the idea of visiting Europe and broadening his
knowledge of current affairs appealed to him. He promised to look up the Cantlies in London, and his former
teacher had hopes of inducing him to resume medical
studies.

A three-month tour of the United States was a complete failure. Nevertheless, Sun's travels thoroughly
frightened the Chinese government. Faced with an apparently indefatigable and mobile agitator who threatened to stoke the fires of rebellion with overseas funds,
Peking took extraordinary measures. Inducements to
help apprehend Sun were advertised in the major cities of
Southeast Asia, and Chinese diplomats throughout the
world were enlisted in the chase. In America they had no
trouble monitoring his journey across the continent since
his "disguise" had been quickly penetrated: the Chinese
legation in Washington had a copy of a photograph he
had posed for in San Francisco. Thus at the end of September, when Sun left New York for Liverpool, the Chinese minister alerted his colleague in London, who immediately asked the British Foreign Office whether Sun
could be extradited upon arrival. The reply was negative,
and on October 1 Sun was in London, in lodgings the
Cantlies had found for him on Gray's Inn Place, not far
from their own residence on Devonshire Street.

Sun's London adventure, which was to be more publicized than perhaps any other episode in his life, began in
conventional tourist fashion. Almost a year had passed
since the Canton plot had miscarried. During that time
Sun had tasted the bitter frustration of a professional
revolutionary searching in vain for a constituency. Now,
seemingly ready for a respite, he turned his attention to
the attractions of London. He also called frequently at
the Cantlies' home. In the meantime, private detectives

hired by the Chinese legation continued to follow him and to file innocuous reports, which were forwarded overseas by the minister. Then, after extradition had been ruled out, the legation chose an unconventional alternative for getting Sun back to China and the stern punishment that awaited him. Unexpectedly, it was Sun himself who provided the opportunity.

Despite his public denials, other evidence, including his private disclosures, indicates that Sun was so incautious as to walk into the Chinese legation of his own accord on at least two occasions. But what is beyond dispute is that on his last visit, on October 11, he was taken prisoner and held for twelve days. Nor is there much doubt that if the British authorities had not intervened, he would have been secretly removed to China for execution.

It appears that neither the sights of London nor the tomes of the British Museum library had kept him from his primary vocation. The urge to spread the revolutionary gospel had proved irresistible, and the search for fellow Chinese and, in particular, Cantonese, drew him to the legation. He must have noticed the building soon after he arrived in London because it was located on Portland Place, around the corner from the Cantlie home. Both Mrs. Cantlie and Dr. Manson had in fact warned him to stay clear of it. Yet Sun had been taught to have the fullest confidence in the British respect for law, and as long as he could not be extradited he felt no cause for alarm. Moreover, he was sure that he could keep his identity hidden. Thus, on October 10 he visited the legation under an assumed name and met a Cantonese employee. It was arranged that he would return the following day; the two would then proceed to Liverpool and meet Cantonese sailors. Afterward, the employee reported Sun's visit to his superiors, who had no trouble in identifying Sun. Plans were then made to detain him when he returned.

The next day Sun's ordeal began. And whether he fell into a trap of his own making or whether, as he later contended, he had been tricked into entering the building and had never been there previously, is immaterial. (Unfortunately, Slater's Detective Agency was unable to give a full account of Sun's activities for both days.) Regardless of how he had entered the premises Sun's detention was a violation of diplomatic privilege. This was to be the verdict of the British authorities who thereby established a precedent for international law. First, however, they had to learn what was happening, and before he got word to the outside, Sun, who was kept under guard in a third-floor room, was terrorized by thoughts of what awaited him in China. He expected to have his "eyelids cut off" and then to be "chopped into small fragments."

His chief captor and the brains behind the "kidnapping" was Sir Halliday Macartney, the secretary of the Chinese legation. Macartney, a Scottish military surgeon who had served in the Chinese army against the Taipings, knew how badly Peking wanted Sun Yat-sen and acted with ruthless efficiency. Three days after Sun's capture he was negotiating for the charter of a ship to transport a "lunatic" to China. Money was no consideration. His principals cabled permission to spend seven thousand pounds. In the meantime Macartney kept intercepting the messages that Sun was trying to send to Dr. Cantlie.

After a week of anguish Sun's powers of persuasion proved equal to the task. He convinced the legation porter, a young Englishman by the name of George Cole, that he was no lunatic but a political dissident similar to "the leader of our Socialist Party here in London." And when the porter still hesitated to disobey Macartney's orders Sun gave him twenty pounds and promised a thousand later if he delivered a message to Dr. Cantlie. Meanwhile, the legation's English housekeeper, in whom Cole had confided, decided to alert Cantlie herself and left an anonymous note in the doctor's mailbox. Sun's friends,

who were already worried over his long absence, now
started to make inquiries, and the next day, October 18,
Cole delivered Sun's note: "I was kidnapped into the
Chinese Legation on Sunday, and shall be smuggled out
from England to China for death. Pray rescue me quick;
a ship is already chartered by the C.L. [Chinese Lega-
tion] for the service to take me to China and I shall be
locked up all the way without communication to anybody
... O! Woe to me!"

After that there was no stopping Cantlie and Manson.
Before the day was over they pestered Scotland Yard, the
Foreign Office and *The Times*. While the bureaucrats
tried to digest their story and *The Times* sat on it, the
doctors dealt with the legation. Cantlie hired a private
detective to watch the building and the next day he had
Slater's Detective Agency on the job. (Thus Slater's, who
worked both sides of the street, was able to keep Macartney informed of the rescue party's progress.) By that
time, however, Lord Salisbury, concurrently prime minister and foreign minister, authorized official intervention. On the evening of the nineteenth, Scotland Yard
started an around-the-clock surveillance of the legation,
and the Thames River police were ordered to watch all
China-bound ships. And Sun, now apprised of his friends'
intervention but still uneasy, sent Cole with another message: "I was born in Hong Kong. I went back to interior
of China about four or five years of age. As legally a
British subject, can you get me out by that?"

The attempted deception was superfluous. On the
twenty-second, the Foreign Office decided to press for
Sun's release. Macartney pleaded for time to get permission from Peking, and Cantlie and Manson, acting on
official advice, applied to an Old Bailey judge for a writ
of habeas corpus against the legation. Though the judge
shifted responsibility back to the Foreign Office, the hearing attracted the attention of the *Globe*. That same day
the paper broke the story in a special edition.

On the twenty-third, Sun's "kidnapping," featured in

the British and world press, was a sensation. Now, the Foreign Office, embarrassed by the exposure of a sinister Oriental plot in the heart of London, made short shrift of Macartney's evasive tactics. That afternoon, under threat of severe diplomatic reprisals, the legation surrendered its prisoner. Reporters and sightseers crowded around as Dr. Cantlie and officials from the Foreign Office and Scotland Yard escorted Sun to safety.

Thus, instead of shipping him home for the "slicing" punishment, the Manchu government inadvertently thrust Sun into the limelight. Their bungled attempt also reinvigorated his determination. If during the year following the Canton fiasco he had sometimes been afflicted with doubts, now he was absolutely certain of his destiny. What had happened, he felt, was no accident but part of the Grand Design that marked him for the role of saving China. ("I owe everything to the great favor of God," he wrote to his former tutor, Reverend Ch'ü. "Through the Way of God I hope to enter into the Political Way.") And on a more mundane level he saw a unique opportunity for bringing his case against the Manchu dynasty out into the open. He believed that the government and people who had been outraged by mandarin machinations in London would readily sympathize with his effort to eliminate the mandarin system in China.

Reporters who interviewed him after a day of recuperation found him a willing and attractive respondent. They were impressed by his personality and completely convinced by his version of the weird doings on Portland Place. Editorial comments and letters from readers were also favorable. And with the help of friends Sun wrote a letter of his own, which *The Times* and other papers published. He thanked the government and the press, and affirmed his renewed faith in "the generous public spirit which pervades Great Britain." Now that he realized "more keenly than ever what a constitutional government and an enlightened people mean," he was "prepared to pursue the cause of advancement, education, and civilization, in my own beloved but oppressed country."

He also took pains to advertise his Christian affiliation. When released he denied having claimed any affinity to the British socialists — which is what the legation porter had declared. Instead, he insisted that he had compared himself to the Armenian Christians, whose persecution by the Turks was at that time arousing public indignation. Though close Chinese friends would rarely see him visit a church during his travels, in London he made a conspicuous church appearance that was duly reported by the press. (Sun himself would later declare: "I do not belong to the Christianity of the churches, but to the Christianity of Jesus who was a revolutionary.") And the *Globe* reported that he would stay in England to help train Chinese medical missionaries.

Months after the "kidnapping" Sun continued to attract favorable publicity. The distinguished Cambridge sinologist Professor H. A. Giles translated a short autobiography he had asked Sun to prepare. A member of Parliament took an interest in Sun and questioned the Foreign Office about the behavior of the Chinese legation and the part played by Sir Halliday Macartney. And in 1897 the publication of *Kidnapped in London* — likewise the result of a collaborative effort — spread his name far and wide. (Sun at this time admitted that he could not write anything "in perfect English without a friend's help.") In describing his political views he was careful not to mention republicanism or revolution, but posed as the leader of the "reform movement of the Young China Party." Nor did he give a completely accurate account of what had happened in either London or Canton. All this made for good public relations. But it failed to win influence where it counted.

In March 1897 he made a direct appeal for Britain's "benevolent neutrality." In return he promised a New

Deal for the British in China — better conditions than they could have ever hoped to extract from the Manchu government. Writing in the *Fortnightly Review* (March 1), and again with the aid of a collaborator, he presented a brief on behalf of the "Reform Party." Boasting that the Chinese army was to "a great extent leavened with sympathizers," he argued that "the benevolent neutrality of Great Britain, and of the other Powers is all the aid needed to enable us to make the present system give place to one that is not corrupt." The ordinary people, he wrote, were neither corrupt nor antiforeign. It was the unholy alliance of Manchus and bureaucrats that kept China backward and shut out the enlightened influence of the West. Under his leadership, he asserted, China would be strong enough to fend off Russia — Britain's chief worry in the Far East — and would allow full scope for British trade and investment. He further promised that in pursuing reform the new government would welcome European advice and administrative assistance.

British policy-makers were of course not taken in by Sun's fictitious claims for his "party." Nor were they swayed by his appeal to Western values and principles. What the diplomats, bankers and businessmen perceived as interests in China had little to do with constitutional government or Christian humanism. Though miscellaneous idealists of the Cantlie and Manson variety saw Sun as the harbinger of a better future for the Chinese people, the British officials who had saved his life considered him a political nuisance and a potential liability. As Britain competed for bases and lucrative concessions, she hardly wished to offend Peking unnecessarily by supporting a conspirator of dubious credibility. In fact, after having reprimanded the Chinese for their behavior in London, Lord Salisbury had been quick to appease them. He had assured the Peking government that Hong Kong would not be used as a base for disturbing the "tranquility of the Empire," and the Colonial Office ordered the governor of the colony to "anticipate and frustrate any revolutionary attempts against the constituted authority in China." Thus "benevolent neutrality" was out of the question. But there was still the British Museum library, and as the glamour of his escapade wore off, Sun became a frequent visitor to that favorite haunt of frustrated political exiles.

According to the private detectives who were still watching him, between December 1896 and June 1897 Sun visited the museum on fifty-nine days and stayed for hours each time. Dr. Cantlie marveled at the wide range of his scientific and political interests. Later, Sun claimed that this intensive reading, coupled with his impressions of the West, inspired the formulation of his famous Three Principles — the simultaneous realization of socialism, nationalism, and democracy. Yet he would also claim that at this time he spent two years "in Europe" studying its "political practices" and making "the acquaintance of its leading politicians." Actually, he spent only nine months in England and did not visit any other European country. Typically of Sun, when for the benefit of his countrymen he would strike the stance of a foremost expert on Western thought and affairs, he could not resist exaggerating the duration and scope of his first Western tour. Nor is there any record of his having met "leading politicians," though he did become friendly with Russian political exiles who also frequented the British Museum. (According to Sun's recollection both he and the Russians underestimated the revolutionary potential of their respective countries. He told them that it would take thirty years for China to have her revolution; the Russians thought that theirs would require a hundred years.)

Nevertheless, it is entirely possible that Sun's first experience of living in advanced Western societies was as instructive as he later claimed. The disadvantages as well as the achievements of modernization were clearly visible. Along with evidence of unparalleled wealth there were slums and conditions of poverty that rivaled those of Canton and Hong Kong. He already knew about socialism, probably through reading the missionary press in Hong Kong. Now he could learn at first hand about the growing opposition to laissez-faire capitalism — how Socialists and Fabians, Single-taxers, Populists and trade union leaders were struggling to eliminate the harmful side effects of unplanned development.

According to his subsequent recapitulation, he concluded that the West could not escape social revolution. It was then, he recalled, that he decided to plan China's progress in such a way as to bypass the pitfalls that Europe, in its blind rush for wealth and power, had not avoided. But whether conceived now or later, the idea of a preventive social remedy, which became an important part of the Three Principles, was not expressed as a political goal until five or six years later. Sun was not prone to theorizing for its own sake. Since he usually tried to fit his appeal to his audience, he did not begin propounding doctrine until student intellectuals came within range of revolutionary agitation. Until then he focused on closer targets.

On July 2, 1897, he sailed for Montreal and then traveled across Canada to Vancouver. It was only when he boarded a ship for Yokohama that the Chinese authorities called off the surveillance that had been maintained throughout his journey. But if his enemies were nervous, Sun too, according to his watchers, was more prudent after the close call in London. Yet he still kept pressing the *hua-ch'iao* for funds to finance another attempt at revolution. Without a clear-cut plan in mind he nonetheless fed optimistic progress reports to overseas supporters. Misrepresenting achievements and prospects, which he had tried in Britain, was to remain a favorite ploy. Though these deceptions would eventually catch up with him, for a long time they were his sole way of maintaining momentum — and a trickle of *hua-ch'iao* money. On this occasion contributions from the American continent enabled Sun to pay an extra hundred dollars and exchange his intermediate-class accommodations for a stateroom on the *Empress of India.* He arrived in Yokohama in early August.

Then, unexpectedly, his all-option strategy began to pay off. During the next few years fate would begin to shift events in a favorable direction, and always prepared to seize the moment, Sun was quick to cooperate.

Initially, he chose Japan as a base of operations because Hong Kong was out of bounds. The authorities there had already issued an order of banishment against him in March 1896, and were enforcing it with added vigilance after instructions from London at the end of October. Sun's threat to appeal "to the English public and to the civilized world," which he addressed to the Hong Kong colonial secretary after his arrival in Yokohama, had no effect. The colony, in fact, was to bar him from legal entry until the Revolution of 1911. But if the British had no use for him, influential Japanese did.

Japan at this time was in the embarrassing position of having created opportunities for imperialism in China that others were better able to exploit. Victory over China had brought Japan recognition as a power in East Asia, but not as a world power. She was isolated, and lacked the military and economic requisites of great-power status. Though now allowed to share in the China spoils — she obtained extraterritorial rights there even before the West had fully surrendered that privilege in Japan — the choicest prizes were out of her reach. This had been made quite clear by the ease with which the Triple Intervention had deprived her of the Liaotung peninsula. Furthermore, though fear of Russian designs on Korea had been an important motive for the China war, victory had not brought security. China was too weak and Japan herself not yet strong enough to counter the Russian threat to northeastern Asia. Eventually, alliance with England would give her a free hand to deal with the Russians. Until then, Japanese who held different views of the national interest and purpose shared the desire to bolster China.

Pan-Asianists, who doubted whether Europeans would ever grant equality to any Asian people, considered it disastrous to cooperate with Western imperialism. Inevitably, they contended, racial ties would pit white man against Asian, and Japan, deprived of her natural allies, would end up the isolated victim of a predatory West. On moral grounds, too, pan-Asianists felt that it was Japan's duty to strengthen and help reform China. Together they could strive for the total liberation of colonial Asia. On the other hand, even those Japanese who wanted to shake off the drag of backward Asia, and who sought identification with the modern West, feared that the premature collapse of China would leave Japan out in the cold, confronted by unfriendly forces on the continent. Therefore the idea of a Chinese renovation under Japanese patronage was appealing. And given the apparent inability of the Manchu dynasty to check the spreading rot, even a lonely conspirator like Sun Yat-sen could not be ignored.

No one was looking harder for a Chinese hero than Miyazaki Torazō, an adventurous pan-Asian idealist who enjoyed the patronage of more realistic politicians. Having already heard about Sun from Ch'en Shao-pai, who had remained in Japan after the Canton episode, Miyazaki rushed off to Yokohama soon after Sun's arrival. Their meeting was the beginning of a long and close comradeship that is still remembered as one of the bright chapters in the unhappy annals of Sino-Japanese relations. Other Japanese were prepared to help Sun for reasons of expediency. Miyazaki's devotion to the cause of Asian solidarity, and to Sun personally, would never be in doubt.

To Miyazaki, Sun revealed feelings and convictions

that he had kept hidden from the British press and Foreign Office. Now there was no quibbling over his aim. He wanted to establish a republic, not merely to overthrow the Manchu dynasty. And instead of inviting European tutelage, he attacked the powers for turning their superior wealth and strength to evil ends. They were preparing China for the "chopping block," he warned, but a swift revolution could save the country and lead all Asia to the "way of humanity." This was the kind of talk Miyazaki wanted to hear. Though they had difficulty communicating because of the lack of a common language, he was convinced that he was in the presence of a man who had the vision and determination to become Asia's answer to Western imperialism.

As with many politicians there was undeniably a good bit of the confidence man in Sun Yat-sen. Given the right situation Miyazaki's candidate for redressing the humiliation of the yellow race could easily reappear as the humble petitioner of European benevolence. Yet there was more here than tactical posturing. Sun believed that the people of Asia had a common cause in resisting exploitation by Europe. He felt that Japan, which was already proving her innovative capacity, and China, whose potential for renewed greatness he never doubted, were natural leaders, partners, for the liberation of the continent. What he envisaged was not just a coincidence of interests but a union of spirit. That Japan would repay her longstanding cultural debt and help China find her way in the modern world was a hope that he shared with most patriotic reformers of his time. Like Sun they were convinced that Japan's recent imperialist venture was a temporary aberration and that Japan's instincts and interests would deter her from following the Western example. But Sun also believed that the West, too, would come to see the folly, as well as the immorality, of imperialism. While posterity has undoubtedly confirmed his judgment that the rest of the world — both East and West

— would be better off if China were strong and intact instead of weak, this was not an easy idea to sell during the heyday of imperialism and Social Darwinism. It was even more difficult to sell himself as the potential leader of a new China. But at this time, and for reasons already mentioned, both Sun and his nationalist goals were not entirely unwelcome in Japan.

Inukai Ki, Miyazaki's influential sponsor, was strongly taken with Sun's personality, and through him Sun was able to meet other leading figures in Japanese politics. For the first time in his life he was getting the attention he felt he deserved. Inukai also had contacts with right-wing ultranationalists for whom pan-Asianism meant Japanese domination of the continent. (Their disciples would assassinate Inukai when he was prime minister in 1932.) There was money in these circles and Sun was seen as a good investment. He was fully subsidized and given a house in Tokyo, where Hirayama Shū, Miyazaki's friend, stayed with him. Since the Foreign Office did not want to antagonize the Manchu government by openly supporting a revolutionary, Sun was listed as a Chinese language teacher for Miyazaki and Hirayama. The name that he assumed, Nakayama, which means "Central Mountain," is read in Chinese as Chung-shan. It was as Sun Chung-shan that he was later best known in China. Also, as a tribute to his memory, his home district of Hsiang-shan would be renamed Chung-shan.

However, Sun was neither the only nor the leading candidate for Japanese support. Ōkuma Shigenobu, Inukai's senior colleague and foreign minister until the beginning of 1898, preferred the gentry reform movement that had been making headway since 1895. Led by the Cantonese K'ang Yu-wei and Liang Ch'i-ch'ao, the scholar-reformers were more closely attuned to the Meiji Restoration model, and also seemed to have more chance of success than Sun. Instead of preaching republicanism, which was not the most appealing prospect to Japanese leaders, K'ang hoped to establish a constitutional monarchy. The young Manchu emperor, with the reign title of Kuang-hsü, was to play the role of his Japanese counterpart. By interpreting Confucianism in an unorthodox, even revolutionary fashion, he tried to use traditional ideology to legitimize radical reform. His big chance came in 1898.

As the imperialist juggernaut moved into high gear the emperor accepted K'ang's blueprint for saving the country. In June he started issuing edicts designed to overhaul the government and other institutions. K'ang's program, which threatened numerous vested interests, proved too potent for his own literati stratum. Rejected by the elite, and having no links to the masses, K'ang and his disciples could only count on the prestige of the emperor. This was insufficient. Backed by the military establishment, conservatives and more moderate reformers rallied around the empress dowager, Tzu Hsi (the emperor's aunt and adoptive mother), who came out of retirement. In September the "Hundred Days of Reform" were over, and the emperor was a virtual prisoner. Six of the radical reformers, including K'ang's younger brother, were executed. K'ang and Liang would have shared this fate had not their prominent Japanese sympathizers, Ōkuma and the renowned Itō Hirobumi, personally supervised their rescue and arranged for sanctuary in Japan.

To the Japanese, who now had both factions on their payroll, the differences between Chinese revolutionaries and radical reformers seemed to be overshadowed by their common goal. Both were enemies of the ruling clique in Peking, and their merger could be expected to give a broader thrust to the forces working for change. Sun, still anxious for literati connections, responded positively to Japanese mediation. So did Liang Ch'i-ch'ao. But his master, K'ang, refused even to talk to Sun and vetoed any suggestion of cooperation. Ostracism by the literati of a lower-class political aspirant and the clash of ambitious personalities only partly explain the failure of the Japanese initiative. It failed mainly because K'ang, who claimed to have a mandate to rescue the emperor, would never budge from his loyalty to the dynasty. And Sun's group could hardly give up the anti-Manchuism which had been its original motive.

K'ang's magisterial attitude also caused trouble within his own faction and hurt his standing with the Japanese. The Japanese gave him a heavy subsidy and in March 1899 he left for Canada, where he formed his Protect the Emperor Association. This was the beginning of the reformers' raids on Sun's overseas territories that would seriously cut into his source of funds. But with K'ang gone, his disciple Liang Ch'i-ch'ao, the greatest Chinese publicist of his time and a peerless expositor of modern ideas, veered toward the revolutionary side. This was an opportunity Sun could not pass up. He leaned over backward in an attempt to widen the breach in the reformist camp. However, a year later Liang was back in K'ang's fold and winning support in Hawaii from people whom Sun had introduced him to. After much vacillation Liang could not overcome doubts about Sun's judgment and capacity for leadership. Sun for his part became distrustful of literati who seemed to lack the resoluteness required for revolutionary action. On the other hand, his Japanese admirers were more attuned to his style. What Chinese intellectuals criticized as Sun's recklessness was the very quality that captivated Miyazaki and other pan-Asian adventurers. They readily followed his lead in fantastic projects, such as the attempt to help the Filipino liberation movement.

Filipino nationalists, who had already been active under Spanish rule, had cooperated with the Americans during the war of 1898. But when it became apparent that the United States intended to retain possession of the Islands, the Filipinos, led by Emilio Aguinaldo, resisted. In the summer of 1898 one of Aguinaldo's agents came to

Japan looking for assistance. Though sympathetic, the Japanese could not risk offending the Americans. Sun, though, responded enthusiastically to the Filipino request. Here was a chance for Chinese and Japanese to join in the Asian struggle against Western domination. And if the Filipino guerrillas were successful, Chinese revolutionaries would have a friendly base for operations against the Manchus.

The Filipinos had money. What they needed were arms and the means of transporting them to the Islands. After their first meeting, Mario Ponce, Aguinaldo's representative, did not hesitate to entrust the whole operation to Sun Yat-sen, so impressed was he with Sun's quiet determination. Behind the scenes the Japanese army gave its approval and assistance, despite the anxieties of the Foreign Office. Friendly business interests helped Sun outfit a munitions ship, which left for the Philippines in July 1899. Enlisted as military advisers, six Japanese, including Hirayama, had sailed earlier. Miyazaki, Sun and other Chinese fighters were scheduled to follow. But the munitions ship, an old Mitsui vessel, sank in a storm off the China coast. The cargo of arms, ammunition and manufacturing equipment was lost, and three Japanese were among the thirteen men who went down with the ship. Sun tried to organize another shipment, but when the Americans were forewarned, the Japanese authorities clamped an embargo on munitions to the Philippines and the entire project had to be scrapped.

Still, Sun's demonstration of pan-Asian solidarity earned the gratitude of Aguinaldo's junta. They presented him with 100,000 yen left from their war chest. This enabled Sun to launch his first propaganda organ, a Chinese daily that Ch'en Shao-pai edited in Hong Kong. Circulated among the *hua-ch'iao*, the *Chinese Journal (Chung-kuo jih-pao)* helped counter the pro-emperor line being spread in the overseas communities by K'ang Yu-wei and his supporters, who were more active in journalism. Thus, by the beginning of 1900 prospects were improving, and Sun could think about another uprising.

He had an arms cache the Filipinos could not use; he had loyal Japanese comrades and leads to Japanese military and political circles; and, thanks to a Hunanese literatus who had defected from the reformist camp, he established his first link with the foremost secret society of the Yangtze Valley, the Ko-lao Hui (Society of Elders and Brothers). In addition, his Cantonese comrades were once more cultivating the Triads of Kwangtung. With these achievements to his credit, and with the publicity he had gained in London, Sun was clearly the dominant figure of his original revolutionary band. His rival, Yang Ch'ü-yün, who had returned to Hong Kong from South Africa in 1898, now agreed that Sun be designated the future "President of the Provisional Government." In the meantime, the regime they hoped to replace continued to skid toward disaster.

Beginning with the German seizure of Kiaochow in 1897 the foreign powers had staked out claims to huge sections of China, where they sought strategic advantages vis-à-vis each other and preferential rights to build railroads, work mines, and engage in any enterprise that promised lucrative returns. These spheres of influence — no less invidious if called spheres of interest — were but a short step removed from outright partition into colonies. And while the specter of dismemberment hovered over the country, it was already being strangled by financial imperialism.

The Sino-Japanese War had turned China into a debtor nation. Indigenous capital was insufficient to finance the war and to pay for the indemnity that was increased in order to compensate Japan for the return of Liaotung. Peking had to turn to foreign bankers, who fell over themselves pushing gold-linked, high-interest loans secured on the government's most important revenues. This meant that China's tax system — already administered in part by foreigners — was working largely for the benefit of foreign bondholders. Within forty months of the war this foreign debt amounted to about fifty million pounds — or nearly three times the annual revenue collected by Peking. Since the value of gold was rising in relation to Chinese currency, actual indebtedness was much greater.

The masses did not grasp the full implications of political and financial imperialism. But they were increasingly aware of deteriorating economic conditions. They were also aware of the missionaries, who despite their good intentions — and good works — were foreigners whose presence had been forced upon the Chinese and whose activities inevitably disrupted traditional social relations. Here was highly visible, ubiquitous evidence of foreign interference that the government was unable to check. As China entered the twentieth century, popular frustration and resentment finally erupted.

THREE

No Helping Hand from Abroad

THE BOXER RISING was a primitive antiforeign outburst. The main victims were Chinese Christians. But while many Manchu nobles and some Chinese officials bet on the Boxers, more level-headed statesmen realized that magic incantations, and swords and spears, were no match for modern arms. They also saw no sense in massacring converts and missionaries, or in eradicating every vestige of foreign influence, including railway tracks and telegraph lines. Yet according to Sir Robert Hart — himself a survivor of the famous siege of the Peking legations — the Chinese world, excluding of course the victims of Boxerism, probably felt that the movement's biggest sin was its failure. The nationalist instincts of the Boxers, though not their atavistic beliefs and methods, pointed toward the dominant trend of twentieth-century China.

The Boxers, so named because of their practice of traditional Chinese boxing or calisthenics, began as an obscure northern secret society consisting of the same type of peasant who had joined the Taipings. Probably an offshoot of the White Lotus Society, the movement was heavily infused with Taoist and Buddhist beliefs, and was intrinsically antidynastic rather than anti-Christian. However, in the spring of 1898 it was mainly antiforeignism that sparked the Boxer revival in Shantung province after a long period of quiescence. This was only one facet of lower-class turbulence, which was on the rise throughout the country. Though maladministration and internally induced economic troubles were the essential causes of unrest, imperialism was a conspicuous contributory factor. The influx of cheap machine-made goods from abroad and the replacement of junks by steamships increased unemployment, and payments on foreign loans necessitated higher tax burdens, of which the peasants bore the brunt. This tax issue fueled major rebellions by the Triads in the southern province of Kwangsi in 1897 and 1898, and similar disturbances afflicted other provinces. Grievances varied according to locality, but risings were increasingly triggered by incidents involving Chinese Christians or missionaries.

The Christians offended their fellow villagers by refusing to participate in and share the expenses of local festivals. Roman Catholics in particular provoked resentment when foreign priests intervened on their behalf in litigation involving non-Christians. Then, in early 1899 Catholic missionaries won the right to be treated as counterparts of Chinese bureaucrats. Thus a bishop was the equivalent of a governor and would not deal with a lower official. By arrogating to themselves privileges of this sort missionaries aroused the ire of local gentry, who were eager to incite the masses against foreigners and their "running dogs," and thereby divert attention from indigenous causes of unrest. Actually, antimissionary riots had been more prevalent in the south. But it was in the north, particularly in Shantung, that antiforeignism flared into a crusade that soon brought the Manchu dynasty into a war with the powers.

Famine had afflicted north China in 1897, and in the

following year the Yellow River flooded and brought additional misery to millions of homeless peasants in Shantung. Coinciding with these natural disasters — whose effects were more severe because of inadequate relief measures — was the German penetration of the province and its exploitation as a sphere of influence. Infatuated with A. T. Mahan's thesis on the role of sea power, the German admiralty had been looking for a base on the China coast, and its choice had fallen on Kiaochow Bay. Conveniently, two German Catholic priests were murdered in Shantung in 1897, and as compensation Germany obtained a lease on Kiaochow and its hinterland. But Shantung also happened to be the native province of Confucius. Its residents were especially sensitive to foreign insults, which the Germans supplied in plenty. The arrogance of their officers, prospectors and promoters, and the zealous efforts of the German bishop of Shantung, known as one of the most energetic servants of church, provoked numerous incidents in the countryside. German reprisals, which included burning down entire villages, were so brazenly brutal as to shock even the sensibilities of old China hands. Kaiser Wilhelm had predicted that "hundreds of thousands of Chinese will quiver when they feel the iron fist of Germany on their necks." Instead, German brutality helped breed Boxerism.

Claiming supernatural powers that made them invulnerable to foreign bullets, the Boxers hoped to frighten "foreign bandits" out of the country by first of all massacring Christian converts. Consequently, the number of Chinese killed by Boxer bands far exceeded the number of foreign victims (counted at less than 250, mostly missionaries). Initially, the Boxers also fought government forces, since they blamed the dynasty for allowing foreigners free rein, but by the fall of 1899 they focused solely on the foreign threat. Expelled from Shantung by a new governor, Yuan Shih-k'ai, who foresaw the dangerous consequences of antiforeign violence, the Boxers ran wild in the metropolitan province of Chihli, where the official atmosphere was more hospitable. Since the antireformist coup of the previous year reactionaries dominated the court and the empress dowager herself welcomed the chance to respond to a grass-roots movement that for a change did not vent its furor upon the dynasty. Now, the Boxer slogan was "Support the Ch'ing, exterminate the foreigners."

Yet, after the murder of a missionary in Shantung on December 31, 1899, five months passed without the loss of a foreign life. The terrorizing of converts, however, alarmed missionaries, and at the end of May, when the Boxers were attacking railways, foreign diplomats decided upon a show of force. An international detachment of some four hundred soldiers was sent to Peking to guard the legations, and by June 3 there were twenty-four warships off Tientsin. Now, escalating fear and suspicion brought both sides closer to open hostilities. An international relief force of over two thousand men, led by a British admiral, set out for Peking from Tientsin on June 10. Then, when rabid Boxer supporters tricked the empress dowager into believing that the foreigners intended to remove her and restore the emperor to power, she saw no reason for restraint. On the seventeenth the foreigners subdued the Taku forts, thirty-five miles from Tientsin, and on the eighteenth, imperial Chinese troops attacked the international column, forcing it to retreat to Tientsin. On the twentieth, the German minister, Ketteler, was shot dead in Peking by a Chinese soldier, and the siege of the legations was under way. On the next day, the twenty-first, China declared war on the foreign powers.

This was only the voice of the pro-Boxer Peking government. In other parts of the empire powerful regional leaders like Li Hung-chang, now governor-general at Canton, realized that China could not win the war and tried to limit the damage. They not only ignored the war declaration but actively enforced peace. While still professing loyalty to the dynasty these realistic officials, who controlled the populous Yangtze Valley and the southern provinces, informed foreign consuls and governments that "rebels" had seized power in Peking and had launched an "unauthorized" war. They guaranteed to keep their domains clear of Boxerism if the powers would keep out their troops and gunboats. Thus the fiction of the Boxer "rebellion" was born and eagerly accepted by the powers. And why not? It meant that belligerency could be restricted to the north. It also meant that treaty obligations, including payments on China's foreign debts, would be honored in the rest of the country. And for the power best placed and most anxious for expansion, war in the north was quite convenient. The Russian minister of war had welcomed the Boxer troubles — "This will give us an excuse for seizing Manchuria."

Peking's embroilment with the powers also seemed like a windfall for Sun Yat-sen. Already working on a plot to unleash the Triads in eastern Kwangtung he now saw all kinds of combinations and alternatives in the offing.

In June, before war had been declared, he received a tantalizing signal from Canton. Liu Hsüeh-hsün, the ambitious literatus who had flirted with the plotters in 1895 and who was now part of Li Hung-chang's entourage, wrote that his chief was considering cooperating with Sun in the establishment of a separate Kwangtung–Kwangsi government. This was probably not so much the governor-general's idea as that of the Cantonese gentry, who were ready for desperate measures in order to keep the region free of both rebellion and foreign invasion. Since his former teacher, Dr. Ho Kai, hoped to get the British in Hong Kong to underwrite the scheme to separate and neutralize the southern provinces, Sun decided to explore Liu's offer. Sailing on a French steamer from Yokohama he reached Hong Kong on June 17. Still banned from the colony, he held a strategy meeting with his friends in the harbor, and three Japanese were delegated to parley with Liu in Canton. Sun then went on to Saigon, where he learned by telegraph that the Canton talks had been inconclusive: Li Hung-chang was awaiting the march of events before making his decision.

There was further bad news in Saigon. Earlier, in the hope of using Indochina as a base for linking up with Triads across the border in Kwangsi, Sun had made a proposition to the French minister in Tokyo. If the French would give him arms and perhaps military advisers he promised to reward them with rich concessions when he set up an independent regime in southern China, the most favored region for the extension of French imperialist holdings. But Paris, no less than London, feared revolution, and the official whom Sun saw in Saigon could not encourage him. In the meantime, Peking had declared war on the powers.

As the affairs of China seemed to be heading toward a crucial turning point, Sun's reformist rivals were also stirred into action. Earlier, reports that the empress dowager was going to have the imprisoned emperor executed led the reformers to schedule a pro-emperor rising in the Yangtze Valley. In Hawaii, Liang Ch'i-ch'ao was using the "Save the Emperor" slogan to raise money from Sun's former backers, and K'ang Yu-wei, in Singapore since the beginning of the year, was enjoying the largesse of a *hua-ch'iao* millionaire upon whom Sun had also cast his eyes. The Japanese had long been urging reconciliation between the two groups, and now, when his rivals threatened to preempt him, Sun authorized Miyazaki to renew negotiations. Miyazaki arrived in Singapore at the end of June, accompanied by two other Japanese.

Having helped rescue K'ang from the clutches of the empress dowager in 1898 Miyazaki assumed that K'ang would trust him. But K'ang panicked when he learned that three hot-blooded Japanese, fresh from a rendezvous with Liu Hsüeh-hsün in Canton, were looking for him.

The exiled reformer, who had good reason for being afraid — he was even higher on Peking's wanted list than Sun Yat-sen — was particularly suspicious of anyone connected with Liu Hsüeh-hsün. That notable was the reformers' archenemy in Canton, and rumor had it that the Manchus had given him a "contract" to eliminate K'ang. K'ang therefore wanted no part of the Japanese, and when they kept insisting upon a meeting, the British police, who were aware of the large price on K'ang's head, took them into custody. Suspicions increased when a baggage search disclosed two "sharp and clean" samurai swords — Miyazaki tried to explain that no Japanese gentleman traveled without one — and a large sum of money.

It is unlikely, however, that Miyazaki was on an assassin's mission, much as that would have pleased Liu Hsüeh-hsün. It would not have fitted in with Japanese policy; nor would it have been consistent with the style of Sun Yat-sen, who preferred using his powers of persuasion. Indeed, if K'ang's murder had been on the agenda Sun would not have quickly followed his friends to Singapore. He arrived there on July 9, accompanied by several Japanese followers and Rowland A. Mulkern, a British soldier who had become fascinated by Sun in London and who had joined the group in Hong Kong.

Instead of finding the way clear for an understanding with K'ang, Sun needed all his eloquence to get the British to release his friends. Because of the de facto war situation he felt free to disclose his plans for the mainland. He told the colonial officials that the first step toward overthrowing the Manchus would be the establishment of an independent southern government. But he warned that fear of partition was liable to provoke the Chinese people to extreme action, and he hinted that Boxerism might spread. He hoped that he could restrain the masses, and boasted that the quiet still reigning in the south was largely due to the moderating influence of his movement, for which, as usual, he claimed an exaggerated strength. Yet he told the British to expect some disturbance, for without it China could not be reformed.

Sir James Alexander Swettenham, acting governor of the Straits Settlements, was not entirely convinced that the Japanese would have stopped with friendly persuasion in dealing with K'ang. Moreover, he did not relish the prospect of Singapore's becoming a base for an uprising in China, especially an uprising in which Japanese were strongly involved. He "remonstrated" with Sun, "pointing out how inexpedient it was for a patriotic Chinese to raise fresh disturbances in China just the moment when it was about to be invaded by foreigners." The authorities therefore issued a five-year banishment order against the Japanese, and were relieved when the whole group, including Sun, left for Hong Kong on July 12.

Hong Kong officials took a different attitude. In early July, Sir Henry A. Blake, governor of the colony, had been informed by a "Chinese gentleman" — probably Ho Kai or a friend, acting on Sun's behalf — that anti-Manchu but not antiforeign risings were on the way. Blake also informed the Colonial Office that Li Hung-chang was "coquetting with this movement," which would welcome British protection. The governor felt that a Li–Sun alliance would be advantageous to Britain because it would guarantee peace in a region close to Hong Kong. Presumably he also preferred that the British rather than the Japanese have an inside track with the revolutionaries, whom he discreetly labeled "reformers." On July 13, when Sun was on his way back to Hong Kong, Blake was ready to let him land and negotiate with Li's representatives. But London would only permit this if Li Hung-chang gave his approval. Thus for the second time in his life the political fortunes of Sun Yat-sen depended upon Li Hung-chang.

The seventy-seven-year-old Li continued to weigh the options. As early as June 18 the court had ordered him to report in Peking. But as long as the Boxers dominated the capital he postponed his departure. He was ready to negotiate for peace, not to help wage war. In early July, when there were signs that his diplomatic skill might be needed, the throne renewed its orders. On July 8 he was reappointed to the key post of governor-general of Chihli, and soon afterward announced that he would leave on the seventeenth.

Hong Kong responded with alarm and indignation. Without Li officials feared that Boxerism would sweep the south. And they were upset by his apparent compliance with a summons from the capital. There, as far as they knew, the unrepentant war party retained control. The Peking legations were still under siege. There was no word from the defenders, and the Western world, panicked by the sudden outburst of antiforeignism, was now ready to believe the worst of the Chinese. On the sixteenth the London *Daily Mail*, relying upon a telegram from a Shanghai correspondent of dubious character, announced that "hordes of fanatical barbarians thirsting for [foreign] blood" had massacred every European man, woman and child in the legations. Even *The Times* was taken in, and on the seventeenth lent its authoritative voice to the chorus of prematurely bereaved Europeans. Demanding "vengeance" for "an outrage without parallel in Western experience," the usually staid *Times* warned against a "universal uprising of the yellow race" and urged a display of force sufficient to deal with the "hordes of northern China." Ten days later Kaiser Wilhelm sounded an even more hysterical note when he bade farewell to his China-bound troops. His foreign minister, Count von Bülow, tried unsuccessfully to censor the speech that exhorted German soldiers to emulate the Huns so "that no Chinese will ever again even dare to look askance at a German."

Soon the world would learn that only seventy-six of the hundreds of besieged foreigners — who included Japanese as well as Europeans — had died. The rest, and several thousand Chinese Christians who had taken refuge with them, owed their lives to the enemy's restraint no less than to their own courage: the order to overwhelm the legations was only halfheartedly executed. As for the vengeance that the West was clamoring for, on the seventeenth the Russians had already exacted a heavy share at Blagoveshchensk on the Russo-Manchurian border. They slaughtered over three thousand Chinese men, women and children, whose bodies floated down the Amur River. This was the beginning. After liberating the legations from the threat of Boxer terror on August 14, the allied expeditionary force, which ultimately numbered forty-five thousand troops from eight nations, would impose its own reign of terror upon the people of Peking and north China.

Meanwhile, in mid-July, at the height of uncertainty and of European apprehensions, Hong Kong pressed for unconventional measures. Governor Blake and his staff wanted to hold Li by force when he passed through the colony on his way north. (Typically, the Kaiser too would later urge that he be captured and held hostage.) But on the seventeenth, the day Li was due, Colonial Secretary Chamberlain forbade any interference with the aged statesman. As it turned out, until he knew for certain that the court wanted peace, and until the powers knew what they wanted, Li was in no rush. After leaving Hong Kong on the eighteenth he sailed to Shanghai, where he stayed for three months before going north to the negotiations with the powers — his last service to China. He died the next year. While in Hong Kong he pleaded for generous treatment of China by the invaders, who had already taken Tientsin and were on their way to the capital. He also hinted that if the powers intended to replace the Manchus with a Chinese dynasty he would not mind becoming emperor. But he showed no sign of wishing to collaborate with southern rebels. Instead, he guaranteed Blake that Canton would remain quiet if the governor repressed agitators in the colony. Thus it was clear that whatever plans Li was considering, Sun Yat-sen did not figure in them.

Sun learned of this while on board his ship, which had arrived in Hong Kong waters at the same time that Li was passing through. Now his choice of options was narrowing. But if K'ang Yu-wei and Li Hung-chang chose to go their own ways, there was still the enticing prospect of latching on to foreign might. Now, as their "avenging" armies were speeding to Peking, Sun, more than at any other time, could expect foreigners to decide the future of China. And when, if not now, could he hope that they would consider an alternative to government by Manchus and mandarins? For a brief period after Li Hung-chang's departure Governor Blake of Hong Kong shared and encouraged these expectations.

But though Blake sympathized with the forces working for change in China, like other Europeans he feared that direct popular action, no matter how accommodating and reasonable its original goals, would ultimately spill over into antiforeignism. Therefore he proposed that Sun's people hold their fire and let the foreign invaders do their work for them. He advised them to petition the powers "in the hope that, when ultimate arrangements are made, their demands will be insisted upon and conceded without the loss of life and property and the general derangement that must follow armed rebellion."

Sun, Yang and other leaders responded by submitting a statement prepared by Ho Kai, who incorporated his favorite Western-inspired political reforms. Claiming to speak for the "People of China" the signatories asked Britain and the other nations to help them change China for the mutual benefit of Chinese and foreigners. They promised to "govern the country righteously," to "get rid of all the corrupt and demoralized officials," and to "take the utmost care of all foreign interests." They proposed to establish a "constitutional central government" headed by a "Ruler President of great respect and popularity." Foreign diplomats would form a "temporary Advisory Board" in the capital and foreign consuls would advise provincial governments. In short, they were again offering foreigners tutelary status in China.

However, despite the exceptional circumstances the offer was no more acceptable to the British than previous ones. On August 18 Blake broached the proposition to Chamberlain and two days later the colonial secretary telegraphed his veto. Even if Sun and K'ang Yu-wei — whose people were also being primed for an uprising — abstained from action, Britain could promise nothing. The governor was ordered to suppress their activities in the colony. And on August 21 British officials were already helping to suppress K'ang's followers in Hankow. The municipal police under their jurisdiction actively cooperated with the moderate governor-general, Chang Chih-tung, when he stamped out the plot that was being organized on behalf of the young emperor. Twenty of the ringleaders were summarily beheaded. Though the unfortunate reformers had made every effort to show goodwill to foreigners, Britain's acting consul-general helped apprehend them because, as he put it, "the overthrow of the constituted authorities would let loose upon us all the disorderly rabble of the three cities [Hankow, Wu-ch'ang, Han-yang], and because the present authorities, who have hitherto striven to maintain order here, are to be preferred to a self-constituted Government of high-sounding aims, but of doubtful experience and ability."

These were the premises of the policy that had throttled Blake's mild flirtation with the revolutionaries and which would continue to favor the "constituted authorities." For imperialism was almost inextricably wedded to the status quo. Obsessed with protecting interests that had been acquired by threat and force the powers instinctively distrusted any release of popular energy and initiative that could lead to changes beyond their control. Moreover, they were too suspicious of each other and too involved in more important arenas of global competition to run the risk of greater commitments in China. Britain, for example, with the largest foreign stake in the country, was so bogged down by the Boers in South Africa that she could only spare Indian troops for the China expeditionary force. The easiest solution for the powers was to support the establishment in China, while in effect they were undermining it. The Boxer settlement was to point up this contradictory role of imperialism.

In September 1901, after months of negotiation and squabbling among themselves, the powers were to saddle the "constituted authorities" — the same Manchus and the same bureaucrats — with a huge indemnity that was determined more by a thirst for revenge than any notion of equity. Amounting to over US$330 million, it more than doubled China's foreign indebtedness. And the burden of annual payments on interest and principal was to be no lighter for those provinces which had abstained from Boxerism. Along with other pillars of the establishment moderates like Chang Chih-tung would have to divert further revenue to foreign creditors, and would have to bear the consequences of increased popular resentment. In effect, by humiliating the "constituted authorities" and by turning them into unwilling agents for foreign bankers, the powers were bringing China closer to revolution. Yet there was hardly much more that foreign interference could accomplish. It could not shore up the establishment indefinitely; and it could never control an indigenous revolution.

But a successful revolution requires an effective organization, and without it, Sun Yat-sen looked for a big, helping hand from abroad. He was still looking in October 1900, when a small, makeshift band of fighters, impatiently waiting for his instructions, was forced into premature action.

The Waichow uprising in eastern Kwangtung, which lasted over two weeks and eventually pitted thousands of peasants against government troops was yet another sign of the latent power of insurgency in the Chinese countryside. This was the second of Sun's attempts at revolution, but it was the first time his fighters actually went into battle and flew the revolutionary flag on Chinese soil.

When it had become clear that neither Li Hung-chang nor the British would provide an alternative, Sun and his friends were left with the independent military option they had been considering since midsummer. The strategy was essentially the same as in Canton in 1895. Triad bands were to form shock troops. Under the direction of leaders of the Society to Restore China's Prosperity, they would seize the Canton nerve center. The key figure in the plot was Cheng Shih-liang, Sun's old friend who was both a Triad member and a Hakka. For several months Cheng lined up Triad notables in his home district in eastern Kwangtung, which was heavily populated by Hakkas — the same sublinguistic group from which the Taiping leadership had originated. This area, in which Waichow was a prefectural capital, was rife with Triads, bandits, smugglers and other unruly elements who were a perennial headache to the authorities. Adding to the volatility of the local population was the resentment caused by the British takeover of part of this area when they extended their Hong Kong holdings in 1898.

Cheng's column was scheduled to create a diversion by drawing loyalist forces from the provincial capital. Canton would then be exposed to a surprise attack led by Sun's recruit from Hawaii, the former planter Teng Yin-nan, who also expected help from converging Triad and bandit gangs. One of the activists in Canton was a new member of the society, Shih Chien-ju, whose recruitment was a sign of the times. Born into a prestigious gentry family, the twenty-one-year-old Shih had become infected with the nationalist fever and looked for foreign learning as a means of contributing to China's salvation. He entered Canton Christian College in 1898. Longing for action, a year later he got in touch with the Canton branch of the East Asian Common Culture Society (Tōa Dōbun Kai), a Japanese pan-Asian project which led him to Sun Yat-sen. Christian converts or products of missionary institutions, like Shih, dominated the leadership circle in Canton, just as converts continued to lead the movement as a whole. Hong Kong, as in the previous plot, was the logistics and fund-raising center. Another new recruit, Li Chi-t'ang, heir to a Hong Kong business fortune, made the biggest contribution, HK$20,000. But not nearly enough money was at hand, and lack of munitions kept delaying the start of the action.

Sun Yat-sen, in the meantime, was working on the Japanese connection. Though the prevailing mood in Tokyo was one of caution — any provocative act was likely to give the Russians an excuse for tightening their grip on Manchuria, the foremost area in Japanese strategic considerations — officials in Taiwan were more adventurous. Rebellion in south China would mesh with their plans for seizing a foothold on the mainland coast opposite Taiwan. In September, while he was in Taipei pursuing this lead, Sun also sent a desperate appeal to Liu Hsüeh-hsün, who was then with Li Hung-chang in Shanghai. In return for a million-dollar contribution Sun was ready to let Liu be "President," even "Emperor," or whatever he wanted to call himself, when the revolution succeeded. Though he hankered for a dynasty Liu doubted whether Sun could sell it to him. Thus another possible trade-off was rejected. Now the success of Sun's strategy depended upon the Japanese.

Meanwhile, the Kwangtung authorities became aware of rebel preparations in the eastern hinterland. Actually, during the long waiting period most of the original band of six hundred fighters recruited by Cheng Shih-liang had gone home. Now his depleted shock force faced encirclement and extermination by the several thousand troops whom the government was cautiously deploying.

Pressed with a telegraphic plea for munitions Sun ordered a temporary dispersal. His instructions arrived too late. On October 6 an eighty-man rebel band, woefully outnumbered and outgunned, routed an advance party of probing loyalist troops. This was the unauthorized yet promising start of the Waichow campaign. Then, the next day fresh instructions from Sun switched the rebel target from Canton, which was west of Cheng's base, to Amoy on the coast in the opposite direction. What had happened was that the Japanese in Taiwan had finally agreed to help with arms, and perhaps a contingent of officers, if Sun's forces got as far as Amoy.

For the next two weeks the improvised army, augmented by thousands of enthusiastic villagers, and armed with captured weapons, kept defeating government troops as it drove through rough terrain that favored guerrilla tactics. But on the twentieth, the insurgents, now numbering ten thousand men with less than two thousand rifles, were finally checked at a point some 150 miles from Amoy. By this time the government had twenty thousand soldiers in the field. Three days later Sun sent a message that abruptly ended the campaign. The Japanese had reneged on their promise. Even if Cheng's army took Amoy, they would not send help. Still not prepared to play a lone hand on the continent, and still worried about the Russians, Tokyo had restrained its impetuous Taiwan officers. Nor was this the only disappointment the Japanese had in store for Sun Yat-sen. After the Philippine project had been aborted he had expected to use the munitions originally earmarked for Aguinaldo's insurgents. Now when he needed them badly he discovered that there had never been any arms cache in Japan. His Japanese agent had embezzled the Filipinos' money.

So Sun's wheeling and dealing during the tumultuous year of the Boxers came to nought. But while wasting energy trying to coax and manipulate extraneous agents, he had, almost inadvertently, tapped for a short time indigenous sources of revolution. Frustrated peasants had massacred Christians and missionaries in other parts of China. In Waichow they marched to a different tune. Here they welcomed an antidynastic movement that blamed their own government for foreign incursions as well as internal misrule. Foreigners, who had expected to see "barbarian hordes" thirsting for Christian and foreign blood, were impressed by the rebels' disciplined demeanor. They studiously stayed clear of missionary stations, and for the most part, refrained from looting villages, which, as foreigners observed, was not usually the case with imperial troops.

In Canton, Shih Chien-ju showed the mettle of that emerging force for revolution, the new breed of gentry-born student nationalists. Hoping to divert pressure from the beleaguered Waichow fighters, he tried to assassinate the highest provincial official, the acting governor-general. On October 28 — actually too late to help the hinterland campaign — he set off an explosion near the governor-general's compound that killed six people but missed his main target. Caught, Shih was beheaded less than two weeks later, despite the appeals of American Presbyterian missionaries.

The Waichow fighters, who had suffered small losses, had in the meantime drifted off into the countryside or fled to Hong Kong. Among those killed by imperial troops was the Japanese who had been Sun Yat-sen's courier. Yamada Yoshimasa, Sun was later to record, was "the first foreigner to lay down his life for the Chinese Republic." Another, and belated, victim was Yang Ch'ü-yün, Sun's former rival and one of the chief organizers of the Waichow rising. On January 19, 1901, a gunman hired by the Canton authorities shot him down while he was teaching an English class in his home in Hong Kong. After Yang's death his former followers broke off from Sun's group. Seven months later the untimely death of

Cheng Shih-liang further reduced the original core of revolutionary plotters and added to Sun's difficulties.

Though Waichow enhanced his reputation for activism, Sun was left without any means of sustaining revolutionary action. Never a coherent organization, his Society to Restore China's Prosperity could not be a suitable vehicle for the new nationalism now sweeping the country.

FOUR

Joining Mainstream Nationalism

IN THE WAKE of the Boxer disaster resistance to reform wilted rapidly. Fearing for national survival, bureaucrats who had balked at radical change in 1898 shed their inhibitions more readily. They found a chastened court in a responsive mood. But the Manchu dynasty, gambling on modernization to save it from falling, faced near impossible odds.

Chinese society was changing in ways that made it less amenable to imperial authority. Given official encouragement, modern learning and modern business and industry made headway and, together with the military buildup, spawned new interests and attitudes that accelerated the erosion of Confucian values. The scholar-gentry, the backbone of the old system, were becoming a more differentiated and restless elite. They began turning out modern investors and entrepreneurs, modern students — both men and women — and, as patriotism dissolved traditional prejudices, even modern army officers.

The weakening of Confucian influence affected the

Manchu dynasty even more severely than would have been the case with a Chinese ruling house. As an alien dynasty it had derived legitimacy largely from its devotion to cultural and institutional orthodoxy. Now it had to satisfy nationalist aspirations. Public opinion, assuming a wider significance in Chinese politics, demanded the "recovery of national rights." Though no government could easily regain what had been lost during the previous half-century, the very reforms the administration authorized inflated nationalist expectations. Nothing illustrated this boomerang effect more dramatically than the overseas student program.

Once they acknowledged the need for change it was natural that Confucian statesmen should give the highest priority to education. Understandable too was the preference for the Japanese path to modern learning, for the use of Japanese textbooks at home and for Japanese schools for overseas training. Conveniently close, Japan had presumably demonstrated how to recover national integrity by combining modern techniques with traditional East Asian values. However, the suitability of the model was illusory. A different tradition and different historical circumstances had enabled an already-changing Japanese society to quickly mount an effective nationalist response to the European challenge, which in any case, concentrated more on China. The new Japanese oligarchy, the product of a shift within the ruling class, used reform to strengthen centralized government. In China, where reform came too late, it bred revolution.

Chinese students, many with traditional literati backgrounds, flocked to Tokyo after the turn of the century. About half were subsidized — either by their provincial governments or Peking. During the peak year, 1906, at least ten thousand, perhaps twice as many, arrived. Most got superficial training in special "diploma mills"; a small minority studied in reputable institutions. And most were originally more interested in getting jobs in the government than in overturning it. Yet few remained indifferent to politics. Even students with a bit of foreign learning tended to lose respect for traditional leaders who lacked it entirely, yet who nonetheless admitted its crucial importance.

In Tokyo students became more aware of China's miserable status and less willing to accept it. They envied Japan's place in the world and admired the militant patriotism of the Japanese people. Drawing facile analogies from Japanese and European history, student nationalists looked for heroic leaders to restore China's dignity rapidly. But compared to Japan's "men of determination," and to the George Washingtons and Mazzinis of the West, China's leaders, despite their stiffening attitude toward imperialism, seemed like gray and prosaic plodders. Who then could kindle a new Chinese spirit and take the nation on a great leap toward international equality? In 1903, when there were over a thousand students in Tokyo, scores of activists claimed that role for themselves.

That year marked a sharp rise in nationalist sensitivity. Actual or perceived threats to Chinese rights, and insults to Chinese pride, provoked feverish responses. In particular, Russia's brutal stand on Manchuria prompted a nationalist demand for action that contrasted sharply with the government's limited ability to act.

In April the Russians suddenly reneged on previous commitments to remove troops that had been occupying southern Manchuria since the Boxer troubles. Now they demanded exorbitant concessions as the price for leaving. Not only China but Japan felt menaced. But it was exactly against this threat that the Anglo-Japanese Alliance of the previous year had been designed. It checked third-party interference and cleared the way for the showdown with Russia that the Japanese public was clamoring for. As war fever mounted in Japan, Chinese students took up the "Resist Russia" theme. Over five

hundred attended an hysterical meeting in Tokyo in May
1903. Orators — notably students sent to study in Japanese military academies — shouted for a "do or die" determination to fight for the Chinese people — but not for
the Manchu dynasty. More than 130 volunteered for active duty in a student army. Women students signed on as
nurses.

Next, a delegation returned to China with the offer to
help roll back the Russians. The mission did not even
earn a hearing. Peking was trying to save Manchuria
through diplomatic and political means; anything
stronger would have risked disaster. On the other hand,
student militancy, with its subversive undercurrents, was
a more immediate, yet still manageable threat. Counter-
moves, like getting the Japanese to outlaw the students'
"army," hardened the impression that the government
feared popular initiatives more than foreign invaders.
Elsewhere, too, nationalists were coming to believe that
revolution was the essential first step toward mobilizing
resistance to imperialism.

The overseas agitators were in close touch with intellectuals in Shanghai. There, modern schools and the relative immunity of the International Settlement and the
French Concession had produced a second cradle for militant nationalism. Shanghai was also China's major commercial center. But the merchants and gentry who were
among the sponsors of large anti-Russian demonstrations
backed off when radical intelligentsia exploited the issue
to agitate for revolution. These radicals, who followed
the Tokyo example and formed the Volunteer Corps to
Resist Russia, made their greatest impact as journalists.

The Chinese press was now enjoying what Lin Yutang
called its "Golden Period." Since 1895 dozens of periodicals and newspapers appeared, notably in Shanghai, the
hub of the new publishing industry, which also featured
translations from Japanese. Most news was bad news and
embarrassed the government. Then, during the inflam-

matory crisis of 1903, the Shanghai radicals started a propaganda war against the Manchu dynasty. That year they published several revolutionary pamphlets and no less than three revolutionary dailies.

The most famous of the newspapers was *Su-pao*. At the end of May it took a brazenly seditious line and poured invective on the Manchus, including the emperor. A month later the government persuaded the foreign authorities of the International Settlement to intervene. The paper was suppressed and its most audacious contributor, Chang Ping-lin, was arrested and held for trial by the Settlement's Mixed Court. Now in his early thirties, Chang was a brilliant classical scholar, one of a number who had switched allegiance from reform to revolution. He had been a leading anti-Manchu firebrand in Tokyo.

The Chinese government also tried to settle accounts with Tsou Jung. Only eighteen years old, Tsou had that year written what was to become the most famous revolutionary tract — *The Revolutionary Army*. It was reprinted a number of times, and hundreds of thousands of copies eventually reached Chinese throughout the world. As in so many other cases, study in Japan and translations from Japanese had enriched Tsou's knowledge of Western ideas. Reading Mazzini, Carlyle, Mill, Montesquieu, Rousseau, and "some Herbert Spencer" had helped convert him to revolution. He and Chang were found guilty of seditious libel, though the foreign imperialists handed out much lighter punishments than those the Chinese government had had in mind. Chang was released from prison in 1906, and Tsou died in the spring of 1905, just a few weeks before his scheduled release.

After the widely publicized *Su-pao* affair, which chagrined the government, the radicals continued to fire vitriolic barbs from their sanctuary in Shanghai. Another revolutionary daily lasted for several months and in December 1903 was followed by a third, the *Russian Affairs*

Alarm, which dealt almost exclusively with the danger to Manchuria. In Japan, too, student scribes were working overtime.

In addition to a powerful revolutionary tract, *New Hunan*, which was inspired by Japanese interest in Russian nihilism, four new student magazines appeared in 1903. Like earlier periodicals they catered in the first instance to student provincial groups and contained many translations from Japanese; these, in turn, were often based upon original German, French and English versions. Most magazines did not last more than several months, but issues were frequently reprinted. Thousands of copies reached the mainland, where modern schools were creating an ever-widening reading public. Though, like the periodicals at home, not all student journals were overtly revolutionary, the focus on modern ideas and current events stimulated radical thinking.

All these publications — books, pamphlets and periodicals that were being churned out in Tokyo and Shanghai — showed how the latest heirs to the Confucian tradition were striving to join the mainstream of world history. Democracy and constitutionalism were popular subjects if for no other reason than that they belonged to the modern trend in politics with which the students wanted to identify. Socialism, even while Chinese capitalism was still emerging from infancy, also began attracting attention. But what undoubtedly made the most potent contribution to revolutionary convictions was the haunting fear of imperialism.

In language charged with emotion student commentators gave imperialism full treatment. They discussed various explanations for its origins — racial competition, greed, lust for conquest, surplus population, and the expanding needs of industrial and financial capitalism. They displayed its brutal results — the direct subjugation or economic enslavement of entire races or nations (the terms, as derived from Japanese, were the same). They cited recent examples — the Philippines and South Africa (where at this time the Boers and not the blacks rated sympathy as victims). And they were certain of its next target.

As they unraveled the record, every aspect of Europe's involvement in China — trade, religion, loans, indemnities, leased territories, and so on — seemed to fit in with a scheme for domination that was reaching its final stage. They warned that few other areas of the globe were still available. And as for the white man's claim to a civilizing mission, they pointed to his plunder of Peking. His complete mastery over China, they concluded, could be checked only by the awakening of Chinese nationalism.

The Social Darwinist perspective, popular then in Japan, gave a strong racial twist to the student understanding of nationalism. According to this view it was as a racial unit, imbued with a spirit of shared destiny, that a modern nation achieved the cohesiveness, the adaptability, and the toughness required for survival. Obviously, this was a view that made it easier to blame alien rulers for China's weakness. That the overthrow of the Manchus was the key to recovery and resistance to imperialism was a seductive argument. Yet it was none other than the foremost expounder of the imperialist danger who tried to refute it.

Liang Ch'i-ch'ao had resumed his journalistic career in Japan in 1898. While in exile he became the most important writer of the post-Boxer decade. No one had a greater intellectual impact upon the new student generation. Based upon Japanese sources but infused with original interpretations, Liang's encyclopedic writings — notably in his magazines, the *Journal of Disinterested Criticism* and its successor, the *New Citizen Journal* — examined the pertinence of the ideas and the social and political processes that shaped modern civilization. Among other topics he analyzed the economic mainsprings of modern imperialism, nationalism, Social Darwinism, socialism, and the ideals and institutions of democracy. For several years he veered close to the anti-Manchu position.

But in 1903, when support for revolution was gaining ground, Liang took a gradualist stand. He feared that revolution would not only open the door to foreign invaders, but would impede the modernization which he saw as the effective response to imperialism. Blaming obsolete institutions rather than the Manchus for China's troubles, he called for popular enlightenment, and he considered constitutional monarchy a reasonable political goal. Ultimately, Liang's main contribution was in introducing criteria for diagnosing China's crisis. He had less success with his prescriptive program. The Manchu government still considered him an enemy and his proposed constitutional reforms too radical. And his student disciples wanted a more dramatic solution. Increasingly, they felt the need for the emotional satisfaction which Liang feared would be the sole reward of an anti-Manchu upheaval. This trend gave Sun Yat-sen the biggest opportunity that had thus far come his way.

However, winning even the conditional approval of radical, gentry-born intelligentsia was not easy. Though he lived in nearby Yokohama Sun had only tenuous contact with the early waves of overseas students who reached Tokyo. Mistrust was mutual.

It was not only gentry prejudice against a lower-class product of missionary schooling that worked against him. Sun had no intellectual credentials, no writings and no sophisticated ideology with which to impress youth who had so much faith in the power of words and ideas. Exaggerating his lack of classical training, some students accused him of being illiterate in Chinese. While his activist record could not be denied, to many it merely projected the image of an "uncultured outlaw." The few who met him face to face were more favorably impressed, but Sun, in common with many professional revolutionaries, still had doubts about the reliability of intellectuals, whose fickleness and snobbery he had already experienced. At the end of 1900, when students in their early twenties began taking an interest in radical ideas, Sun at thirty-four already had two revolutionary conspiracies and a dramatic escape in London to his credit. For the next few years he preferred plying familiar routes rather than plunging into the theoretical discussions that occupied students and émigré intellectuals.

In Yokohama, where he enjoyed the companionship of a Japanese mistress, Sun passed the time uneventfully. He read up on military strategy and especially on the Boer War. He apparently hoped to apply Boer guerrilla tactics in his next campaign but was short of money. His overseas resources, which were being successfully raided by his rivals, K'ang Yu-wei and Liang, supplied only the bare minimum. However, by the end of 1902 he was on the move again, this time in search of French support for a projected invasion of south China from Tongking. Renewing contact with the French minister in Tokyo, Sun received an introduction to officials in Indochina. He passed through Hong Kong, where he collected HK$1,000 from a friendly businessman, and reached Hanoi in February 1903. Though he again promised the French preferential rights if he succeeded in establishing a revolutionary regime in south China, they once more vetoed the use of the colony as a rebel springboard. Sun stayed in Indochina for six months. All he could show for the lengthy visit was the recruitment of eight *hua-ch'iao* — including three tailors — who formed the Hanoi branch of the Society to Restore China's Prosperity. In the meantime the young intellectuals were creating nationalist storm centers in Tokyo and Shanghai. When he returned to Japan that summer Sun began giving them more serious attention.

Now, too, more students visited him in Yokohama, and some urged him to form a new organization. He was still not ready, but since the Manchu government had stopped private students from attending Japanese military academies, Sun decided to set up a secret military school of his own. Helped by Japanese officers — one of them a specialist on the Boer War — he offered an eight-month course on military science and the manufacture of arms. Only fourteen or fifteen students — predominantly fellow Cantonese — enrolled, and the school, opened in the summer of 1903, closed after several months. Nevertheless this was a beginning of an approach to a new audience.

Although the oath administered to his cadets incorporated the principles of the Society to Restore China's Prosperity, it was more explicitly republican. He also added a new plank — "equalization of land rights." This slogan expressed for the first time his idea of a preventive social revolution that had apparently been germinating since his visit to the West in 1896–97.

It was also time for a contribution to the booming nationalist press. In November 1903 he published a short essay, "On the Preservation or Dismemberment of China," in the Tokyo student journal *Chiang-su*. Addressing Chinese readers for the first time since he had written to Li Hung-chang in 1894, Sun revealed strong anti-imperialist feelings that until now had only been shared privately with friends like Miyazaki. When appealing for European support Sun blamed Manchu obscurantism for depriving China of the purported benefits of foreign trade, religion and investment. Now, adjusting to the student wavelength, he accused the Manchus of selling out China to foreigners. He praised the Boxers' spirit and condemned the late Li Hung-chang — whose patronage and partnership he had sought — for having failed to drive out the foreign invaders. But if the Manchus and "Han traitors" who served them were incapable of defending China, Sun was confident that once aroused, the people themselves would foil any attempt to partition the country. He warned would-be partitioners — both Europeans and Japanese — that the Chinese, no less stubborn than Boers and Filipinos, were too numerous to be subdued.

Yet he claimed that foreigners were not necessarily imperialists. Many Europeans, he said, admired the character of the Chinese people, and Japanese Sinophiles realized that "preservation of China means self-preservation." Much depended, he indicated, upon what policies China pursued. And what was his own policy? He promised to explain later. Before bidding for leadership of the student movement Sun wanted to build up his assets overseas where the hope of finding *hua-ch'iao* money and friendly foreigners never ceased to attract him.

Arriving in Hawaii in the fall of 1903 he discovered that Liang Ch'i-ch'ao, who had visited the Islands earlier, had blurred the distinction between reform and revolution and had stolen his following. In responding Sun revealed a hitherto untapped talent for political debate — and no lack of demagogic style. He addressed large *hua-ch'iao* audiences and also used the press to argue the merits of a republic as against those of constitutional monarchy. When China imports locomotives, Sun contended, she does not choose the earliest but the latest models. Why then in choosing a new political structure should she reject the newest model — a republic — and settle for constitutional monarchy? A people capable of destroying absolute monarchy, he said, could easily go a step further. As for the fear of foreign intervention, he claimed that the very act of revolting would earn international respect: "If the people . . . could rise and overthrow the worthless . . . Manchu government, every country would respect us." Echoing student pamphleteers he accused the Manchus of pacifying the country on behalf of foreigners and of presenting them with large chunks of Chinese territory.

Six months of campaigning brought only "several tens" of new recruits. Since the Society to Restore China's Prosperity was beyond rehabilitation, Sun inducted them into the "Chinese Revolutionary Army" and had them sign the same written oath that he used for his cadets in Japan.

For the first time in seven years he had a chance to be with his family. Though his brother was still taking care of their mother and Sun's wife and three children on Maui, he had suffered financial losses and could no longer bankroll Sun's political activities. Sun now had to depend more on the sale of "patriotic bonds" — redeemable after the revolution at ten times their purchase price — and other fund-raising devices, such as peddling Japanese silk.

While in the Islands, Sun joined the local branch of the Triads, hoping that this would give him leverage with the Cantonese in the United States. In order to ease his way past the American immigration authorities, whose ruthless enforcement of Chinese exclusion laws was notorious, he prepared affidavits ostensibly proving that he had been born in Hawaii.

Sun arrived in San Francisco in early April 1904, and was detained a few weeks until his credentials passed muster in Washington. Next came seven months of frustration. Deprived of basic civil liberties — including the right to become naturalized American citizens — the *hua-ch'iao* may have felt like "men without a country," and many were probably exhilarated by Sun's confident platform manner and his promise of a powerful home government to protect their interests. But their commitment to revolution and willingness to risk reprisals against their families fell far short of his expectations. Even a dollar or two from each of the seventy or eighty thousand Triad members would have brought in a sizable sum. Instead, he raised US$4,000 in the San Francisco Bay area — where a Chinese professor at the University of California gave him strong support — and then spent it all on a fruitless coast-to-coast tour accompanied by the titular head of the secret society. He was practically penniless when he reached New York in December. His old friend, the medical missionary Dr. Hager, visited him at a Chinatown Christian mission and noted the absence of Sun's customary bounce and optimism.

While in New York he met Chinese students, among them Wang Ch'ung-hui, whose father, a Cantonese Christian pastor, was an old friend. Now a student at Yale Law School, the younger Wang helped Sun write a pamphlet, *The True Solution of the Chinese Question.* This was Sun's first appeal to Americans.

As in previous statements to both Chinese and Europeans Sun maintained that an anti-Manchu revolution would benefit the West as well as China. For obvious reasons he dropped the militantly nationalist line he had been taking with Chinese audiences. The Manchus, therefore, were no longer weak-kneed appeasers of foreigners but progenitors of the antiforeign spirit that "culminated in the Boxer trouble." And the United States was not the imperialist conqueror of the Philippines but one of China's "nearest neighbors," with legitimate commercial interests in the East. A Chinese revolution, Sun argued, would serve these interests and also be in accord with American sentiments. Though he claimed that revolution was imminent, and was the exclusive responsibility of the Chinese people, he asked for sympathy and support from the civilized world in general and from the United States in particular "because you are the pioneers of Western civilization in Japan; because you are a Christian nation; because we intend to model our new government after yours; and above all, because you are the champions of liberty and democracy. We hope we may find many Lafayettes among you." The pamphlet, printed in ten thousand copies, had no greater impact than previous appeals to foreigners.

At this time, when Sun's one-man campaign had come

to a standstill, the student revolutionary movement likewise stalled. In 1904 returned students and intellectuals, who in the previous year had formed a subversive organization in the middle Yangtze Valley province of Hunan, failed in their attempt to launch an uprising with the help of secret societies and army officers. In the Shanghai and lower Yangtze Valley region a separate organization of student revolutionaries was still too feeble to do much on its own. The time was ripe for a coordinated effort under an experienced leader. Sun Yat-sen was not only available, but had no other hope of extending his political life. At the end of the year he readily accepted an invitation from student militants in Europe.

In London, his first stop, Sun had a revealing exchange with Yen Fu, the pioneer translator and interpreter of Western ideas and the leading Chinese apostle of Social Darwinism. In the last decade of the previous century he had been in the forefront of the intellectual transformation that had affected Liang Ch'i-ch'ao and other progressive literati. But now, in his early fifties, Yen was even more opposed to revolution than Liang, though his relative conservatism was rooted in very modern, nontraditional thinking. Because he was firmly committed to Western models, and specifically to that of England (he had studied there in the 1870s), he rejected the notion of a unique stage-skipping timetable for China's progress. When he told Sun Yat-sen that the Chinese people were not yet ready for a republican revolution because their "knowledge is at a low state," Sun replied, "How long can a man wait for the [Yellow] river to clear? You, sir, are a thinker, I am a man of action."

Action was also what students wanted, and none more so than several hotheads from the central Yangtze Valley region. They had been sent to Europe because the authorities wanted them as far from home as possible. In early 1905, when Sun was staying with British friends in London, the students sent him money for a trip to the continent. Meeting with them first in Brussels, he spoke on nationalism, democracy and socialism, and unveiled a plan for China's future constitutional system. The students had no serious objections to Sun's program. But they did object, and quite strongly, to his proposal for revolutionary strategy.

Whenever he courted potential supporters or allies, Sun made extravagant claims for his other prospects. In this instance he extolled the fighting qualities of the secret societies, whom he said were the best bet for building revolutionary power. The students, however, pointed out that lower-class fighters had proved unreliable in the past, and insisted upon giving priority to their own people, some of whom were already infiltrating the modern army. Eventually Sun agreed that intellectuals were fit to lead the revolution, and that they would be the main target for political agitation. This was presumably what he had already had in mind, but by feigning reluctance hoped to deflate student self-estimations and enhance his bargaining position.

On this basis he became the leader of a "revolutionary party" consisting of sixty recruits in Brussels, Paris and Berlin (altogether there were only about one hundred students in the three countries). Sun had them swear loyalty to his four-plank program, but postponed the choice of a formal name for the organization until the main body of overseas students in Tokyo could be consulted. Then, before he left Europe, he was once more victimized by the capriciousness of intellectuals: all but fourteen of his new recruits had second thoughts and withdrew. Still, the handful of Hupeh extremists who remained loyal recommended him to their friends in Tokyo. There, Sun realized, his ability to impress non-Cantonese, intellectual enthusiasts of revolution would face the crucial test. Meanwhile he intensified his efforts to cultivate international goodwill.

In the spring of 1905 he visited the secretariat of the

Socialist International in Brussels and apparently sold its leaders a fictitious account of the Chinese "socialist movement" and an astonishing analysis of China's social structure. An organ of the Second International subsequently described him as the "chief of the Chinese Revolutionary Socialist Party" whose aim was "to build a new society *without any transition.*" This was possible, it was reported, because according to "Comrade Sen" there were no significant class distinctions in China: "There are few poor people . . . but there are even fewer who are really rich," only a "few or no great landowners." Sun also said that Chinese guilds were already socialist. But his most preposterous claim was that "there are 54 socialist journals in Chinese."

While wooing socialists Sun did not neglect the other end of the political spectrum. In Paris he visited the Ministry of Foreign Affairs twice and revived proposals made earlier to French officials in the Far East. This time he offered to help counteract the growing influence of Japan, which was then trouncing France's ally, Russia, in the war that had begun the previous year. Japan, he said, had lost interest in his movement. He was therefore willing to let France replace her as his major patron. The Quai d'Orsay was still skeptical and made no commitments, but some French intelligence officers welcomed the prospect of using Chinese revolutionaries to keep track of the ubiquitous Japanese.

Thus Sun saw the Russo-Japanese War as an opportunity to diversify the search for foreign help. The war also fortified his faith in the ultimate validity of pan-Asianism. Twenty years later he still remembered being struck by the contrast between Western and Eastern reactions to Japan's success. When Admiral Tōgō annihilated a Russian fleet at Tsushima in May 1905, Europeans were shocked. Some were fearful for the future of the white race. Sun found this was true of many Englishmen, despite the Anglo-Japanese Alliance. "As the English saying

goes," he remarked, " 'Blood is thicker than water.' "
And later, when his steamer passed through the Suez
Canal on the way to Japan, an encounter with Arab laborers revealed the war's exhilarating effect on Eastern
nationalism. Never before in modern times had Asians
defeated a European power, and the Arabs, at first mis-
taking Sun for a Japanese, made a fuss over him. Japan's
victory, they said, was a triumph for all the colored peoples of the non-Western world. Now they were more confident of eventually throwing off Western domination.

Further east, of course, the war's repercussions were
even more pronounced. Nehru recorded the exuberance
of young Indian nationalists. And though Japan's own
continental policy was not above suspicion, her prestige
among Chinese was never greater.

Thus Sun's endorsement by Japanese pan-Asianists at
this particular time was important for building a bridge
to student nationalists. His close friend, Miyazaki Torazō,
whose autobiography — first published in 1902 and translated into Chinese a year later — had already drawn favorable attention to Sun by dramatizing their joint
adventures, was his chief lobbyist. And influential student leaders probably trusted Miyazaki more than any
other Japanese. On July 19, 1905, the day Sun arrived in
Yokohama, he was in Tokyo singing Sun's praises. He
portrayed Sun as a peerless leader whose international
fame would bring credit to the revolution. Soon afterward he introduced Sun to the key people, including
Huang Hsing and Sung Chiao-jen, leaders of the all-
important Hunan group. The two, who had climbed the
first rung of the traditional scholarly ladder before turning to revolution, did not have to be convinced of the
need for a wider combination of antidynastic forces.
(The Hunanese plot had failed the previous year.) But
should Sun be the unifier? These first, crucial meetings —
where the presence of Miyazaki and another of Sun's
Japanese confidants gave him moral support — focused on

the strategy of revolution rather than its terminal goals. Sun did most of the talking and stressed the unity theme. Separate revolutionary risings, he warned, would invite internal chaos and that most dreaded of disasters — foreign intervention. But he was confident that a united effort would ensure a smooth transition and keep foreigners at bay. As in Europe he made the most of his secret-society connections but once more agreed to give primacy to intellectuals. They were needed, he said, to exert a "civilizing" influence upon the Triads' "destructive" tendencies.

The Hunanese leaders went into a huddle to consider Sun's call for a merger. Failing to reach a consensus, they decided to let individual members of their Revive China Society choose for themselves. But the overriding urge for concerted action was working in Sun's favor. "Revolution means conspiracy," a pro-Sun student had argued earlier, and no one else matched Sun's experience and versatility in practicing the conspiratorial vocation. As for his rhetorical skill, this would soon be demonstrated by the enthrallment of large student audiences.

The next day, July 30, seventy student militants representing seventeen of the China's eighteen provinces — Kansu had not sent any students abroad — gathered to hear Sun's plea for a new organization. The meeting took place in the premises of the most important Japanese ultranationalist organization — the Black Dragon (Amur River) Society. Among other reasons for encouraging revolution in China, the society hoped that the overthrow of the Manchus would leave a vacuum in Manchuria and enable Japan to create a continental boundary on the Amur River. Uchida Ryōhei, who had founded the society in 1901, was one of Sun's active collaborators. The venue of the meeting, plus the presence of Uchida, Miyazaki and another Japanese adventurer, supplied conspicuous confirmation of Sun's Japanese connection.

The Hunanese leaders now gave unequivocal support

and Sun's motion carried the day. It was decided to form the Chinese Alliance (Chung-kuo T'ung Meng Hui). (The official name in English was "The China Federal Association.") Following the procedure adopted in Europe, individual members pledged loyalty to Sun's four aims — "expulsion of the Manchus, restoration of Chinese rule, the establishment of a republic, and equalization of land rights." The election of officers was scheduled for the next meeting, when the Alliance was to be formally launched. However, Sun had already broken through the literati ostracism that had kept him on the fringe of Chinese politics during the first decade of his career. The news that well-known student leaders had endorsed him sent ripples of excitement throughout the community. On August 13 hundreds crowded into a Japanese restaurant to hear his first major speech to the Tokyo students.

Sun rose to the occasion and, with a slap at the apostles of gradualism, exhorted his audience not to sell China short. He spoke of the country's unmatched potential for greatness — a vast area containing the world's largest population, and a rich culture that for thousands of years had been the envy of the world. Though China had temporarily fallen behind, there was no reason, he said, why she could not once more surpass Europe, America and Japan. He belittled the foreign threat. Though foreigners were itching to "carve China up like a melon," they "trembled with fear" at the slightest sign of popular resistance. But he did not anticipate a head-on clash with imperialism. It would be sufficient, he said, for the Chinese to demonstrate their renewed vitality by overthrowing the Manchus. Foreigners would then quietly shelve their designs for aggression. What was essential, however, was the leadership of "men of determination." In the past he was alone; now the students were joining him. And how should they plan the nation's future?

Repeating his locomotive analogy Sun urged them to choose a republic — the newest and best of political models. Other countries, he declared, had undergone "natural progress," but China, progressing "artificially," could achieve in twenty or even fifteen years what had taken Japan thirty. Here was an early adumbration of the "great leap" concept that would be so dear to Mao Tsetung. The assertion that prescient leaders, armed with a blueprint of the future, could modernize China quickly appealed to the students' elitist predilections as well as their nationalism. With his extreme voluntarism and insistence that China was a special case, Sun caught their mood more accurately than the reformers did. By projecting the pace of Chinese progress according to universal, rational criteria, the reformers offered the grim prospect of continuing to lag behind others. Sun held that an enlightened elite could transcend social and cultural obstacles, ignore precedents from world history, and restore China's claim to preeminence. This came out clearly in his peroration:

Everything can be managed by men of determination. They will introduce what the ordinary people do not understand. If their thoughts are elevated the qualifications of the ordinary people will be elevated. . . . It is incumbent upon us as men of determination to choose the most civilized form of government in the world. . . . If in one transformation we can stir people's hearts, civilization will come in a hurry, and in only ten years the word "independence" will as a matter of course be stamped on people's brains. . . . In the future every country will want to come and learn from China. . . . We are determined not to follow evolutionary change, but insist upon artificial change with its faster progress. I want you gentlemen to save China by choosing from the top.

Sun made a big hit, and again, Miyazaki and another Japanese "man of determination" were on hand to endorse him.

A week later, on August 20, the Alliance was officially established when over three hundred students met at the home of a Japanese politician who had interests in Chinese coal mines. Sun was elected head (*tsung-li*), and Huang Hsing, who drafted the organization's regulations, became his second in command. The head office in Tokyo was to have three departments whose names were evocative of the branches of the American government. Having already enrolled several hundred students representing almost every province in China, the leaders planned on creating branches throughout the mainland. They also decided that *Twentieth Century China*, a recently formed student magazine, mainly under Hunanese auspices, would be their organ.

Thus China's first multiprovincial, "modern" political party was born. It had a rudimentary organization, an ideology, and a program for propaganda and action. As a political organization it was much more formidable than Sun's earlier, makeshift combination of Cantonese rebels. The students who formed the Alliance did not have their social roots in treaty ports and missionary institutions but in well-placed families from the interior of China. That Sun Yat-sen, the longtime outcast, was suddenly able to heave himself to the top of this student movement was a remarkable personal achievement. It was also an achievement that reflected the fears and inhibitions, as well as the impatience, of the young nationalists.

Actually, Sun brought little of tangible value to the Alliance. In what was ostensibly a merger of separate groups, the others, from the central and lower Yangtze Valley regions, contributed much more. Only a few members came from Sun's Society to Restore China's Prosperity. (Yet the three Japanese admitted to membership, Miyazaki, Hirayama Shū and Kayano Chōchi, were his personal followers.) Nor did Sun make any significant ideological contribution. Nationalism and republicanism were already winning slogans. Though sympathy for socialism — or more precisely, a distaste for laissez-faire capitalism — was evident, Sun's particular formula for achieving socialism, which was his only original programmatic contribution, was least acceptable to the students, who were not quite sure what "equalization of land rights" meant. Though Sun improved his image and showed that there was more to him than the artful conspirator, he did not entirely dispel the old doubts about his learning. He was a moving speaker, and his optimistic and resolute bearing could be infectious, but he did not command intellectual authority. The new intelligentsia — who carried over some of the prejudices of the old — valued him more for his reputed expertise in managing a revolution than for his ideas. He was the senior revolutionary, and supposedly adept at harnessing secret society fighters and overseas wealth. He was also sure that he could steer the revolution clear of foreign gunboats.

Given the obsessive fear of imperialism, this was an important consideration. The young nationalists had decided to postpone the reckoning with their external enemies until after they had overthrown the Manchus and achieved internal consolidation. What was needed, as the scholar Chang Ping-lin had already argued in 1903, was a quick takeover that would avoid giving foreigners an excuse for intervening. And if foreigners had to be temporarily placated, Sun Yat-sen's presumed dexterity in handling them was considered a crucial asset. Who else had traveled so widely and worked so hard at winning foreign approval, and who seemed better able to neutralize the foreign threat? Even so, Sun's accommodative nationalism and his readiness to co-opt foreigners would not always go down well with the tougher-minded, mainstream nationalists who joined him in the Alliance.

Sun's status as leader, therefore, was definitely qualified. His was largely an instrumental or conditional type of leadership. He had to deliver the quick and easy results he had promised. And with its leader mainly a functionary, the Alliance lacked the unity and discipline of a truly transcendent party that becomes "an end in itself, instead of remaining in the domain of ways and means." Thus it would have trouble enough trying to fight the dynasty, let alone replace it.

FIVE

The Revolution of 1911

WHILE THE REVOLUTIONARIES were getting organized in Tokyo, post-Boxer reformism entered a swifter, telescoped phase. For the second time in a decade a demonstration of Japanese military might stimulated change in China. The defeat of Russia — which took place on Chinese territory — was seen as proof that constitutional government was stronger than autocratic. In 1905 the court authorized a study of foreign constitutions. Next, that same year, came the momentous decision to abolish the traditional civil service examinations. This removed the main prop of the Confucian system and weakened the incentive for studying the classics. Though the shortage of funds, teachers and texts affected its quality, modern education expanded faster. The government encouraged private contributions for education and the practice of converting religious property into schools. Officials also sent more students to Japan. There, as at home, the new learning continued to kindle subversive ideas (they also flowed from Russia — the revolution of 1905 excited intellectuals throughout Asia). However, student revolutionaries were not the only threat to dynastic integrity. Nationalism and modernization generated pressures that without being overtly revolutionary whittled away at the center's authority. Though established through Peking's initiative, chambers of commerce became instruments of gentry and merchant power in the provinces and, like other new local institutions, reinforced the long-growing trend toward regionalism. Regionalism was also a vehicle for nationalism. Local leaders stepped to the forefront of the struggle to recover sovereign rights.

Not that Peking was indifferent. Foreign diplomats and business promoters found that the spirit of post-Boxer nationalism also animated official policy. But the government was too tightly shackled by foreign debts and too weak militarily to push the rights recovery movement as hard as nationalists demanded. The anti-American boycott, launched in the summer of 1905, illustrated Peking's dilemma.

Provoked by renewal of discriminatory immigration laws — which now applied to the Philippines and Hawaii as well as the United States proper — students and merchants led China's first antiforeign boycott. A Shanghai merchant expressed the mood shared by many coolies and uprooted peasants who were the main victims of anti-Chinese exclusion laws: "When our government proves itself unable to protest . . . the people must . . . do so." The people maintained the boycott for over six months. The government, pressured by the Americans, helped bring it to an end.

Antiforeign incidents mounted. The powers blamed Peking and resorted to gunboat diplomacy. This further provoked nationalist anger against the foreigners and the dynasty they intimidated.

But while nationalism drew broad, multiclass support, the reform efforts that it stimulated mainly served the elite and antagonized the masses. Pushed by modern, urbanized gentry, who still had links to the traditional landlord sector, the reform program tilted heavily in favor of the already rich and powerful. It meant little to the peasants — except higher taxes and rent, which in some cases were not even invested in reform but simply lined the pockets of "bad gentry."

Educational reform catered chiefly to children of the same gentry or of established families that produced overseas students. The new schools, whose location favored town dwellers, were usually too expensive for the masses. In any case, the peasants did not always see the advantages of modern learning. For many it still bore the stigma of imperialism, under whose auspices it had first been introduced. The new schools sometimes provoked rioting, especially when temples or monasteries were taken over. Nor did other reforms send peasants into raptures of joy. Self-government organs were dominated by local elites, and modern police and military forces were busier protecting elite interests than in resisting foreign enemies.

It was clear that China was changing (much to the astonishment of foreigners, who never believed it possible). It was also clear that the gentry were the big winners—and at the expense of the masses as well as the central government.

Rural conditions had long been deteriorating as a result of land hunger. They worsened more rapidly as Confucian moral norms and central bureaucratic controls became less effective in checking the predatory habits of landlords and usurers. Absentee landlordism, more prevalent as commercial opportunities lured gentry to the cities, hardened the terms of rural tenancy. And economic development, which was being carried out without concern for peasant welfare, aggravated rural poverty. Modern domestic industry and foreign imports crippled rural handicraft industries, the traditional supplement to agriculture.

This combination of new and old causes of rural distress brought a sharp increase in banditry, rioting and secret-society uprisings. Usually directed against the gentry and local authorities, spontaneous peasant outbreaks did not directly threaten the dynasty. But they strained its dwindling financial resources and further damaged what was left of its prestige. Moreover, ferment in the countryside was accompanied by urban unrest.

Though growing, industry could not nearly absorb all the refugees from village poverty who poured into the cities. Unemployment and brutal labor conditions — evocative of the worst abuses of the early industrial revolution in Europe — spread misery and disorder. As in nineteenth-century Europe, old-style artisans and manual laborers resented the machines that displaced them. And they resented the foreigners who introduced the machines. For where the Chinese experience was different was in the close connection between economic and nationalist grievances.

Having won the right to engage in manufacturing in the treaty ports after the Sino-Japanese War of 1894–95, foreigners now controlled a large share of the modern industrial sector, which included the textile and other light industries, public utilities, mining, shipping and railways. As a result, the modern Chinese working class, though small, poorly organized, and lacking a strong class consciousness, responded quickly to nationalist agitation. Strikes, usually triggered by political issues, broke out more frequently.

Sun Yat-sen's Alliance accordingly made its appearance at a time of rising potential for revolution. There was a power drain at the center of government, disaffection among intellectuals, and a readiness for desperate action among the masses. As this situation unfolded, there were two tasks for the revolutionary movement. The first was to speed up the collapse of the incumbent government by inciting and exploiting outbreaks of violence. The second and more important was to prepare itself for becoming an alternative government. While the Alliance had some success in meeting the first challenge, it failed badly with the second.

Lacking a total commitment to its leader at the outset, the organization never achieved the cohesiveness required for a sustained drive to power. Nor did the shift from the Society to Restore China's Prosperity to the more sophisticated Alliance cause a substantial change in Sun's style: he still bet on extraorganizational forces for sparking an antidynastic chain reaction. In October 1905 he went abroad to resume the search for money and foreign allies, while in Tokyo the two-month-old Alliance rested on a shaky foundation that perpetuated regional loyalties.

Rather than Sun himself, the provincial recruiters he appointed exercised authority over individual members. These recruiters became increasingly independent, and the students, who were scattered throughout Tokyo, associated mostly with fellow provincials. They had little to do with the head office, which would itself be immobilized for long stretches when Sun and other leaders were absent. However, the Tokyo group did perform the important function of publishing the Alliance's monthly organ, now called *People's Report* (*Min-pao*), with which Sun was only tangentially connected.

Until closed down in 1908, this magazine, printed in as many as ten thousand copies, most of which were mailed to the mainland, was a powerful vehicle for revolutionary propaganda. Moreover, it was responsible for rebutting the criticisms of Liang Ch'i-ch'ao. Writing scholarly essays in his *New Citizen Journal*, published fortnightly in Yokohama, Liang was still trying to dampen student enthusiasm for revolution. Though by this time he had little chance of success, because of his personal prestige and journalistic skill he could not be ignored. Sun, lacking the time and talent for written polemics, did not answer him directly. He sounded the big themes, discussed some of the details with student followers, and then let them defend the Alliance's program.

What exactly was the program? In his introduction to the first issue of *People's Report* (November 26, 1905), Sun for the first time used the broader terms "nationalism," "democracy" and "socialism" to describe the aims included in the party's membership oath. (Sun used the classical term *min-sheng*, "people's livelihood," to denote his version of socialism.) Though his confidant, the Cantonese law student Hu Han-min, did the actual writing, the tone and thrust of the arguments were unmistakably Sun's. This was another projection of the "great leap" motif. He urged that China catch up with the West by adopting nationalism and democracy "without delay," and that she surpass the West by achieving socialism. Economic development had saddled the West with frightening social problems, but "China may more easily get rid of them since they have not yet deeply affected her. . . . If we can nip economic evils in the bud, we may, by one stroke, reap the benefits of both a political and social revolution. Thus we may outdistance the Western powers." Sun concluded: "In every community there are a few farsighted intellectuals who can urge it to the road of progress."

Hu Han-min elaborated upon Sun's ideas when he defined the journal's "Six Great Principles" in the April 1906 issue. The first three, "the overthrow of the present evil government, establishment of a republic, and land nationalization," covered domestic goals. The others dealt with foreign policy. They pledged support of world peace and Sino-Japanese cooperation, and asked the foreign powers to support the revolution. This last point was coupled with a promise to honor the international commitments of the Manchu government.

The most authoritative policy statement was the Program of the Revolution — a collection of proclamations and regulations that were to be issued when the revolution broke out. Drafted by the Tokyo headquarters and mimeographed in 1906, the program was distributed the following year when Sun began to stage uprisings. Besides explaining the aims of the revolution, it fixed guidelines for the behavior of the revolutionary army. The purpose was to assure the local population — including government officials and soldiers — and foreigners that the rebels were reasonable men who wanted to minimize violence and restore order as quickly as possible. The Proclamation to Foreigners, originally written in English by Ike Kyōkichi, another of Sun's Japanese friends, promised to protect foreigners and honor existing treaty and loan obligations. But it warned against pro-Manchu intervention.

According to the Proclamation of the Military Government — the first item in the Program — the ideals of the revolution were liberty, equality and fraternity. (Later Sun would compare his Three Principles both with this French revolutionary slogan and Lincoln's "of the people, by the people, for the people.") The Proclamation also explained some of Sun's specific proposals.

"Equalization of land rights" — the means for establishing "a socialist state" — simply meant that the government would expropriate increases in land values during the expected postrevolutionary development boom. Sun incorporated the ideas of Henry George — the single tax — and especially those of John Stuart Mill, who had proposed taxing the "future unearned increment increase" of land values, that is, increases that did not result from the efforts of individual landowners but from the growth and development of society at large. The idea was to prevent land speculation of the kind that had earned easy fortunes in the West, especially from urban property. In limiting the socialist content of his program to this taxation device Sun ignored agrarian injustice and worried more about the impoverished state of the entire economy.

Yet Sun may have entertained a more drastic land policy. He had briefed Hu Han-min, and Hu had come out flatly for "land nationalization," which would "wipe out the power of the landlord from the Chinese continent." However, with Liang Ch'i-ch'ao accusing him of trying to incite the lower classes, Sun stuck to the more innocuous formula, especially in official pronouncements. Even that sounded too radical for some of the gentry-born students. Also to be considered were the fears of the rich overseas merchants he was soliciting.

More importantly, the land-value taxation method enabled Sun to claim the socialist label while disclaiming any threat to existing property relations. For just as he preferred a nationalist revolution that would not antagonize foreigners, he preferred a social revolution that would not provoke class conflict. What he was advocating, then, was the prevention of the need for a Western type of social revolution in China. The future unearned increment tax was admirably suited for this preventive function. It fitted in with Sun's basic contention, namely, that China could turn her backwardness into an advantage and be one revolution ahead of the West.

The Program also included Sun's plan for achieving constitutional government in three stages: first, three years of martial law; second, six additional years of military government, but with a provisional constitution that would encourage self-rule; and third, promulgation of a constitution and the popular election of a president and parliament. In other words, there was to be a nine-year interval between the passing of the Manchus and the establishment of a full-fledged republic. Why nine years? Perhaps Sun recalled the Japanese example, for in 1881 the Meiji emperor had promised a parliament for 1890. Though Sun had already thought about a transitional period, Liang Ch'i-ch'ao's criticism was an added incentive for scheduling it. Ridiculing Sun's juxtaposition of locomotives and forms of government, Liang contended that a temporary period of "enlightened despotism" would best suit the needs of the Chinese people and prepare them for the next step, constitutional monarchy. At this time, Sun, committed to a crash program for overtaking the West, made only a token concession to the concept of graded political progress. Later, after the disappointing results of the revolution, he would turn his projected second stage into an indefinite period of political tutelage under one-party rule.

In December 1906 Sun put the final touch to his platform. Addressing over six thousand students who had gathered in Tokyo to celebrate the first anniversary of *People's Report*, he unveiled the "five-power" constitution he had discussed earlier in Europe. The subject was timely because the Manchu government had recently declared its intention of adopting a constitution in the future. After its study mission returned from abroad, the Manchus, not surprisingly, favored the Japanese model, which had in turn followed conservative German theory. What Sun offered was an improved version of the more liberal American constitution.

He proposed converting two traditional Chinese institutions — the censorate and the recently scrapped examination system — into independent branches of government and adding them to the American "three powers" (executive, legislative and judicial). The supervisory organ, he explained, would compensate for the Americans' failure to provide an impartial impeachment process. The examination agency would examine the qualifications of all prospective officials — candidates for election as well as appointment. This would remedy another defect of the American system, for Sun had found that demagogues who played on the emotions of the electorate often defeated better-qualified candidates. The West, he reminded his listeners, had first learned about civil service examinations from China and had then developed them further. Now the West would again learn from

China. He boasted that the "five-power" constitution was a breakthrough in political theory and would set a new standard for the entire world. But was perfecting the American constitution relevant to building revolutionary power in China? For that matter, how relevant was Sun's entire program?

His Three Great Principles of nationalism, democracy and socialism (the term Three Principles of the People came into vogue later) embraced the main political impulses of the modern world, and indeed, were so comprehensive as to leave hardly anything out. Nor was Sun the first Chinese to discover them. However, in translating these slogans into specific policies Sun skirted the most rankling issue — imperialism — and the potentially most explosive — peasant exploitation. Neither, of course, could be tackled by an abbreviated, one-stroke revolution. But the Manchu issue could. Thus, on the one hand Sun tried to show what an easy target the tottering dynasty made, and on the other, invested exaggerated importance in its removal. It was as if the Manchus were the main impediment to fulfilling nationalist aims and to the adoption and even refinement of the latest Western institutions. This modernizing posture distinguished Sun from traditional antidynastic rebels. Promising to "choose the good fruit" of modern civilization and to "reject the bad" enabled him to score some points with the new intellectuals. Yet it was precisely when he tried to be original that he was least successful in convincing them. Many paid only lip service to the innovations — the "five-power" constitution, the "three stages," and "equalization of land rights" — in which he took so much pride.

But whatever the doubts about Sun and some of his substantive proposals, the idea of revolution had an intrinsically winning appeal. This gave *People's Report* a decisive edge in the two-year debate (1905–1907) with Liang Ch'i-ch'ao's *New Citizen Journal*.

Both sides looked beyond China's experience and tra-

ditional beliefs. Relying chiefly upon Japanese translations, both invoked foreign precedents and the prestige
of foreign pundits. Actually, basic goals and conceptions
were not far apart, which made the argument more acri-
monious and often logomachic. Both claimed faith in the
idea of progress and in democracy. Both favored socialist
measures for controlling the abuses of capitalism. (Liang,
like Sun, relegated the danger of acute social problems to
the future industrial era, and felt that China's big problem was underdevelopment, not inequality.) There was
even common acknowledgment, though pro forma on
the part of the revolutionaries, of the need for a temporary
period of authoritarian, tutelary rule. The real argument
was over timing and priorities, and above all, methods.
These issues made the debate more than a simple extension of organizational rivalry.

Liang attacked revolution from two directions. Citing
appropriate foreign scholars and historical examples, he
tried to show that, in general, revolutions did more harm
than good. Then he examined China's particular circumstances and found that the preconditions of a viable
republic were still missing. And, emphasizing the anti-
imperialist component of nationalism more than the anti-
Manchu, he gave high priority to internal unity. He
warned that revolution was likely to encourage foreign
aggression.

Among the host of writers who replied in *People's
Report*, the most faithful expositors of Sun's ideas came
from his hard-core Cantonese following: Hu Han-min;
Hu's fellow law student Wang Ching-wei; and Wang's
brilliant nephew Chu Chih-hsin. Others took more individual lines, but still, the general pattern of argumenta-
tion and underlying value choices showed how accurately
Sun had gauged the student temperament. On one front
writers disputed Liang's external evidence. They challenged either his reading or choice of foreign sources and
rejected his interpretation of historical data. They insisted

that revolution, not gradual change, was the universal lubricant of progress. On another front they disputed his internal evidence, arguing that Chinese tradition was not so incompatible with democratic and other modern tendencies. In this way they reduced the gap between China and the West. As for Liang's prediction that revolution would provoke outside interference, China, they contended, was potentially stronger than he imagined, and foreigners less addicted to imperialism. And finally, they resorted to Sun's favorite argument: an enlightened elite could overcome all objective constraints and ensure Chinese exceptionalism.

But if the revolutionaries took refuge in extreme voluntarism, Liang — at least during the grand debate — was also unrealistic, and in the opposite way. He was overly concerned with external precedents from which he distilled an ideal formula for sequential change. In effect he was saying that change had to take place under optimal conditions or not at all. But the optimal conditions are never present anywhere, and in China orderly reform was as remote a possibility as an all-purpose, one-stroke revolution. In the summer of 1907 Liang stopped publishing *New Citizen Journal* and, encouraged by the new winds blowing at home, shifted his attention from expository journalism to practical political work. But while his moderate stance cost him influence among the students, the Manchu government, despite its reconciliation to the idea of constitutionalism, still found him too dangerous and wanted no part of him. Four years later, on the eve of the revolution — which finally made it possible for him to return to China — Liang changed his mind again and endorsed violent action, just as he had in 1900. During the interval the popular propensity for violence grew fast — much too fast for the organizational capacity of his opponents, the confirmed revolutionaries.

The P'ing–Liu–Li uprising of December 1906 was one of the most significant of these spontaneous outbursts. While Chinese intellectuals in Japan were analyzing the constitutional theories of obscure German jurists, peasants and workers in south-central China made a suicidal attempt to overthrow the establishment. The scene was the same Hunan–Kiangsi border area where Mao Tse-tung would recruit peasant fighters some twenty years later, and the causes were worsening economic conditions and recent famine that aggravated long-standing grievances against the gentry. Secret societies, assisted by student agitators — including some who had returned from Japan — supplied the leadership. Under the imposing title "The Revolutionary Vanguard of the Southern Army of the Chinese National Army," twenty thousand peasants and miners and other discontented elements picked up whatever weapons were available, including farm tools, and fought a guerrilla war against government troops from four provinces. But while sharing resentment of gentry and officials, the rebels lacked a common positive goal. Due to student influence some of their slogans and proclamations paralleled the Alliance's propaganda: anti-Manchuism, protection of foreigners, republicanism, and "equalization of land rights," which was sometimes put more bluntly as "rob the rich and aid the poor." But they also marched to slogans calling for the restoration of an ethnic Chinese emperor.

Fighting an unplanned and uncoordinated campaign with primitive weapons, the "army" still managed to stay in the field for one month. Its defeat was followed by brutal reprisals that took the lives of thousands, sometimes in the most barbaric manner: "Killed and wounded rebels were cut into and their livers removed by the troops, who ate them mixed with their grub."

The P'ing–Liu–Li incident, which joined some student revolutionaries with a wide range of nongentry elements, revealed the depths of the masses' bitterness and their potential for self-sacrificing struggle. It also revealed that the struggle would be futile if it were not backed up by an organization equipped for mobilizing, directing and sustaining popular dissent. The Alliance, only a little over a year old, could not fill that role. According to one report, the Tokyo headquarters first learned about the uprising from the Japanese press. Some members rushed back home, but the authorities there clamped down tighter on student activities. *People's Report* was banned in China and suffered a loss of circulation.

The Hunan–Kiangsi outburst gave Sun Yat-sen another incentive for speeding up his own activist campaign. Since the birth of the Alliance he had spent most of his time chasing after money in Southeast Asia. He had also renewed pursuit of the French option.

En route to Saigon in October 1905 he had an eight-hour meeting with a French intelligence officer during a stop in Shanghai harbor. What ensued was an example of the mutual bluff that characterized Sun's negotiation with foreigners. Wanting to use Tongking for a strike into southern China, Sun "charmed the French officer and persuaded him that the revolutionary movement was on the brink of success." And the Frenchman, Major Boucabeille, who hoped that the revolutionaries would supply him with a "ready-made intelligence network," exceeded instructions and gave Sun the impression that France would back him. As a result, Boucabeille sent three officers, accompanied by Sun's liaison people, on a fact-finding mission to south China. Their reports convinced him that Sun had not exaggerated the extent of anti-Manchuism. But when he developed real sympathy for revolution and recommended that France support Sun, his superiors balked. Where one of Boucabeille's agents fanned the revolutionary sentiments of Chinese soldiers by drawing comparisons with the French Revolution, higher echelons bowed to the protests of the Manchu government. More importantly, they realized that the underlying nationalism of the antidynastic movement would not only clash with French interests in

China, but could spill over into Tongking and infect their Vietnamese subjects. The French government aborted Boucabeille's mission in October 1906; but this was not the last they would hear from Sun Yat-sen.

Yet, if the French foresaw the incompatibility of China's resurgence with the continuation of classic imperialism, so, really, did Sun Yat-sen. He said as much to a foreign friend, the adventurous Russian Narodnik known as Dr. N. K. Russel, who in 1905 had begun publishing a Russian-language paper in Nagasaki. That same year — on the eve of his own departure for Saigon via Shanghai — Sun met Russel through a Japanese belonging to the expansionist Black Dragon (Amur River) Society, which cultivated both the tsar's enemies and those of the Manchus. In November of the following year — after the French shied off — Sun wrote Russel that he was very skeptical of the latter's efforts to get capitalist support for the Chinese revolution. Why, he asked, should American capitalists "commit commerical suicide" by helping China modernize? Sun was certain that the slightest sign of China's industrial progress would send Western capitalists "screaming about the so-called Yellow industrial peril." As for Russel's prediction that China's revival would accelerate Western social revolutions — a prevision of Lenin's thesis — Sun replied that the less capitalists knew of this, the better. He still believed, however, that the "regeneration of one-fourth of mankind would benefit all mankind." But he was afraid that it would be a long time before Westerners had any sympathetic understanding of China's problems.

Even so, he would continue to woo foreign capitalists — with greater desperation and no better results. As for the *hua-ch'iao*, the wealthiest continued to disappoint him, but contributions from clerks, petty shopkeepers, peddlers and laborers helped keep his career alive.

Right after the formation of the Alliance, Sun had two million dollars (HK) worth of bonds, in denominations of HK$1,000, printed in Yokohama. He had other bonds printed in English and French, but there is no record of purchases by the Europeans for whom they were intended. In February 1906 he left for Singapore and established what eventually became a major branch of the Alliance. He returned to Tokyo in April and a month later was on the move again. He organized branches in various towns in Malaya and revisited Saigon. But *hua-ch'iao* sympathizers wanted him to promise early uprisings, preferably in their native provinces of southern China, before investing money. The students, too, were impatient for action: had not Sun always insisted that it would be easy to overthrow the dynasty? In October he returned to Japan for what was to be his last stay for several years.

After defeating Russia, Japan could play major-league power politics. She inherited Russian concessions in southern Manchuria, and the powers recognized her paramount role in Korea. Now that she belonged to the imperialist establishment and participated in the squeeze on Peking, Japan had less need of Chinese revolutionaries, whose links with her own socialists and anarchists were in any case disquieting. In late 1905 the government began hounding Chinese student activists, and in February 1907 took more drastic steps. They expelled thirty-nine students from Waseda University and, complying with Peking's request, got rid of Sun Yat-sen.

Rarely has a host relieved himself of an unwelcome guest so elegantly. Sun's friends, including the head of the Black Dragon Society, convinced the Foreign Ministry that it would pay to keep some lines open to the most notorious enemy of the Manchu dynasty. Official sources provided Sun with a cash present — amounting to 5,000 yen (US$2,500) or, according to one report, at least ten times as much — and an expensive farewell banquet. A Japanese broker added another 10,000 yen. Sun accepted these gifts without consulting his colleagues and departed voluntarily on March 4 for Indochina.

Though he left 2,000 yen for *People's Report*, which was pressed for funds, this did not satisfy Chang Ping-lin, who since August had been editing the journal. The leader of the Chekiang–Anhwei clique, Chang had never shared Sun's foreign orientation nor respected his claim to intellectual prowess. When he learned the details of Sun's deal with the Japanese, he accused him of being a traitor and an embezzler of revolutionary funds. Earlier, a dispute over the design of the revolutionary flag had pitted Sun against Huang Hsing, the popular Hunanese. Both quarrels revived dormant antagonisms, partly based upon regional and personal ties, and partly on policy orientations.

Huang and another Hunanese leader finally blocked what had become a widely supported move to replace Sun as leader. They knew he needed all the money he could get for the impending military campaign, the success of which required unity. Nominally, unity was preserved, but the cracks, papered over diaphanously, grew wider. Sung Chiao-jen remained skeptical of Sun's southern orientation and went to Manchuria for a fruitless attempt to organize a revolt around the Mounted Bandits, the local counterpart of the gangs that Sun had been co-opting.

Cut off from his old base of operations in Japan just when pressure to produce results was rising, Sun found a new one, even better situated for striking out at the Manchus. Either through the negligence of French officials or their deliberate disregard of higher policy, he operated in Hanoi for almost a year — from March 1907 to January 1908. He and his lieutenants managed to stage four uprisings across the border; there were two more after he left. These six unsuccessful attempts cost at least HK$200,000, most of which came, directly or indirectly, from his own fund-raising efforts.

In Kwangtung, as elsewhere, the threshold of violence had dropped considerably, and Sun planned on hitting several sore spots simultaneously. The previous year he had met Triad leaders in Singapore who were already working on an uprising in their native prefecture of Ch'ao-chou in eastern Kwangtung. He co-opted them into the Alliance and dignified one with the title "Commander of the Chinese People's Army in the Eastern River Valley." In Ch'in-chou, at the western end of the province near the Tongking border, an antitax protest of sugarcane planters — in this case, supported by some local gentry — flared into open rebellion in May. Another factor in the conspiratorial equation was the expected defection of two officers heading army units sent to stamp out the tax rebellion.

Dispatching emissaries across the border and attempting to maintain liaison via Hong Kong, Sun was unable to control the march of events. The army officers missed their cue and in the middle of May battered the peasant rebels. In the east the Triads did not wait for orders from the "Commander," who was waiting in Hong Kong for orders from Hanoi. In the course of rescuing two of their comrades who had been arrested for unruly behavior at an opera performance, seven hundred Triads captured the poorly defended town of Huang-kang on May 22. Several days later, the rebels, having grown to a force of two thousand, ventured out of the city and were defeated by a smaller but better-armed government contingent that, on the twenty-seventh, recaptured Huang-kang. During the five days they held the town the rebels distributed Sun's Program of the Revolution and conducted themselves accordingly. The seventy to eighty thousand residents of Huang-kang suffered much more at the hands of returning government troops. Besides looting and destroying property, the soldiers executed many passive participants along with Triad activists.

The next attempt also took place in eastern Kwangtung, at Hui-chou, where Sun, in 1900, had instigated his second uprising. The local leader, a Triad who had joined the Alliance in Singapore, was not present when several hundred of his followers attacked a market town near Hui-chou on June 2. For almost two weeks they fought a running battle with four battalions of loyalist troops before retiring to the countryside with relatively small losses. The Triads this time dusted off their old slogan calling for the restoration of the Ming dynasty. And some of their leaders reverted to old deceptions. Supplied with cash by Sun's agent in Hong Kong, they disappeared before the fighting began.

By now Sun had spent all his money, including remittances from Singapore. He tried to coax more from local *hua-ch'iao*. He also had a secret benefactor in Paris, Chang Jen-chieh, whom he had met in 1905. A wealthy businessman and onetime commercial attaché at the Chinese legation, Chang hobnobbed with anarchists and was later a staunch patron and mentor of the young Chiang Kai-shek. He had promised to help Sun, and he never let him down. During the Hanoi period he sent HK$60,000.

After three months Sun and Huang Hsing tried again in western Kwangtung, where remains of the tax rebellion were still smoldering. Their principal lieutenant was another Triad and bandit chief whom Sun had recruited. While Sun stayed in Hanoi, Huang went to the scene of action and even infiltrated the government army. On September 4 the defection of some soldiers enabled several hundred Triads to capture the town of Fang-ch'eng, west of Ch'in-chou. But the high-ranking officers again refused to collaborate and fighting ended ten days later.

An integral link in Sun's strategy — and another reason for his concentrating on the southern coastal region — was a scheme to smuggle munitions from Japan. In the summer he had Kayano Chōchi buy arms and ammunition. After delays, partly due to interference from the suspicious Chang Ping-lin, Kayano got the shipment off in October. Too late for the western Kwangtung episode, it could have been used for a projected rising in the east. The ship reached the coastal rendezvous, but miscalculations and police surveillance prevented unloading. Sun now trusted his Japanese friend Miyazaki more than his Chinese colleagues in Tokyo. He secretly appointed Miyazaki the revolutionary army's sole financial and supply agent in Japan, and authorized him to negotiate with "capitalists . . . at his discretion." And in December Sun would authorize another Japanese friend, Ike Kyōkichi, who was with him in Hanoi, to raise funds and obtain supplies for the revolutionary cause. In the meantime, a restless faction in the Alliance formed a separate organization in Tokyo, the Common Advancement Society, whose members undertook subversive work in the Yangtze Valley. Sun now depended mainly upon the Cantonese and Japanese who comprised his personal following.

He sent Wang Ching-wei on an extensive tour of Southeast Asia and promised to reward heavy contributors with lucrative concessions as soon as the capture of the key city of Nanning, in Kwangsi province, enabled him to establish a military government. (Kwangsi had been the starting point for the Taipings' historic march to the Yangtze and central China.) Wang, the persuasive political writer who had defended Sun's ideas in *People's Report*, was also an inspiring orator. His trip eventually paid off, but the big entrepreneurs still did not bite.

It was in southern Kwangsi, close to the western Kwangtung region where his people had been active, that Sun scored a minor success: for the first time since 1895 he was able to step on Chinese soil and, for the only time, to have a direct hand in military operations against the Manchu dynasty. On December 3, eighty ex-soldiers-turned-bandits captured the strategic fortress of Chennan-kuan with surprising ease. Right on the Kwangsi–Tongking border, this was the tangible success local *huach'iao* had been waiting for. That night, Sun and Huang, whose entourage included the Japanese correspondent Ike and an "opium-smoking French artillery captain" on leave, reached the fortress by foot after taking a train to the border. With the Frenchman in charge of the one cannon in working order, they were able to repel a loyalist counterattack the next day. If Sun had had enough money he might have bought off the local commander. Instead, all that he and his party could do was rush back to Hanoi — they arrived on the fifth — and hope to return with rifles and ammunition before large Manchu reinforcements arrived. The *hua-ch'iao* responded generously, and a French banker dangled the prospect of a 20-million-franc (US$4 million) bond issue if the revolutionaries took an important city. Somehow Sun managed to buy weapons quickly and even ship them by train. And somehow the Hanoi authorities decided to let the shipment through after customs had held it up for a day. But the fighters, already surrounded, could not receive the goods. On the eighth they crawled out of the fortress and crossed the border.

Lasting less than a week, the Chen-nan-kuan adventure ended Sun's use of Hanoi. The French, besides being pestered by Peking, were worried about the rise of Vietnamese anticolonialism, which they attributed to Chinese revolutionary influences. The governor-general published an order of banishment, and on January 25 Sun was put on a boat for Singapore.

Huang Hsing, the Alliance's boldest commander, led another uprising at Ch'in-chou from the end of March to the middle of April. Bandits and Triads again participated, joined by *hua-ch'iao* from Hanoi and Haiphong. And finally, on April 30 a small, secret-society band captured the town of Ho-k'ou in Yunnan, just over the Tongking border. Within days defecting police and army units swelled rebel ranks to several thousand. Peking was alarmed and French promoters again showed interest, but only as long as the movement seemed likely to seize a large chunk of the mineral-rich province. That possibility faded on May 12, when the French also expelled Huang

Hsing. By the end of the month, the uncoordinated rising, which had depended too heavily on mercenaries, fell apart. The government commander actually made better use of nationalist sentiments, and gained the support of miners who blamed the French for introducing labor-saving equipment. More money might have bought more time for the rebels, but in Singapore wealthy *hua-ch'iao* turned down Sun's offer of a ten-year monopoly of Yunnan mining rights in return for a HK$100,000 loan.

The six failures were not insignificant. Starting with tiny secret-society and bandit gangs, Sun and Huang Hsing had been able to incite uprisings that generally drew popular support, including that of some government troops. Their Triad recruits usually fought bravely and behaved well, and on several occasions tied down thousands of loyalist troops for weeks. Yet at best these engagements amounted to localized rebellions whose expansion depended too much upon conspiratorial contrivances and contingencies. What was missing was the mass agitation that a disciplined organization could have provided. (Sometimes Sun's forces did not even acknowledge affiliation to the Alliance.) But it was not only Sun Yat-sen who preferred short cuts. In the lower Yangtze Valley a separate group of revolutionary intellectuals tried the same route and were even less successful. In July 1907 their attempts to start uprisings with secret societies in Anhwei and Chekiang failed, but resulted in the assassination of a provincial governor and the martyrdom of two revolutionary leaders, including a heroic young woman.

Far from causing a change of strategy, the failures of 1907–1908 deepened Sun's conviction that money was the key to successful revolution. Nor could anything shake his belief that he carried the fate of the revolution — indeed, the fate of China — in his hands. During the next few years, while a fragmented Alliance slipped further out of control and dedicated followers lost heart, he kept up the quest for funds — even when it meant going against the main current of Chinese nationalism.

While he was still in Tokyo, Sun and his closest followers took a soft stand on the Japanese threat to Manchuria — unlike Sung Chiao-jen, who supported the Chinese case against the Japanese in a Manchurian border dispute. Then, in early 1908, when Sun's fellow Cantonese led China's first boycott against Japan, he tried to help the Japanese resist.

The incident that touched off a wave of nationalist indignation began off the coast of Macao on February 5. A Chinese gunboat seized a Japanese freighter, *Tatsu Maru II*, which was trying to smuggle arms, probably for a private Chinese dealer. The Japanese, aping long-established imperialist practice, treated an attempt to enforce Chinese sovereignty as an insult to national honor. After rejecting China's offer to submit the dispute to arbitration, the Japanese issued an ultimatum demanding acceptance of humiliating terms, which included a demonstrative apology, punishment of an officer who had lowered the Japanese flag, and an indemnity. The government, as usual, had no alternative but to comply, but the people, as in the furor over American immigration policy, acted on their own to defend China's national honor. Cantonese merchants, supported by gentry and students, and thousands of ordinary citizens, including housewives, declared a boycott of Japanese goods on March 20. The press, now a power in China, spread the news; crowds threw Japanese goods into bonfires and sang specially composed "hymns of national disgrace." Lasting until the end of the year, the boycott intensified popular political awareness and encouraged what its leaders called "civilized" forms of protest.

Its economic effect, however, was less than that of the 1905 anti-American boycott since it was confined mainly to south China, Hong Kong and some overseas communities. Still, the boycott disturbed the Japanese because of their heavy dependence upon the China market. At this time China took more than a quarter of total Japanese exports and the bulk of modern industrial exports. Chinese businessmen used the opportunity to push native goods and develop their industrial competitive power.

As a young student in Hong Kong, Sun Yat-sen had been deeply impressed by the patriotism of dockers who refused to service a French ship that had bombarded Foochow. In 1908, twenty-four years later, when he looked at grass-roots patriotism from the narrow vantage point of a professional revolutionary, Sun found it expedient to work against the boycott. In the first place he and his followers were themselves too closely involved with Japanese gunrunners to make a fuss over the *Tatsu Maru* case. Secondly, though persona non grata in Japan, he had received favors from Japanese in the past and still had hopes for the future. Uchida Ryōhei, who had interceded with the government to get Sun a generous send-off, now wanted a favor in return. Delegated by the Foreign Ministry to enlist Chinese dissidents against the boycott, Uchida found the revolutionaries receptive. While Liang Ch'i-ch'ao and his people actively supported the boycott — Liang worked on the *hua-ch'iao* in Japan — the revolutionaries were able, with difficulty, to get an antiboycott resolution passed at a stormy student meeting in Tokyo. And the Alliance's Hong Kong organ, run by one of Sun's personal followers, was the only paper in south China that opposed the boycott.

At the end of April, in replying to Uchida's telegraphic plea for help, Sun exaggerated the results of his antiboycott campaign in Southeast Asia, and asked if Japanese businessmen would give him 300,000 (yen?) so that his party could "smash" the boycott in Canton. He blamed his rivals — the K'ang-Liang constitutional monarchists — for the Canton agitation, and claimed, apparently without basis, that they were heavily subsidized by provincial officials. However, Sun was not able to wheedle any money out of the Japanese. His efforts on their behalf, which were probably not too effective, cost him and his followers prestige among the Cantonese nationalists. This was one of Sun's worst years. Failure to deliver the victory he had promised slowed down the flow of *huach'iao* funds and he had trouble trying to resettle six hundred fighters who had been deported to Singapore by the French after the Yunnan campaign. Moreover, a rival faction in the Alliance started raising money independently in Southeast Asia. There was also bad news from Japan. In the fall the government closed down *People's Report* and appeared to have definitely ditched the revolutionaries. In Tokyo student morale dropped and the Alliance ceased to function as a unit. A despondent Sung Chiao-jen took to drink and opium.

In Singapore Sun worked tirelessly to shore up his position in Southeast Asia. With the help of Wang Ching-wei and Hu Han-min he created new branches in Malaya and one in Bangkok, which he visited in November. But he barely met expenses and had no hope at all of raising the huge sum that he was determined to have before starting another uprising. Thus, when a French broker sent word that he might float a 10-million-franc loan in Paris, Sun jumped at the chance. He had to wait months, though, before remittances from Bangkok and Rangoon provided travel expenses. He left Singapore in May 1909 and spent the whole summer in Europe. The Paris deal fell through and in London a broker raised hopes that later proved groundless. In October, supplied with travel money by friends in Paris and Brussels, he sailed for New York.

During the past year the loss of momentum in the revolutionary camp did not relieve pressure on the Manchu dynasty. Modernization, to which it was finally committed, and nationalism, whose aspirations it could not completely satisfy, continued to work against it. In August

1908 the government outlined its plan for constitutional rule, which was to be fully implemented in nine years. (Like Sun, the Manchus chose the Japanese timetable.) The convening of provincial assemblies the following year spurred demands for a faster retreat from absolutism. Meanwhile, the death of the empress dowager Tzu Hsi on November 15, 1908, the day after the shadow emperor died, removed the strongest Manchu personality from the scene. By the end of 1909 death had also taken the last of the old-guard Chinese officials who had been piloting the dynasty through crises since the latter half of the nineteenth century. Their most able successor, the fifty-year-old Yuan Shih-k'ai, had been dismissed at the beginning of the year. Thus, at a time of heightening tension between the central authority and the provinces, and of escalating unrest among the masses, an infant boy two and a half years old sat on the throne; his father, a weak Manchu prince, was regent; the imperial family was riddled with dissension and lacked the benefit of experienced Chinese advisers.

Though saddled with troubles of his own, these unmistakable signs of dynastic decline prompted Sun to consider another stab at his favorite target, Canton. While delegating operational plans to his lieutenants in Hong Kong, he conducted his fourth coast-to-coast tour of the American continent. He formed party branches and scrounged for dollars in the Chinatowns of the United States and Canada. His reception this time was better because there was less opposition from his rivals, the constitutional monarchists. The death of the Kuang-hsü emperor, on whose return to power K'ang Yu-wei had always relied, and K'ang's problematic handling of funds had taken the luster off the reformer's prestige. Still, Sun raised only HK$8,000, not the HK$20,000 he had promised his people in Hong Kong, and far less than the amount he really considered necessary for guaranteeing success. Though outwardly as confident as ever, Sun realized that financing on the scale he dreamed of would never come from *hua-ch'iao* laundrymen, even if they contributed their life savings, as some of them did. For this reason he never gave up the hope of tapping the foreign money market. If bankers all over the world were jockeying for the right to lend money to the Manchu government, why could not some of them bet on the revolutionaries? Before Sun left America he thought that he had finally made the right connection. While he had been looking for angels in Paris and London, several American promoters, no less imaginative than he, were already looking for someone like him — a Chinese leader who could promise them control of China's resources and economic potential in return for help in overthrowing the Manchu dynasty.

The progenitor of the scheme, later called Red Dragon, was Homer Lea. A frail, eighty-eight-pound hunchback, Lea was a racist and militarist of the fiercest Social Darwinist breed, and an amateur strategist. Though lacking any formal military training, he dreamed of leading armies (as a student at Stanford he had plotted campaigns on battle maps strung across the walls of his dormitory room). Lea was obsessed by fear of impending disaster for the Anglo-Saxon "race." He saw waves of immigrants diluting America's Anglo-Saxon virility, and the colored races swamping the British Empire. In 1909, when he was thirty-three years old, Lea published a book, *The Valor of Ignorance,* which earned him praise in professional military circles. Thirty-two years later it was recalled that in his book Lea had predicted the strategy of a Japanese attack against the United States. But if he feared and hated the Japanese he had a paternalistic interest in the Chinese. He studied their history and language, and, through Chinatown friends, became associated with K'ang Yu-wei. As K'ang's military adviser with the rank of "lieutenant general," he drilled the Chinatown youths he had organized into companies of "Reform Cadets." These were the only soldiers he actually led. In 1900 he persuaded K'ang's supporters in San Francisco to send him to China. There, his plan to attack Canton from Macao with "a coolie army of 25,000" never materialized. Lea probably met Sun Yat-sen in the States in 1904, the year Sun issued his appeal for "American Lafayettes." But Lea still preferred working with the more popular K'ang, on whose behalf he tried to drum up government and business support. Also, boasting that he could deal effectively with Chinese "jingo" elements who were responsible for the anti-American boycott, he unsuccessfully lobbied for the post of U.S. consul-general in Canton.

In 1908 the "General" began drawing up plans for an anti-Manchu expedition, with Americans supplying the officers and money. His co-conspirator was Charles Beach Boothe, a retired New York banker then living in South Pasadena. Their informant on Chinese affairs was none other than Yung Wing, the Yale-educated native of Sun's home district of Hsiang-shan. Now eighty years old, Yung was living in Hartford, Connecticut, but still had political ambitions. In the fall of 1908 Boothe enlisted the aid of W. W. Allen, a consulting engineer and a member of the Union League Club of New York. Allen, who helped Lea get his book published by Harpers, was a hardheaded businessman and less optimistic about the project than the two Californians. But he agreed to act as their link to the eastern financial hierarchy. He estimated the cost of the revolution at $9 million, including expenses for Lea's army and for bribing Manchu forces. He proposed raising $5 million from American investors — constituting an "Outside Syndicate" — and the rest from Chinese sympathizers. The "Combined Syndicate" would have formal control of the project and divide profits proportionately, but voting control, and hence, real power, would be in the hands of the Americans: Allen could not get used to the idea of "Orientals" disbursing

"Occidental" money, but did not mind their "reaping some of the harvest." Investors would be guaranteed ten percent annual interest on their investment after the revolution; these payments would come from unpledged revenues, if there were any left, of the Chinese government. The big rewards were to come from concessions granted to the syndicate by the revolutionary government. These included a ninety-nine-year concession to build and operate all Chinese railways, control of a central bank, a twenty-five-year coinage concession, and a monopoly of China's mineral resources.

The conspirators needed a Chinese figurehead, and had at first thought of K'ang Yu-wei. But Allen disqualified him when he learned that K'ang was accused of investing $800,000 — collected from *hua-ch'iao* supporters — in Mexican streetcars, and of registering the investment in the name of his daughter, a student at Barnard College. Next on the list was the recently dismissed Yuan Shih-k'ai, but there was no way of getting in touch with this "tower of strength." In January 1909 Allen also mentioned the name of Sun Yat-sen, who, he had heard, was another "tower of strength" but mainly in the Canton region. Later in the year, while in Europe, Sun read *The Valor of Ignorance* and wrote Lea that he hoped to see him in the States.

Sun arrived in New York in November, and later met Allen through Yung Wing. Though he liked Sun as a person, Allen emerged from their meeting with strong doubts about his capacity and credibility as a leader. He advised against relying on Sun, and declared that until the revolutionaries were better organized and disciplined, "it would be an insult to the intelligence of any capitalist to ask him to risk his money in this project." As currently constituted, Sun's movement, he concluded, was only capable of mounting sporadic and easily quelled uprisings.

The latest of these abortive risings had in fact taken

place in Canton on February 12 and 13, 1910. As on so many other occasions, Sun's people could not stick to the arranged schedule but were forced to move prematurely. However, what was unique about this operation — which was meagerly financed, mainly from Hong Kong — was that for the first time mutinous soldiers made up the main revolutionary force. Several thousand soldiers in the Canton region were said to have joined the Alliance, and a hundred of them were killed in the fighting. The subversion of modern army recruits — most of them with better backgrounds and education than the traditional Chinese soldier — spelled danger for the dynasty and opened up a whole new line of strategy for the revolution. There was also evidence that dissatisfaction with the government now crossed class barriers: not only peasants but some gentry and merchants sympathized with the mutineers. Sun Yat-sen recorded this, the seventh of the Alliance's military operations, as the ninth attempt that forces under his command had undertaken since 1895.

Sun at this time was on the West Coast of the United States, where he met Lea and Boothe. The Californians, unlike Allen, were impressed by Sun's inflated catalogue of revolutionary forces — "10 million" enrolled in various secret societies and "30,000" intellectuals and students in his own party plus a number of cooperative divisions of the regular army. (These figures, of course, were nowhere near the truth. The Alliance, even a year later, could have had no more than ten thousand members, including perhaps three thousand students and intellectuals of whom several hundred constituted the party's active nucleus.)

Satisfied that they had found the right man, Lea and Boothe came to an agreement with Sun on March 14. As "President of the Federal Association of China [the Alliance]" Sun appointed Boothe "sole foreign financial agent" with full powers to negotiate loans, receive money, and sign agreements on behalf of the organization. Boothe could disburse funds "in such manner as may be authorized . . . by the president," and Lea, as "Commanding General," could also requisition funds from Boothe. But there were never any funds.

Earlier, Allen found that Wall Street was cool toward China investments in general, let alone toward a speculative venture of this sort. In February 1909, J. P. Morgan, whom he identified as "a big man who shall be nameless . . . *the One,* of all others, whom I should prefer to have behind me in a venture of this sort," was not interested. Nor were lesser financial lights. Then, when his friends overruled him and dealt with Sun, Allen became less active. In the summer of 1910 Morgan's final refusal to get involved — delivered over coffee and cigars at the Union League Club — virtually ended Allen's role in the conspiracy.

But though aware of Allen's failures and loss of enthusiasm, Boothe and Lea kept feeding Sun optimistic reports — as baseless as those he fed them. The Sun–Lea operational plan called for establishing a staging area along the Tongking border and included a list of desiderata for an American-led expeditionary force. Instead of the $3.5 million he had originally asked Boothe to raise, at the end of March Sun asked for $10 million, which he promised to pay back in double. He also promised investors exclusive concessions and assorted plums, including appointments as collectors of customs in provinces captured by the revolutionaries.

Though, as already noted, Sun doubted whether American capitalists would "commit commercial suicide" by contributing to China's development, he saw no harm in trying to lure them with attractive bait. There was no question in his mind that the new China could easily sever demeaning ties to foreigners. Meanwhile, he felt that no price was too high for acquiring the means to power. Nor in dealing with foreigners did he hesitate to work both sides of the street.

At this time, for example, the engagement of the Japanophobe Lea as his "General" did not shut out the possibility of a special relationship with the Japanese. On March 24, when he was sailing to Honolulu from San Francisco, he wrote Lea asking whether the U.S. War Department would be interested in having Japan's secret mobilization plans, and sent him a list of "twelve documents of a certain military Power." (In January a member of the Alliance had tried to sell Japanese army plans concerning Manchuria to the Russians.) But in June Sun was courting the Japanese Ministry of War.

There were in fact many strings to Sun's bow. While in New York he and an American broker discussed a scheme for cornering the Malayan tin market. This deal, on which Sun would have earned a middleman's commission, required the cooperation of Chinese mine owners. They did not cooperate. Nor by claiming to have this and other fund-raising projects in the pipeline was Sun completely successful in fighting the despondency that afflicted his comrades. The latest victim was Wang Ching-wei. Dismayed by the string of military failures and the bitter internal opposition to Sun Yat-sen, he hoped to save the movement from complete collapse by becoming a martyr. In April he failed in an attempt to assassinate the prince regent and was imprisoned.

In the middle of June, following a two-month stay in Hawaii, Sun returned to Japan after an enforced absence of three years. His arrival in Yokohama, which was not kept secret, brought inquiries from the Chinese minister, to whom the Japanese responded evasively. At a Japanese cabinet meeting the war minister's view prevailed and Sun was allowed to remain. Assuming Hawaiian identity he stayed in Tokyo as "Dr. Alaha" until the Chinese legation exerted pressure. According to his letter to Boothe, Sun decided to relieve the Japanese government's "uneasiness" and, ten days after his arrival, left of his own accord, though he claimed that "friends in connection with the war department" wanted him to stay a little longer. In New York Allen wondered why.

Always ready to hedge their bets, Japanese generals may have been persuaded by Miyazaki to take another look at Sun. But relations with his own people in Tokyo worsened. During a sharp confrontation Sun challenged the opposition to go its own way. For some time now he had been doing exactly that himself: while in America he had formed new branches under the name "Chinese Revolutionary Party" rather than "Alliance," a name that had never pleased him. He had also arbitrarily reworded the membership oath and started using the slogan "Three Principles of the People." Formally, the Alliance did not break up at this time, but Sun's critics rejected his Cantonese strategy and began planning independent action in their home region, the Yangtze Valley provinces. However, the influential Huang Hsing still backed Sun and was one of the seventeen provincial leaders who signed a power of attorney that Sun mailed to Boothe from Japan. Confident that with enough money government troops in the Canton area could be subverted, Huang dismissed the idea of having American officers lead the revolutionary army.

In July the Singapore *hua-ch'iao* became less hospitable because of Sun's failure to stage a successful rising and because of charges of embezzlement that a rival had leveled against him. Sun shifted his headquarters to Penang. There, for one of the few occasions in his life, he lived with his wife and children — except for his nineteen-year-old son, who was studying in Hawaii. Vowing that this would be his last attempt to unseat the Manchu dynasty, he waged an ingenious fund-raising drive that offered something for everyone, according to their tastes and pocketbooks. He put up for sale, in the name of the future republic, rights of citizenship, business concessions, terms of office in parliament and, for the highest price, statues and parks named after the donors. This multifaceted appeal to the *hua-ch'iao* — to their patriotism, their resentment of discrimination, and to their dreams of wealth and honors — is recorded in a speech that Sun delivered in Penang at the end of October.

The idea of revolution, Sun declared, was in accord with the teachings of China's ancient sages, who approved of the overthrow of despotic rulers. Later, other countries — England, Turkey, Japan, and most recently, Portugal — found prosperity through revolution. This was the way for China to gain an equal footing with powerful nations. Under the Manchus, he warned, she faced partition, or conquest like Korea. And the *hua-ch'iao*, even if wealthy, would continue to suffer indignities.

A Chinese millionaire from Java had told him of a humiliating experience. He had stayed late visiting a friend and had forgotten to bring his pass and a lantern, without which — according to Dutch regulations — a Chinese could not stray farther than a mile or two from his home at night. But a Japanese could. So the millionaire hired a Japanese prostitute who was living next door to take him home. Sun concluded: "A Chinese millionaire is regarded in Java as lower than a Japanese prostitute. This is because our government is too weak to afford protection to Chinese living in foreign lands."

The *hua-ch'iao*, Sun insisted, were missing the boat by pursuing riches through trade in foreign lands. At home, revolution would provide fantastic opportunities. People like "Roosevelt, Rockefeller and Morgan" did not gain their wealth through trade but from "assistance to . . . revolutionaries in various countries." Given China's incomparable natural resources, the *hua-ch'iao* could earn "100 times more than they could get from trading" if they helped the revolutionaries.

The big moneymen were still not convinced. Nor, Sun gradually discovered, were American investors. In September he began pressing Boothe for interim funding, but his "financial agent" was unable to deliver half a million dollars, not even the $50,000 Sun had asked for as a private loan. In November Sun wrote that unless he received money within three months his forces would take independent steps. If successful, these measures would require changing the terms of their agreement. Further pleading and predictions of an early triumph failed to produce a penny. In March 1911 Sun asked Boothe to return the power of attorney, and in April Boothe admitted that Red Dragon was a dead project.

The reason for the urgency of Sun's appeals was that in November, when Huang Hsing and other leaders joined him for a strategy conference, plans for the next assault on Canton had jelled. Sun's credibility was stretched to the limit and he could no longer postpone action. And when the prospect of getting millions from foreigners faded, he and his comrades lowered their target to HK$130,000, which they could only get from their perennial standby, the *hua-ch'iao*. However, the British now decided that Sun's activities could no longer be represented as "educational." After being apprised of his October speech, the governor of the Straits Settlements had a subordinate "intimate to Dr. Sun . . . that his further presence in the Colony was considered undesirable." Now barred from British, French and Dutch territories, and from Japan and Siam, Sun sailed for Europe in December.

He spent a week in Paris. Hoping to impress French politicians he lived in an expensive hotel, but no one showed up. He had better luck with the *hua-ch'iao* of Canada. After brief stops in New York and San Francisco he arrived in Vancouver in February 1911. For four days running he packed in audiences of over a thousand in a Chinese theater. Working through Triad lodges in Vancouver, Victoria and other towns, he sold HK$70,000 worth of bonds in return for the usual promises of rewards after the revolution. This money, plus HK$15,000 from sales in the United States and Hawaii, was remitted to Hong Kong, the headquarters for the next Canton rising. Scheduled for April 13, this was meant to be the Alliance's supreme effort.

It was also a uniquely self-managed operation. The outsiders whom Sun Yat-sen usually co-opted were less prominent. Led by Huang Hsing and a former army officer, the Alliance mobilized its own personnel, including veteran student members who volunteered for suicidal combat duty. Students also stirred up grass-roots support and spread propaganda stressing the government's inability to resist foreign interference. Party members, including women, smuggled arms from Japan, Indochina, Siam and Hong Kong. These were deposited in secret cells throughout Canton. According to the plan, several hundred volunteers were to start the action from various quarters in the city. New Army units and bandit gangs were primed for responsive risings. After seizing Canton, the revolutionaries, who coordinated plans with comrades in the Yangtze Valley, intended driving northward.

For the first time funds were not lacking. The *hua-ch'iao* of Southeast Asia contributed over HK$100,000. Responding to appeals to save China from foreign domination, these overseas supporters, still predominantly wage earners and small shopkeepers, willingly parted with their meager savings. Some returned home to risk their lives in the action.

For weeks ominous rumors kept the authorities on edge. Then, on April 8, five days before the action was to start, an impulsive comrade from Singapore, a former miner "imbued with the revolutionary doctrines of Dr. Sun Yat-sen," assassinated a Manchu general. The authorities took extra precautions — and none too soon. They confined untrustworthy troops to barracks and removed the bolts of their rifles. The revolutionaries now considered postponing the action indefinitely. But they were too deeply committed, and moreover, could not afford disappointing overseas supporters. On April 27 after much hesitation, Huang Hsing, who had taken charge in Canton a few days earlier, led 130 men in an attack on the governor-general's office. Armed with pistols and homemade bombs, they scored a deceptively easy success. Repeated cancellations had sowed confusion and prevented coordination. Potential mutineers in the New Army were not alerted. Neither they nor most of the bandit gangs participated. Though the rebels fought with "absolute fanaticism" — while loyalist troops were inclined to panic — within a few days the government had the situation in hand. Rebels and suspicious characters were decapitated or strangled. But public indignation forced the authorities to stop their house-to-house search.

Revolutionary tradition immortalized "72 martyrs," but actually close to a hundred rebels were killed, largely through execution after capture. Most were recent peasant and worker recruits; twenty-nine were active members of the Alliance, including nine students from Japan. Huang Hsing was wounded and narrowly escaped capture.

Sun Yat-sen was in Chicago when telegrams from Hong Kong brought the bad news and a plea for funds to help the survivors. He rushed to San Francisco and sold bonds to the Triads for the sum of HK$15,000; Hawaii sent HK$5,000. Money, however, could not make up for the crushing blow to the party's Canton network, and the damage to morale. In England news of the defeat and fear that China would be partitioned drove a gifted student pamphleteer to suicide. Despair temporarily immobilized Huang Hsing and others who had been closely involved. In America Sun Yat-sen was less visibly affected.

He too had his gloomy spells and only the previous year had spoken of giving up politics and returning to medicine. But these lapses were few and brief. After this latest disappointment — "our tenth defeat" — he quickly resumed the old routine. In May he visited Washington and failed to get an appointment to see Secretary of State

Knox. Then he canvased the Triads on the West Coast. The lodge leaders refused to form a company for selling shares in future mining rights, but accepted a joint organizational setup with the Alliance. Sun kept encouraging his comrades, and by August began sending money to Hong Kong.

His optimism was justified. Though the Alliance had taken a beating in Canton, the rising and the assassination that preceded it cast a long shadow of fear over officials in the southern provinces. For weeks some were afraid to step out of their compounds. The public grew more contemptuous and the armed forces less reliable. In the summer a British intelligence report predicted strong support for the next anti-Manchu operation in Canton. By that time the issue that would finally precipitate the downfall of the dynasty was already agitating the people of Kwangtung and the Yangtze Valley provinces.

Railways spearheaded the imperialist penetration of China. For political no less than for economic reasons, after the Sino-Japanese War foreign powers built and operated railroads in their spheres of influence. Some also policed and developed so-called railway zones or areas—whole strips of territory virtually free from Chinese jurisdiction. After 1900, when the Chinese themselves went into the railroad business, they turned to the international money market, which subsequently supplied nearly 80 percent of the capital invested in government railways. Chinese ownership was purely nominal. Foreign lending syndicates demanded and obtained actual control. They supervised construction, purchased materials — usually from their own countries, and for a commission — audited expenditures and receipts, and managed operations. Since the Chinese received only 90 to 95 percent of a loan's nominal value, the syndicate, which usually floated the loan at close to 100 percent, started off with a good profit margin. Some contracts guaranteed them fixed percentages of future net profits. Payments on interest — usually 5 percent — and principal were secured by twenty-to-fifty-year mortgages on the railways or their earnings. Even after 1905, when the Chinese obtained better terms, lenders could still get respectable returns with minimal risk. Since Europe had surplus capital, European bankers, working in tandem with diplomats, competed for contracts and, when necessary, put political pressure on Peking. The one railroad constructed entirely by Chinese engineers and with Chinese capital equaled the quality of any built by foreigners. And the cost per mile was almost 30 percent less.

Small wonder, then, that the redemption of foreign railway concessions became a major target of the rights-recovery movement. In some cases the popular outcry against foreign loans and centralized ownership enabled provincial railway companies to raise considerable sums toward redemption. But these were indeed isolated cases. There was simply not enough indigenous capital available for long-term, relatively low-interest investments. In 1905, when gentry and merchants prodded the government into buying back an American concession to build the Canton–Hankow line, it had to borrow money from the Hong Kong colonial government. The Morgan interests, who had held the concession, made a profit of several million dollars. Provincial companies then undertook to build this and another trunk line connecting Hankow with Szechuan. Together they were known as the Hukuang railways. After several years the sale of shares and special tax levies brought in only a fraction of the capital required. And some of that was lost through speculation. Construction proceeded at a snail's pace.

In 1908 Chang Chih-tung, the last of the great Confucian statesmen, was put in charge. Since the provinces were making a mess of the Hukuang project, Chang favored nationalization and centralized control. He also saw no way of avoiding the use of foreign capital for creating the great arteries required for China's economic development and defense. After settling their own differences British, German and French bankers initialed a loan agreement with him in 1909. The Americans, led by President Taft himself, pushed their way in. In May 1910, what was now a four-power banking consortium agreed to float a £6-million loan — later raised to £10 million — for the Hukuang railways. J. P. Morgan, who was at this time turning up his nose at Sun Yat-sen's proposition, organized the American group.

Chinese entrepreneurs — the most influential people in the provinces concerned — were furious, and not only because of genuine feelings of patriotism and provincial pride. They themselves hoped to profit from railway development, or more precisely, from access to the funds collected for railway development. The government hesitated as the newly convened provincial assemblies, dominated by these gentry businessmen and returned students, charged that the loan was a step toward partition by the foreign powers. Soldiers joined the protest. The masses, though less concerned with investments than with the grim struggle for existence, were easily incited by students and gentry, but not always amenable to their control.

Chang Chih-tung at least had a reputation for integrity. His death in October 1909 left Sheng Hsüan-huai, the most notorious wheeler and dealer in the empire, as the government's main figure in railway affairs. He was appointed head of the Ministry of Communications in January 1911. Opponents of the loan raised charges of corruption and focused their attacks on him personally. The consortium powers would not let the government off the hook, and in May Sheng finally signed the contract. At the same time the government announced that it would buy out provincial stockholders and nationalize the railways, which would be subjected to the usual control provisions insisted upon by foreign lenders. Though some Chinese shareholders were promised eventual return of their money — but with little profit — those in Szechuan were not to be compensated for losses due to the provincial company's speculative investments.

For technical reasons railway centralization made sense, and a government that enjoyed the people's confidence might have overcome objections with little trouble. But the Manchu dynasty had by now exhausted public confidence. Too weak to stifle demands for political reform, the imperial family was too frightened to share real power. In October 1910 the newly formed National Assembly — half its members were selected by provincial bodies and half by the throne — exceeded its consultative function and demanded a shorter timetable for establishing parliamentary government. The court gave in and promised a parliament for 1913. The Assembly then attacked the Grand Council — the Manchu-dominated body that advised the throne — and demanded its replacement by a cabinet. Again the court made compliant noises, but in May 1911 unveiled a cabinet packed with incompetent Manchu nobles headed by an aged and venal prince. This was the cabinet that was supposed to steer the nation's constitutional development. Its composition was a blow to the dynasty's credibility and a slap at Chinese ethnic pride. Thus the court succeeded in alienating its gentry constituency throughout the country while in Szechuan railway agitation cascaded.

Thousands attended emotional mass meetings organized by the Railway Protection League. A general strike developed; tax payments stopped. Instead of trying to appease railway investors the government, goaded by the foreign powers, decided to stand firm. (In August a worried British consul in Szechuan suggested a compromise to placate local railway interests; his superiors "hauled him over the coals.") In September the governor-general arrested the gentry ringleaders, and troops killed thirteen demonstrators in front of his office. Disorder broke out in China's largest province.

Here was an opportunity for organized revolutionaries.

But the Alliance, the oldest and largest of the antidynastic combinations, was not able to seize it. It was only on July 31 that Sung Chiao-jen and others from the Yangtze Valley who were skeptical both of Sun's southern orientation and his overall leadership established the party's Central China Office in Shanghai. They hoped, some time in the future, to start uprisings in their home provinces. However, the storm clouds burst sooner than expected and caught them unprepared. As late as October 7, when the Szechuan disturbances seemed to be subsiding, they decided that "arrangements for revolts . . . should be slowed down."

In Hupeh other revolutionary groups were unable to wait. The Common Advancement Society — the offshoot of the Alliance that had been formed in Tokyo in 1907 — recruited members from the local secret society. Another group, hiding under the name "Literary Society," enrolled several thousand soldiers in the New Army. Like the Alliance both groups were led by students. Unlike the Alliance they constituted self-contained fighting bodies whose leaders were not preoccupied with a search for funds or foreign allies. Their ideological formulations were even looser than those of the Alliance. They had a vague commitment to republicanism, but what really fired them was a determination to get rid of the Manchu dynasty. This was good enough at a time when the Manchus had antagonized all strata of Chinese society, though not always for the same reasons. Most important, these fighting forces were concentrated in China — not overseas — and flexed for action at the right place and at the right time. The two organizations came to a working agreement in September. While maintaining loose liaison with the Alliance leaders in Shanghai and Hong Kong, they scheduled their own revolt for mid-October.

The action started off like many of the Alliance's enterprises. It ended quite differently. On October 9 an accidental explosion in their arms cache in Hankow, on the north bank of the Yangtze, set the police upon the conspirators and forced them to act prematurely. Led by noncommissioned officers, mutineers seized the armory at Wuchang, on the south bank, on the tenth — the date subsequently celebrated as the opening of the revolution. The next day rebel and loyalist forces, each numbering several thousand, fought a hard battle that ended in a rebel victory. The Manchu governor-general and his top military commander fled to Hankow. The rebels controlled Wuchang, and the next day easily took Hankow and Hanyang, thus completing the capture of the three Wuhan cities — the political and industrial heart of the middle Yangtze region, one of the most important in the country. The subsequent recapture of Hankow and Hanyang by imperial forces did not stop the anti-Manchu trend. Two months after Wuchang most Chinese provinces, including the entire south, opted for revolution.

The uprising at Wuchang turned out differently from that at Canton mainly because the whole country was more ready for revolution. Between April and October the government had skidded disastrously on the railway and constitutional issues. Also, the Hupeh conspirators had been more successful in subverting the New Army, so they faced better odds than previous insurgents. (They may also have benefited from the earlier shift of troops from Hupeh to Szechuan because of the railway riots.) And finally there were purely chance events, like the early seizure of the arsenal and the panicky flight of civil and military officers.

Thus, forces that had little to do with the Alliance and nothing to do with Sun Yat-sen set off the chain reaction he had always hoped for, and which, it turned out, he could not control. No outstanding leader was available at Wuchang. The mutineers had to drag a brigade commander — Li Yüan-hung — out of hiding and force him to assume the military governorship of Hupeh. On October 11 he proclaimed Hupeh part of the "Chinese Republic." A few days later he cooperated actively when it was clear that respectable gentry who controlled the provincial assembly backed the new government. The pattern was repeated elsewhere. Trimmers in the imperial army and bureaucracy joined with gentry constitutionalists in repudiating the Manchu dynasty. Only in Kwangtung, the Alliance's stronghold, and in a few other provinces, did its own people seize power, at least temporarily. At Wuchang the arrival of Huang Hsing and Sung Chiao-jen at the end of October did not change the situation. Li Yüan-hung, the gentry's choice who only a few weeks earlier had signed proclamations of the military government with a pistol at his head, retained overall leadership. Huang, as commander-in-chief of the revolutionary forces, was his subordinate.

The Alliance's eclipse by gentry and militarists was not solely due to a failure of organization. Revolutionary leaders shared Liang Ch'i-ch'ao's fear that a dragged-out civil war would invite foreign intervention. This was a strong inducement toward keeping the masses in check and giving way to respectable provincial power holders who shared the negative aim of eliminating Manchu rule. Foreign warships — there were sixteen at Hankow alone within days of the outbreak — patrolled inland waters and the China coast.

Foreigners had their own nightmare — a resurgence of "Boxerism" — and they sighed with relief when the revolution assumed a moderate guise, both in its internal and foreign policies. A week after the Wuchang rising the Hankow consuls rewarded moderation by declaring neutrality. Though the Manchus had been accused of cringing obeisance to foreigners, their accusers could not have been more scrupulous in protecting foreign lives and property, and in maintaining foreign privileges. A British consul thought it "extraordinary" that revolutionary troops *"walked* beside the Shanghai-Nanking railway line" rather than use the trains, which they could have easily commandeered. The British inspector-general of the Chinese Maritime Customs happily noted that the revolutionaries, though hard pressed for funds, did not interfere with customs collections — which were pledged to meet foreign loan and indemnity payments. He was surprised by their "sweet reasonableness." This should have been no surprise. More than anything else this generation of Chinese leaders feared partition by foreign powers. Many believed, and not without justification, that few things could be done in China without foreign approval and credits. And no one believed it more than Sun Yat-sen.

Sun read about the Wuchang uprising in a newspaper while he was sitting down for breakfast in a Denver, Colorado, restaurant. Instead of returning directly to China, he took the long route via Washington, London and Paris. He felt that foreign attitudes would be decisive — for the fate of the revolution and probably for his personal position as well. Though Sun was still the best-known revolutionary — the British minister to Peking credited him with being the revolution's "prime mover" — his role as a leader, never unqualified, had by now become almost redundant. He read in the press that he was slated for the presidency of the future republic. He realized, however, that only an outstanding achievement abroad — the field in which he always claimed special skills — could put him in the running. Besides stopping the consortium from advancing funds to the Manchus, he hoped to land a loan for his own party and return to China bearing the stamp of foreign approval.

Sun spent a few days in Washington, where Secretary of State Knox turned down his request for a secret meeting. This did not stop him from making fantastic claims in London. There, at the end of October, he met Homer Lea, who was finishing his latest jeremiad, *The Day of the Saxon,* which warned that German power threatened Britain's supremacy. With Lea's help Sun got the support of Sir Trevor Dawson of Vickers, Sons and Maxim. Dawson, under the impression that Sun would shortly be "President of the Chinese United States," expected orders for arms and munitions. He saw the foreign secretary, Sir Edward Grey, on November 14 and submitted Sun's statement and a memorandum signed by Sun and Lea. Sun's party, it was stated, wished to make an "Anglo-Saxon alliance with Great Britain and the United States." Sun claimed to be in "close touch" with the United States "through Senators Root and Knox" and was willing to have Grey check with Washington. He said that he could get a £1-million loan, presumably from America, if the British government agreed. He needed Britain's friendship and support, and promised to act under the advice of her government, whose nominee he would appoint as political officer. He promised Britain and the United States preferential treatment if his party came to power and he assumed the presidency, which he "believed to be a certainty." He would place the navy under the command of British officers subject to his own orders, and would accept British advice regarding any agreement between China and Japan. His sworn supporters in China, he stated, included thirty to forty thousand of "the best educated students" and thirty-five million members of secret societies.

Grey was not taken in by Sun's claims nor enticed by his offers. The Foreign Office had already tabbed Sun as an "armchair politician and windbag." Besides, Britain was satisfied with developments and needed no prompting from Sun to stop lending money to Peking. On November 8 the consortium bankers had already decided not to advance funds from recently contracted loans until a responsible government took charge. They had no reason to believe that the revolutionaries, who controlled most of the country and its treaty ports, would act irresponsibly toward foreigners. The foreign secretary told Dawson — and permitted him to tell Sun — that Britain would remain neutral. He also said that "there seemed to be one good man on the side opposed to the revolutionaries, Yuan Shih-k'ai, whom we all respected." "All" included not only the British and most other foreigners, but a good part of the anti-Manchu camp, especially its recent gentry adherents. Even key members of the Alliance were sounding out the possibility of giving Yuan the presidency if he obtained the Manchus' abdication and opted for a republic.

Yuan did have an impressive record. And the British were especially grateful for his effective stand against the Boxers. Though his shrewd maneuvering in the dangerous world of Peking politics had earned him enemies, he was an able administrator and an outstanding modernizer who had even scored some success in resisting imperialist encroachments. He had built the Peiyang (Northern) Army, China's best-trained and most modern force, and still exercised considerable personal control over it. When the revolution erupted, the Manchu court, which had dismissed him in 1909, swallowed its pride and called him back. Yuan held out for full military powers, which he received on October 27. In November he was also named premier as the dynasty hastily met demands for constitutional government. At the end of the month, after his forces pushed back the revolutionaries on the Hankow front, where thousands were killed in the severest fighting of the revolution, both sides were ready for the armistice that the British now suggested. As the alternative to interminable fighting, foreigners and influential Chinese counted upon Yuan's political talent to bring about a negotiated settlement. So too, when his European gambit failed, did Sun Yat-sen.

While he was in Paris (November 21–24) holding fruitless talks with bankers and politicians, including Georges Clemenceau, Sun wired revolutionary leaders in Shanghai that either Li Yüan-hung or Yuan Shih-k'ai — both of whom were being considered as presidential candidates — would be acceptable to him. Accompanied by Homer Lea and several Chinese comrades, Sun sailed from Marseilles on November 24. En route he received a wire from Sir Trevor Dawson informing him that the British would not object if he stopped off — but only briefly — at Hong Kong and other colonies. That was all they would do for him.

When he arrived in Hong Kong on December 21, Hu Han-min and other Cantonese followers urged him to hold out for complete victory. Instead of continuing to Shanghai — where peace talks had begun a few days earlier — they wanted him to consolidate the Alliance's Cantonese base and prepare for a showdown with Yuan's army. Sun refused. He did not want to jeopardize the easy revolution he had predicted and which, he had always contended, was the only kind China could afford. Resumed fighting, he warned, might induce foreigners to intervene, as they had done against the Taipings. While sharing his friends' suspicions of Yuan, Sun argued that they could use him to remove the Manchus. Yuan's military power, he admitted, might eventually pose a problem, but he was not too worried because he, Sun, had the "people's hearts." The hard-liners were convinced, and in any case would have had little support. Along with the nonparty people who dominated the anti-Manchu combination, most of the Alliance's leaders still favored continuing negotiations. Even Wang Ching-wei, another of Sun's Cantonese disciples, actively wooed Yuan after being released from a Manchu prison. Moreover, Chinese opinion was reinforced by foreign, and especially British, opinion. No less an authority than G. E. Morrison, the London *Times* correspondent, warned the republicans that it would be hopeless to expect early recognition by the foreign powers if they were led by someone like Sun Yat-sen, or anyone besides Yuan Shih-k'ai, who "alone could obtain the confidence of the Powers."

Sun arrived in Shanghai on December 25. Rumor had

it that he had brought a large sum of money, but he announced that he had not brought "a farthing," only "a revolutionary spirit." That he was the senior and most-publicized enemy of the Manchu dynasty was undisputed. He received a hero's welcome and, probably more by accident than design, the honor of launching the republican regime.

Since mid-December, while waiting for Yuan Shih-k'ai to come around, provincial delegates in Nanking had been haggling over the leadership of their provisional government. One group favored Huang Hsing; another, Li Yüan-hung. Sun's arrival resolved the dispute. On December 29, with delegates from sixteen of the seventeen provinces represented voting for him, Sun was elected provisional president of the Chinese Republic. However, he immediately notified Yuan Shih-k'ai that Yuan could take over if he declared allegiance to the republic. In the meantime Sun would retain custody of what was left of the "revolutionary spirit."

SIX

Defending the Spirit of the Revolution

SUN TOOK OFFICE on January 1 and for the next few months presided over a weak and money-starved provisional government. Control of the armies that had spontaneously deserted the dynasty tended to stop at the provincial level, where military and gentry leaders rejected not only Manchu rule but any form of strong, centralized government. In his prerevolutionary planning Sun had anticipated the danger of this centrifugal pull and the regional warlordism to which it would eventually lead. But there was no way now of enforcing his Program of the Revolution. The three stages and Sun's other devices, like the five-power constitution, were forgotten — even by his comrades — when provincial delegates deliberated in Nanking.

Though the scenario was not his, Sun played the part assigned him. He stood in for Yuan Shih-k'ai but took little interest in administration, which he never liked, and delegated it to others. Perhaps, when peace talks stalled for a few weeks, the hope of playing a larger role revived. At the end of January, however, several northern generals jumped on the republican bandwagon. Yuan then convinced the imperial family that further resistance was futile and the child emperor abdicated on February 12. The revolutionaries promptly carried out their part of the bargain. Sun submitted his resignation the next day, and two days later the Nanking assembly elected Yuan provisional president. He was inaugurated on March 10 — not in Nanking, which, at Sun's insistence, the assembly had picked for the site of the capital, but in Peking, where Yuan claimed his presence was needed to keep his troops in line. On April 1 Sun formally vacated his office, and the assembly moved to Peking, now designated the capital of the republic. Despite lingering suspicions of Yuan, leaders of the Alliance were generally satisfied. They knew of course that the revolution was incomplete. To what extent was not so obvious at the time.

The peasants, who had joined the revolution in the hope of gaining relief from landlords and tax collectors, were suppressed. Yet without a social revolution at home, international equality would remain a distant dream. The gentry–bureaucratic elite had not been replaced but had joined with militarists. At the heart of this combination was a time bomb: rampant warlordism would wreck both republicanism and traditional gentry power.

Nonetheless, what happened in 1911 was significant. While the revolution did not install a stable alternative, it completed the break with the most enduring political tradition the world had ever known. And it left a legacy of frustrated hopes that would fuel the next stage of China's modern revolution.

Later, Sun would try to divest himself of responsibility for the deal that made the republic the hostage of Yuan and his generals. He would retroactively reproach his comrades for having abandoned "revolutionary fundamentals" and for having turned him into a puppet. That the party, which had never marched faithfully to his tune, paid even less attention to him in 1912 is true. What is highly unlikely, though, is that he would have steered a different course had he been in full control of the party. For the Alliance did not control the revolution. And, as has already been emphasized and as Sun himself intimated to Hu Han-min, no Chinese in his right mind could have ignored the foreign powers.

Actually, few foreign policy-makers, with the possible exception of some Japanese, seriously contemplated active intervention. Remembering the Boxer rising, they were afraid of provoking the Chinese masses. Revolutionary leaders, on the other hand, remembered the consequences of Boxerism and were afraid of provoking the foreigners. They accordingly kept a tight rein on the masses, which they were inclined to do anyway for purely domestic reasons.

However, foreigners did not have to intervene physically in order to bring about a negotiated solution. Their money power was sufficient. Deprived of major sources of income the governments of both Nanking and Peking were practically bankrupt. Foreigners appropriated customs receipts, which were pledged to meet payments on loans and indemnities, and provincial leaders siphoned off potential income from the land tax. A revolution that drew its strength from a mobilized peasantry might have broken the power of local notables and enabled a central authority to benefit from surplus agricultural production — whatever it amounted to. Because that kind of revolution did not take place — and by definition an easy revolution precluded social conflict — no one could form a viable government and pay off the hundreds of thousands of army recruits without increasing China's dependence upon foreign bankers. And the bankers would not respond until the Chinese themselves got together and formed a government that could mortgage what was left of the country's resources.

Before the final settlement the republicans did raise

some money, even a considerable amount, from the same sources that Sun Yat-sen had been cultivating for the previous sixteen years. Still, this would not be enough to meet their swollen needs. The *hua-ch'iao*, including formerly dubious tycoons from Southeast Asia, came through generously when the dynasty began collapsing. According to Sun they contributed HK$600,000 during his three-month stint as a provisional president. His Triad fundraising apparatus in America sent six Curtis airplanes and an American mechanic. Together with a Greek pilot, they constituted a republican air force that never got off the ground, but one that added to the revolutionaries' prestige. Total overseas remittances from October 1911 to early 1912 were about HK$2.4 million. Much, however, did not go to the revolutionaries' headquarters but to the *hua-ch'iao* home provinces of Kwangtung and Fukien. As for the needs of the Nanking government, its budget for March alone amounted to HK$5.4 million, most of which was earmarked for the army.

Sun's other traditional source — the Japanese military-industrial complex — shipped arms to both sides during the fighting. While peeved at their British allies for bypassing them, Japanese policy-makers were not sure what type of Chinese government was best for Japan. However, there was considerable support for the view that a disrupted China offered a better chance of getting the share of imperialist spoils that Japan felt had so far been denied her. Sun's Mitsui connections loaned the republicans HK$450,000. But bigger Japanese loans, to be secured on railroad, shipping and industrial properties, were blocked by British and other consortium bankers, and by Chinese stockholders. Sun also made an unsuccessful attempt to frighten Americans into helping him by informing them of purported Japanese offers. Only at the end of February, when the bankers started advancing money to Yuan, did Nanking get help toward paying off its troops and meeting other urgent needs. And though

Sun tried, he would never be able to fully compensate the *hua-ch'iao* who had purchased his bonds.

But if the other foreign powers, notably Britain, used their influence to press for a negotiated solution — and thus helped put a brake on the revolution — it should again be pointed out that they were not directly responsible for frustrating Sun Yat-sen's personal ambitions. On their own the Chinese people, or at least those Chinese whose opinions counted, disqualified him. Sun did not have the ability and background they required of a leader. Members of his own party who had originally credited him with practical fund-raising talents now considered him an impractical idealist. Yen Fu, probably the most profound Chinese thinker of the time, called Sun "harebrained." But Yen probably thought the same of anyone who insisted that China was ready for a republic. Even so, Sun suffered from a particularly glaring credibility gap. The habit of making extravagant claims and promises suited his previous role as the revolution's chief drummer overseas. It did not suit a head of state. Soon after the outbreak of the revolution, while Sun was still abroad, one powerful gentry leader suggested that as a roving ambassador Sun could help the republic earn international recognition. The suggestion reflected the opinion that whatever talent Sun had was better applied away from China.

Then, too, there were Sun's old handicaps — his low social status and lack of a classical education. Without these handicaps other leaders of the Alliance had better rapport with gentry converts to republicanism. Probably many members of the elite shared Yuan Shih-k'ai's private view that Sun was only "half-Chinese." Since Sun had spent most of his life abroad, there was substance to Yuan's charge that Sun knew little of China. Also disquieting was Sun's choice of friends and advisers. Japanese flocked around him in Nanking, where he also had in tow the American Japan-baiter Homer Lea. How indeed could people trust Sun's judgment if he displayed a dubious character like Lea as his military adviser? (After Sun's resignation Lea returned to California, where he died in November 1912 at the age of thirty-six.)

By deferring to Yuan, Sun enhanced his own prestige. Ironically, this was one of the few occasions in Sun's life when so many Chinese and foreigners credited him with statesmanlike behavior. He gained respect not only for contributing to a peaceful settlement, but for appearing to have acknowledged his inadequacies.

Yet, at the time, Sun appeared quite happy in the role of an elder statesman who had forsworn a quest for personal power so that he might better serve the national interest. Under the circumstances he had in fact not done so badly for himself. Despite his questionable performance as a revolutionary leader, luck had combined with persistence to catapult him into national, even international, prominence. Sun was the most newsworthy personality the revolution produced. The globe-trotting conspirator whom the world had first noticed as the hero of a hairbreadth escape in London finally came home to preside over the surrender of his enemies and the establishment of Asia's first republic. Less knowledgeable foreigners overestimated his influence. Missionaries — though a few were dismayed by reports of his less than faithful observance of Christian doctrines regarding church attendance and marriage vows — generally hailed him as a major force for Christianizing China. A usually perceptive missionary even wrote that "Sun had unquestionably done more than anybody else to bring about the recent changes in China." An influential American magazine described him as "The Father of the Chinese Revolution," and Calvin Coolidge would later recall seeing in Sun a "combined Benjamin Franklin and George Washington of China."

For the first time in his life Sun could display for home audiences the oratorical style he had developed abroad,

and the personal charm even his detractors acknowledged. The crowds that turned out to hear him, and learn
more about him, were impressed. Sun could hold them
for hours, not with emotional harangues but with a quiet,
deliberate manner that emphasized his sincerity and his
faith in China's future. Projecting the image of a disinterested patriot, Sun at last achieved a public standing of
sorts. Though less than he had originally aimed for, it is
easy to understand why he accepted it.

For Sun to have admitted at this time that his party
had abandoned him, and that the leadership of the republic was in the wrong hands, would have meant dis-
paraging his own accomplishments and depreciating the
value of his personal sacrifices. Nor would it have been
easy to ignore the national interest as well as the chance
for unity and progress under Yuan. Thus, both egotistic
and patriotic motives stopped him from trying to play the
spoiler. And few would have followed him if he had. It
would also have been incompatible with his nature simply to pack up and sulk. Instead, it seems that Sun, who
had tried so hard to bluff others, now convinced himself
that his optimism had been vindicated, that he had
guided the revolution to a safe haven, and that his duty
lay in contributing to the task of reconstruction.

During the first year of Yuan's presidency, though Sun
retained titular leadership of the party, he chose to ab-
stain from active participation in politics. His colleagues
were happy to honor his wish. But when he told them
that the party should stay out of the contest for political
power and, instead, concentrate on promoting education
and industrialization, they refused to follow his example.

Soon after the birth of the republic various groups,
including dissident offspring of the Alliance, began forming political parties. The Alliance, shedding its secret,
conspiratorial character, got a head start in the new game
of politics, and in early March 1912 convened a party
congress that drew close to five thousand people. The

congress endorsed a new constitution and program, and chose Sun Yat-sen as the party leader. Huang Hsing, the real hero of the armed campaign against the dynasty and the administrative mainstay of the Nanking government, was named one of two deputy leaders. The other was Li Yüan-hung, the revolution's reluctant Garibaldi, who soon formed another party, one more supportive of Yuan Shih-k'ai. (There would be much party-hopping and many cases of multiple affiliation.) The congress defined the Alliance's major aims as the consolidation of the republic and the promotion of people's livelihood, that is, Sun's brand of socialism. A more explicit nine-point platform included support for state socialism, equal rights for women, and international equality.

Despite its more progressive posture the Alliance, like its competitors, catered to an elitist, gentry constituency. By restricting membership to educated adults who could afford the enrollment fee and annual dues — however modest — the party shut the door against the majority of the people. The masses, moreover, were only dimly aware of the significance of the revolution. (In April villagers living less than twenty miles of Peking still did not know of the republic's existence and thought that Yuan Shih-k'ai was the new emperor.)

Thus there were no mass parties, and Sun Yat-sen had never expected the Alliance to become one. During his provisional presidency he had declared that "the mob had no opinions" on important political issues, but "was guided on such questions by the active spirits of the nation. Wherever the latter led the mob would follow." Unfortunately, the "active spirits" were not to assume the benevolent tutelary role he had originally envisaged for his own party. And even his party found it expedient to tone down its relative radicalism.

The erosion set in when the Alliance opened its ranks to assorted timeservers who had ditched the Manchus at the last moment. Further attenuation of its program resulted from the absorption of several minority parties whose votes were needed in the parliament. Pushed through by Sung Chiao-jen, the amalgamation produced a new party, the Kuomintang (Nationalist Party) on August 25, 1912. (One of the reasons for rejecting the name Democratic Party was that the Democrats had been losing so many elections in the United States. The pro-Yuan party, formed in May, was called the Republican Party.) Sun was elected head of the Kuomintang's executive committee, but delegated the office to Sung Chiao-jen.

The price paid for expansion was the abandonment of slogans that smacked of social leveling or that threatened relations with foreigners. The party discarded its demand for equal rights for women, and instead of "striving for international equality" it pledged support of "international peace." State socialism was out, and only a generalized statement favoring a "people's livelihood policy" — but not Sun Yat-sen's definition — remained.

There was one issue, however, upon which Sung Chiao-jen and other party activists would not compromise. They were determined to enforce constitutional rule. The provisional constitution, ratified in March 1912, combined the American and French systems. Parliament and the cabinet were supposed to balance presidential power. But factional squabbling immobilized the parliament, and friction developed between Yuan and the Western-educated premier, T'ang Shao-yi, who had recently joined the Alliance. Four other members of the party, including Sung Chiao-jen, served in his ten-man cabinet. T'ang ran into trouble when he bypassed the consortium and negotiated a small loan with an independent foreign syndicate. Humiliated by the consortium powers, who forced him to cancel the loan, and by Yuan, who disregarded the balancing provisions of the constitution, T'ang resigned at the end of June. Sung Chiao-jen and the other members of the Alliance left the cabinet a few weeks later. But Yuan's opponents still considered him indispensable. They only wanted to subject him to constitutional restraints. The formation of the Kuomintang in August was considered the first step toward party government. The next was to be the national elections, scheduled for the winter.

While Sung Chiao-jen was devising this strategy for taming Yuan's authoritarian tendencies, Sun Yat-sen gave the president unqualified support. Praising Yuan went hand in hand with magnifying the accomplishments of the revolution. Radiating buoyant optimism after his resignation, Sun proclaimed that the revolution, while causing less disruption than any traditional dynastic change, had achieved the two aims of nationalism and democracy. All that remained, he said, was to fulfill his third principle, people's livelihood, now consisting of "equalization of land rights" and state socialism, that is, government ownership of railways and other utilities. Since his slogan still aroused fears, Sun gave it special attention in the speeches he delivered throughout the year. Skeptical property holders were told that they had nothing to worry about: "Socialism is a preventive against the emergence of capitalists. . . . It is exactly like guarding against an illness." Sun also lectured on less controversial subjects, such as patriotism, education, local government and railway building.

The high point of this new, nonpolitical phase of Sun's career was a month-long visit to Peking (August–September). Sun came at Yuan Shih-k'ai's invitation, and at the same time attended the inaugural meeting of the Kuomintang. No mean manipulator himself, Yuan gave Sun full honors and even listened sympathetically to discourses on the single-tax theory of Henry George. And to make sure that Sun would stay out of politics, Yuan appointed him director of national railway planning, a job that provided him with an office in Shanghai, a handsome monthly stipend, and little else except the illusion of being engaged in a grand enterprise.

Convinced that railways held the key to China's economic development — and her transformation into the leading power of the world — Sun had decided in the summer that he would devote himself entirely to this field. His approach, as made public in June and July, was utterly impractical, if not ridiculous. This was a subject on which he would let his imagination, never easily restrained, run absolutely wild. "Choosing from the top," as usual, he took the United States as his model. Without railways, he said, America had been as poor as China. But with money borrowed from abroad the United States had built a 200,000-mile railway network and had become the wealthiest country in the world. China, Sun urged, should follow this example. But since she was five [*sic*] times as large as the United States, China needed one million miles of railways so that *she* could become the strongest power on the globe. This goal, he said, could be achieved in ten years! (China at this time had less than six thousand miles of railways; during the next sixty-five years, including several decades of Communist rule, about another twenty-five thousand miles would be added.)

W. H. Donald, an Australian journalist who later became an adviser to Chiang Kai-shek, recorded his reaction when Sun first divulged his scheme. He "brought forth a large map," Donald wrote, "about six feet square, and when Sun had spread it out upon the floor I saw evidence of a most convincing nature that Sun is not only mad as a hatter, but that he is madder." Undaunted by topographical obstacles Sun had simply taken his brush and "filled in every province and dependency [including Tibet, Mongolia and Sinkiang] with as many lines as he could cram there." Donald concluded: "He is mad, not because he drew the map, for with money and an abundance of time, every line he drew, and more, could be built, but

Sun has the audacity to think that because he drew the thing foreign capitalists would give him sufficient money to build the whole lot within from five to ten years!" It was equally naive to expect Chinese nationalists to accept the control provisions which foreign bankers, even if they agreed to finance further railway building, were sure to demand. It was upon this issue, it will be recalled, that the Manchu government had foundered less than a year earlier. In September Sun lowered his sights to the more modest goal of seventy thousand miles of railways which would still have required loans totaling several billion dollars, or ten times the amount of outstanding railway debts. He had agents solicit foreign financiers, among whom the venerable J. P. Morgan was again a key target. None of these efforts were successful, but Sun continued to deliver the bombastic pronouncements that in less credulous circles would earn him the nickname Big Gun (big noise) Sun.

Only in his old stamping ground, Japan, were people in high places willing to encourage his grandiose plans. For at this time Japanese expansionists had no other card to play. Yuan Shih-k'ai, whom they had never trusted, used Britain, despite the Anglo-Japanese Alliance, to fend them off. While Russia had an inside track with Outer Mongolia, which had proclaimed independence during the last days of the Manchu dynasty, and the British reaped advantages when Tibet loosened its ties to China, Japan had so far gained nothing from the revolution. And though admitted to the consortium — along with Russia — in June 1912, the Japanese could not compete with European capital.

Thus when Sun came to Japan on a state visit in February 1913 and stayed over a month, his hosts fawned on him. They gave him use of a private train, suites in the Imperial and other expensive hotels, and entertained him at banquets attended by political, financial and military dignitaries. Discussions about the use of Japanese capital to develop Chinese industry led to the formation of the

China Industrial Company. Sun was to be president, and Mitsui, Mitsubishi and other *zaibatsu* were to supply the funds. (However, by the time this was announced, in June, Sun would not be in a position to participate.)

A talk with Katsura Tarō, the acting prime minister, whose third cabinet had fallen a few days before Sun's arrival (February 13), revived the old pan-Asian dream. A soldier-politician and the bête noire of Japanese liberals, Katsura warmed Sun's heart when he urged that China and Japan work together for the liberation of India and the awakening of the nonwhite races of the entire world. Japan, he said, would then "never have to worry about land for colonization and commerce, and would never pursue the crude policy of conquest." Katsura also warned him against Yuan Shih-k'ai, but advised him to wait until he was better prepared before challenging Yuan. Sun promised Katsura that he would try to suppress anti-Japanese boycotts in China.

In speeches to Chinese students and *hua-ch'iao,* as well as to Japanese, Sun emphasized the pan-Asian theme. He claimed that China, a continental power, and Japan, a maritime power, were as mutually dependent as "lips and teeth." On the other hand he warned that a Russian orientation spelled only danger for China: what had happened to Mongolia was a portent of more serious aggression. Because of her ingrained isolationism he discounted the possibility of America's help. He also classed the United States with the European imperialist powers against whom China needed Japan's help. This kind of talk naturally pleased the Japanese. They gave Sun the impression that he had not only scored a diplomatic triumph, but had bought some personal insurance in case of a clash with Yuan Shih-k'ai. News from home suddenly pointed up the necessity of such insurance.

On March 20 Sung Chiao-jen, the thirty-one-year-old leader of the Kuomintang, was shot by a hired gunman in

Shanghai and died two days later. The assassin, who had been reputedly paid £200, and his accomplice were soon arrested. Documentary evidence linked the killing to the premier, Yuan's man, and a cabinet secretary. Though conclusive proof that Yuan himself had ordered the assassination was not found, few people doubted his involvement. This was not the first nor would it be the only murder that served his political needs.

Sung was shot when he was about to entrain for Peking and cash in on the Kuomintang's stunning victory in the elections held in December and January. Under his leadership the party had won large pluralities in both houses of parliament. Though the electorate had been restricted to the small minority who had property or educational qualifications, a Chinese election would never come any closer to meeting democratic standards. And since Sung, who had become more openly critical of Yuan, intended to use the parliament to put the president in his proper, constitutional place, or even to replace him, he had to be eliminated.

Yuan, sharing the popular conviction that he was the only man who could hold China together, refused to be hampered by legal or other restraints. An outstanding reformer and progressive under the monarchy, he never considered the new form of government more than window dressing: political opponents were a nuisance and had to be neutralized through flattery, bribery, intimidation or murder.

Enraged as the finger of guilt pointed toward Yuan's entourage, the former revolutionaries who constituted the nucleus of the Kuomintang thought of forcing a showdown, but hesitated because of their military weakness. Sun, who had been foremost among those who had credited Yuan with honorable intentions, vacillated. When he returned to Shanghai on March 25 he was still so intoxicated by the prospect of Sino-Japanese cooperation that he did not mention the Sung Chiao-jen affair in a press interview. Instead, he announced his discovery of Japan's ostensibly true aims: "What Japan wants is not territory in China, but increased trade," which, he pointed out, could only be obtained by pursuit of a peaceful policy. But a week later a Kuomintang organ was urging him to assert forceful leadership and preserve the accomplishments of the revolution. Sun, and also Huang Hsing, preferred legal means of punishing the guilty, though they sent out feelers to potential military allies at home, and also in Japan. The response was not encouraging.

In the meantime, Yuan Shih-k'ai brought to a successful conclusion his long negotiations for a major loan from the consortium. On April 26, the day that the complicity of his people in Sung's murder was publicly confirmed, the foreign powers gave Yuan a vote of confidence — and also imposed unprecedented control provisions. The Reorganization Loan, as it was called, was supposedly for £25 million. But China was credited with only £21 million and was committed to paying back almost £68 million by 1960. Of the £21 million, moreover, a large share was earmarked for repayments to foreign banks and never left Europe. The Americans had withdrawn from the consortium in March because the new president, Woodrow Wilson, found that the loan conditions — which gave foreigners the right to supervise disbursement of funds — touched "very nearly the administrative independence of China itself."

Given the government's financial straits the loan, though offensive to nationalist sensibilities, was unavoidable. But in violation of the provisional constitution, Yuan did not request parliamentary approval. It was on this constitutional issue that the Kuomintang, still reluctant to resort to arms, chose to challenge him and, at the same time, to leave the door open to conciliation. Yet the party kept putting on pressure. In May Sun Yat-sen appealed to the foreign powers not to subsidize the destruction·of parliamentary government. But Yuan got the money and made his moves accordingly. In June he dismissed three Kuomintang military governors, and in the beginning of July shifted troops to battle positions. On the eleventh a Kuomintang general responded by starting what became known as the "second revolution." Sun Yatsen, whose despondency was aggravated by the death of his eldest daughter, supported the rising, but Huang Hsing again took the more active role. Military affairs were not considered Sun's forte. Despite unofficial Japanese help the revolution never had a chance of succeeding and collapsed in September. (According to an unverified Japanese source Sun and Huang agreed to a Mitsui executive's offer to supply them with 20 million yen and equipment for two divisions in return for a promise to cede Manchuria. The project was said to have been vetoed by the Tokyo government.)

Yuan won, not only because he had the superior military machine and the foreign money to oil it. He also had more support from the public, which was not all that fired up by the cause of pure republicanism. While the nation still faced external dangers higher priority was given to the preservation of national unity. Even some veteran revolutionaries opposed this second round of fighting, and Kuomintang moderates, now comprising a fractured remnant of the original party, continued to sit in the Peking parliament. Liang Ch'i-ch'ao, back in China since October 1912, was among the Kuomintang opponents who extended Yuan credit, even when he ran roughshod over representative government. Liang, it will be recalled, had previously warned against the premature adoption of republicanism.

On October 6 Yuan pressured the parliament into electing him president — an office that he had been holding on a provisional basis. The next day the major powers — except for the United States, which had already done so in May — officially recognized the republic, which met their demands on the Tibetan, Mongolian, and other issues. Yuan, who had started terrorizing and executing members of parliament during the second revolution, expelled Kuomintang legislators on November 4 and outlawed the party. In January 1914 he suspended the parliament and in the following months assumed dictatorial powers.

Since August 9, 1913, Sun Yat-sen had taken refuge in Japan. Public opinion there was sympathetic, and he had close friends among the ultranationalists like Tōyama Mitsuru, who provided him with lodging. But the government now had less use for him. Pressure upon Yuan Shih-k'ai had yielded railroad concessions in Manchuria and Inner Mongolia. Still dissatisfied, pan-Asianists had to wait for another opportunity to unleash Sun Yat-sen. Yuan, on the other hand, emerged from the second revolution with even more solid support from Europeans, led by the British. Sun Yat-sen's stock in these quarters fell to a new low.

The Westerners who the previous year had praised him for what they felt had been a patriotic act of self-abnegation now accused him of disrupting stability in the pursuit of personal ambition. Comparisons with George Washington, declared a missionary journal, had been premature, and a distinguished American missionary attributed to Sun "that lack of balance of mind, which had long been obvious except to the color-blind." Some aspects of Sun's behavior during the next few years would cause others to share this view.

As he brooded in Japan, Sun saw himself as a multiple victim — victimized by the party, then by Yuan Shih-k'ai, and finally, by the Western democracies that had turned their backs on him and on the principles they cherished at home. Someone of lesser resilience and self-confidence would now have concluded, as did many Chinese and foreigners, that his political career, shot through with disappointments, had finally reached a dead end. Sun took failure in a different way. He resolved to prove that his life's work had not been in vain and that success was incomplete because he had not had sufficient power. In a letter to an American sympathizer the following year, Sun disclosed that he was "busily preparing for another movement. This time I shall conduct the whole affair personally. . . . The first Revolution broke out before I could reach China. . . . In the second Revolution I did not take part, for I thought that many there were quite competent to carry out the work to a successful conclusion. . . . But too many cooks spoiled the broth!" In internal correspondence he was less sparing of his comrades and bluntly accused them of having blocked him on both occasions. Now he demanded absolute loyalty and obedience. He created in Japan a new, secret, handpicked organization designed to overthrow Yuan and take custody of the nation's destiny until the promulgation of a democratic constitution.

The Chinese Revolutionary Party, as it was called, resembled both traditional secret societies, with which he was familiar, and the Leninist model, which he would later try to emulate. He was elected head, with the old title of *tsung-li,* but with much more authority. Established in July 1914 the party attracted only a fraction of the former revolutionaries and very few of the most prominent. Huang Hsing was among those who refused to join, the main reason being Sun's insistence that every member swear obedience to him personally, not just to the party's program. Also found objectionable was his demand that each member be fingerprinted. Replying to critics who claimed that autocratic rule of the party was not compatible with its democratic aims, Sun cited a European authority: "Dr. [Robert] Michels," he wrote, "says that even the political parties most dedicated to popular rule have to be obedient to the will of one man.

... It is apparent that no matter what the party, all must be obedient to the dictates of the party chief. And how much truer this is in the case of a revolutionary party which has to be obedient in carrying out military commands." Among the exiles who accepted this definition of political leadership was the twenty-seven-year-old Chiang Kai-shek. Chiang, who soon after Sun's death in 1925 would dominate the Kuomintang, had joined the Alliance in 1908, when he was a military cadet in Japan. He had later participated in both revolutions. At this time, however, he was not yet part of Sun's inner circle.

The party's program included Sun's familiar slogans — democracy, people's livelihood, the five-power constitution and the three stages. Sun made a significant change in this last item. Instead of a transition of nine years between the seizure of power and the full establishment of representative government, he scheduled an indefinite period of party rule — now called government by tutelage.

What was strangely missing from this program was the principle of nationalism. That it had been left out of the 1912 party platforms is more understandable. Since the immediate thrust of the revolution had been directed against the alien Manchu dynasty, the revolutionaries had wanted to stress their achievement of this component of nationalism and to avoid giving foreigners reason to interfere. But what Chinese really wanted was no secret. A British diplomat spelled it out for London in May 1912: "The idea of 'China for the Chinese' would seem to be gaining ground. Students returning from Japan, America and England all share the ardent desire to control the settlements and concessions in China and abolish extra-territoriality. They complain of the treatment of Chinese by foreigners at Shanghai and other treaty ports, and wish to keep in their own control the finances, railways, and other enterprises of China." Duly noting this intelligence, a Foreign Office higher-up registered his irritation: "I don't like . . . the 'China for the Chinese' idea."

The "idea" nevertheless spread as the republic, instead of earning relief from imperialist pressure, was squeezed tighter. Yuan tried to ease the pressure by playing off foreigners against each other in the time-honored Chinese fashion. He was of course limited in what he could do, and not the least by his own myopia. Because of his disdain for popular political action, he could not fully capitalize upon nationalism. Sun, on the other hand, went directly against the nationalist trend because of his frantic search for funds.

In 1914 dissension among the original revolutionaries infected overseas sympathizers and slowed down contributions. Though as southerners the *hua-ch'iao* had no love for Yuan Shih-k'ai, they were also solicited by Sun's ex-comrades who had been more prominent in the second revolution. And whereas in plotting against the tottering Manchu dynasty Sun had counted upon the capture of a single province to start a chain reaction, in Yuan he faced a well-armed enemy whose defeat, it seemed, required much more money for buying arms or — this was Sun's preference — for bribing troops. And since Britain was squarely behind Yuan, Sun turned to other countries for money, and especially to Japan, which he never considered just another country, but the natural partner of a resurgent China. So at this low point of his career Sun did not really change his style of conducting revolution. It was just that his single-minded desire for revenge upon Yuan, who had betrayed the republic that was to have been the crowning achievement of Sun's career, made him even more reckless.

In May 1914 Sun wrote to the Japanese prime minister, Ōkuma, and promised Japan, in return for help to the "Republican Army," a virtual monopoly of Chinese commerce and greater profits than England was taking out of India. Sun's generous offer — comparing Japan's projected gains with those that America received by helping Panama gain independence — did not move the Japanese government. It was still waiting for what its foreign minister had once called a "psychological moment" to realize its aims in China. But Sun's letter was published in China and, to put it mildly, did him little credit.

In August Sun began dunning a Californian, James Dietrick, who had earlier showed interest in his railway project. Sun's bait was franchises for opening department stores throughout China or, alternatively, for undertaking various industrial projects. His only condition was that his future government own half the shares in these enterprises. Extending for almost two years, Sun's correspondence with Dietrick resembled the one he had conducted with Homer Lea's partner, Charles Boothe. Again, he started off by asking for millions, went down to a few hundred thousand, and when he ended up with nothing, demanded the return of a power of attorney which the American, like other agents in the past, had received. In the meantime Sun's prospects in Japan had brightened. After August 1914 the "psychological moment" Tokyo had been waiting for drew near.

The outbreak of World War I diverted international attention from China. Invoking the Anglo-Japanese Alliance, Japan declared war on Germany on August 23, and Britain, which needed Japanese naval help in the Pacific and Indian oceans, could not stop her ally from using the opportunity to move in on China. In November Japanese troops captured weakly defended German holdings in Shantung. Though Britain and Germany also violated Chinese neutrality, the Japanese went much further and occupied half the province. In December they announced that since they had had to fight to evict Germany, they were under no obligation to return the leased territory to China. And on January 18, 1915, Japan delivered the

Twenty-one Demands to Yuan Shih-k'ai. This was her long-delayed bid for the preeminent imperialist role in China.

The demands, divided into five groups, dealt mostly with economic concessions. On the whole, these were no more invidious than the ones European imperialists had already extracted. Among other things Japan wanted confirmation of the right of succession to German privileges in Shantung, extension of her own special positions in Manchuria and eastern Inner Mongolia, and a share in running the major industrial complex of central China. Group five, however, included demands for Japanese political, military and financial advisers in the central government, a joint police force, and a dominant role in the development of Fukien province. This section, which seemed to be a blueprint for reducing China to protectorate status, was ominous enough. But the way the Japanese presented the whole package — enjoining Yuan to secrecy, and hinting that if necessary China would be clubbed into complying — magnified the sense of danger and the insult to Chinese pride.

The news was leaked to the press a week later and created an uproar the like of which imperialism had never evoked before. Nor at any previous time in modern Chinese history was public opinion so widely expressed. Newspapers — their total circulation was now close to forty million — and mass rallies called for firm resistance. An anti-Japanese boycott was started in late March, and for the first time revealed the true potency of this weapon, practically the only one in China's arsenal. Though anti-Japanese agitation, like all political activity, affected only a small part of the population, the growing labor movement was also involved.

Yuan was not the man to lead a popular nationalist movement, but public indignation strengthened his negotiating hand. The Japanese had more guns and the advantage of unique international circumstances. In early March they began landing thirty thousand troops in China to augment their existing garrisons, a measure permitted by treaty arrangements. Their diplomats, however, were no match for the Chinese in what the British minister called "a typical Oriental fencing match." By keeping foreign diplomats informed, the Chinese got even the British to oppose group five — which threatened their own rights in China. For months Yuan and a staff of professional diplomats quibbled and stalled until the frustrated Japanese issued an ultimatum on May 7: either China agreed within two days or Japan would take the necessary "steps." By this time the Japanese had scratched group five, and on May 9 China accepted most of the other demands. But the ultimatum and its acceptance brought public furor to a crescendo. May 7 and 9 were designated "Commemoration Days of National Humiliation."

The concessions and investment opportunities that Japan finally got could probably have been obtained more quietly at that time since Western capital, tied up elsewhere, was less competitive. Instead, by reviving the old imperialist tactics in the most heavy-handed and brutal manner, Japan touched off a new, volatile and uncompromising phase of Chinese nationalism, with herself as its chief target. Japan would retain this distinction for most of the next thirty years.

While most patriotic Chinese, including many of Sun's former comrades, either lined up behind Yuan or abstained from obstructing him while he resisted Japan, Sun stood on the other side. Disregarding Huang Hsing's warning "not to get rid of a tiger to let in a wolf," he continued to give the highest priority to his feud with Yuan. Though he argued that Yuan had in fact invited the demands in order to gain Japanese support for his suspected ambition to become emperor, in secret Sun offered the Japanese similar exclusive privileges. On March 14, 1915, while the Japanese were putting pressure on Peking, Sun had sent his proposition to the Tokyo Foreign Office. In return for help in removing "the evil government of China" he invited Japanese tutelage in political, military and economic matters. This was a renewal of the pan-Asian idea, for Sun proposed that Japan forgo other alliances and assist China in getting rid of extraterritoriality and the rest of the unequal treaty obligations.

For Tokyo's purposes, however, there was as yet no need for arming Sun. But the threat to do so enhanced its leverage on Peking. Though the details of Sun's offer were not publicized, it was no secret that he had become the unwitting pawn of Japanese expansionists. His very presence in Japan while other Chinese rushed home to defend the nation infuriated former supporters. One veteran revolutionary, H. H. Kung, took the charitable view that Sun was a misguided patriot suffering from mental strain. In a letter to Yuan's Australian adviser written in April, Kung said that despite Sun's good intentions, the Japanese were able to manipulate him because of his "mistaken ideas." He went on: "Some think that his dangers and anxieties have affected his nervous system." Sun was now an isolated and discredited figure. Then, in August, his enemy made a fatal mistake. Yuan, as Sun had warned he would do, began orchestrating a campaign to make himself emperor.

Personal ambition alone does not explain Yuan's decision. Since republicanism had not struck roots among the masses, he hoped that a new dynasty would provide a focus for national unity and facilitate centralization. Nor was administrative centralization the mere whim of a despotic personality. Yuan saw it as the condition for realizing nationalist goals and furthering internal development. Where he went wrong was in assuming, first, that the ordinary people who were more familiar with the imperial tradition would go out of their way to revive it when his government had done nothing to relieve peasant distress. Second, he mistakenly identified support for his stand against Japan with support for the personal accumulation of power that a restored monarchy would give him. The gentry were already balking at his centralizing measures. And so were some of his generals. Furthermore, most Chinese intellectuals equated republicanism with modernization. They would resist any attempt to turn the clock back. In short, Yuan, as Sun Yat-sen put it, had "mounted a tiger." Sun's plan for destroying him with Japanese assistance suddenly seemed more feasible. Sun also had a new wife to inspire him.

On October 25, 1915, Sun married a beautiful young woman who worshipped him and shared his conviction that he was still destined for great things. Soong Ch'ing-ling (Rosamonde Soong) was twenty-three years old, twenty-six years younger than Sun, and the daughter of one of his best and oldest friends, Charles Jones Soong. In 1913 Soong and his family had fled with Sun Yat-sen to Japan, where the eldest daughter, Ai-ling, continued to serve as Sun's English-language secretary. When she married H. H. Kung in 1914, her sister Ch'ing-ling, a recent graduate of an American university, replaced her. Ch'ing-ling's marriage to Sun supplied the love and companionship that his first marriage, arranged during his youth by his parents, had lacked. Sun's first wife, who had given birth to his three children, was also a Christian, and Sun's second marriage, without having divorced her, upset the Chinese Christian and missionary communities. The marriage also cost Sun the friendship of Charles Jones Soong, a devout Methodist. Yet it later enhanced the influence of the Soong family. The third and youngest sister, Mei-ling, married Chiang Kai-shek in 1927, and she and Ch'ing-ling, as Sun's widow, their brother T. V. Soong, and brother-in-law, H. H. Kung, would all be prominent in politics, though not always on the same side. There were no children from Sun's second marriage.

In the autumn of 1915, when Yuan's dynastic aspirations drew rumblings of discontent, Sun reaffirmed his determination to pursue an independent course and not to repeat the mistake of 1911. He aimed at putting himself and his party in sole control. Urging his followers to seize key points, he declared that he would not cooperate with defectors from Yuan's camp. However, on their own Sun's people, among them Chiang Kai-shek, were unsuccessful. In November they assassinated Yuan's commander in Shanghai, but failed in an attempted naval uprising there in early December. At the end of the month Liang Ch'i-ch'ao's supporters started a rebellion in Yunnan, in southwest China. The real anti-Yuan movement had begun, but not under the leadership of Sun Yat-sen.

Now the Japanese, as Sun had hoped, became more active. Though in principle Japanese leaders preferred a monarchy to a republic in China, Yuan's elevation to the emperorship at this time would have been tantamount to a vote of confidence to resist Japan. Thus, beginning with a diplomatic initiative against the projected monarchy in October, the Japanese kept in step with the indigenous anti-Yuan movement. Britain and her European allies, with troubles of their own, could not interfere. They needed Japan more than they needed Yuan. Besides, they had originally welcomed him as the guarantor of stability. Now he caused instability. In December the Japanese army sent a high-ranking officer to Shanghai to assist rebel movements. In January 1916 the government decided not to recognize the new Chinese dynasty, slated for inaugural that year. Sun Yat-sen's turn finally came in February.

At the time the southern rebels were still encountering stiff resistance, the Japanese decided to subsidize Sun. This was handled unofficially through the industrialist Kuhara Fusanosuke, a shadowy figure operating in military and pan-Asian circles, and a friend of General Tanaka, the army's deputy chief of staff. Tanaka, who as prime minister in the late 1920s would be known as a hard-liner on China, was one of the main architects of the anti-Yuan strategy. From February 20 to April 27 Kuhara gave Sun a total of at least 1.4 million yen (US$700,000) in loans, the last one being transmitted by Tanaka. But Sun would have to show tangible results before getting more money. The Japanese did not rely upon him exclusively, as he had hoped.

On March 7 the Tokyo cabinet decided to go all out for Yuan's removal and to pave the way for establishing hegemony over China. For this purpose it was also decided to give belligerent status to the southern rebels, led by Liang Ch'i-ch'ao's disciple, and to spread money among all anti-Yuan factions. The same Kuhara loaned a million yen to one of Yuan's old enemies, a former high official who was cooperating with the southern rebels. Another businessman, Ōkura, advanced a similar sum to a Manchu prince, a longtime candidate for a puppet role in Manchuria, where Japanese officers pressed for a more audacious policy.

Yuan was in any case marching toward extinction, but Japan made it happen faster. After he canceled the monarchy on March 22, an emboldened Chinese opposition wanted him out entirely, and then in April the Japanese struck their hardest blow. They persuaded the international commission administering China's salt tax to withhold the revenue that remained after deductions for loan and indemnity payments. Without money Yuan could not slow down the defection of bureaucrats and soldiers.

Sun Yat-sen, trying to direct operations from Tokyo, was now more worried about Yuan's other opponents than Yuan himself. He warned his followers that unless they seized the initiative China might fall into the hands of a "second or third Yuan Shih-k'ai." He sent money to bribe troops, pleaded with the American *hua-ch'iao* to send volunteers, planes and pilots, and shipped arms through the good offices of the Japanese military government in Shantung. (It would turn out that Japanese dealers had unloaded obsolete weapons.) On April 27 he left for Shanghai to take personal charge. By this time, probably at the insistence of the Japanese, he gave up the idea of going it alone and instructed his people to cooperate with nonparty elements. Though he warned against advertising the Japanese connection, it was highly visible, especially in Shanghai and Shantung. In Shanghai Sun himself stayed at the home of an official of the Japanese South Manchurian Railway Company. His bodyguard was a young officer who some twenty years later would command Japan's expeditionary force in Shanghai.

A significant military success might have lured more Japanese money, but Sun's fighters failed to bring it off. Claiming that only 5 million dollars stood between him and the capture of Peking, Sun made a final, futile plea to his American friend Dietrick. At the same time, recognizing that his rivals had again stolen a march on him, Sun called for unity of all forces committed to republicanism. But on June 6 Yuan, already preparing to flee Peking, died of uremia. What followed was not a revival of republicanism, but a period of regional warlordism starring Yuan's former protégés in the Peiyang Army. Nothing approximating centralized rule would be seen in China for the next twelve years.

Japan, by helping to bring China closer to chaos, scored gains, but only for the short term. Continental hegemony, Japan would find, could not be obtained through proxies, and bullying tactics only stiffened Chinese resistance. Eventually the Japanese imperial army would have to fight the Chinese people. For their country was not for sale. It never had been and never would be.

Neither Sun Yat-sen nor those among his rivals who had also accepted Japanese aid intended to be puppets. All were hoping to exploit Japan for their own immediate ends. Still, Sun had been by far the least discreet in courting Japan, especially during the furor over the Twenty-one Demands. He moreover sincerely believed in pan-Asianism, based upon a true mutuality of interests, just as he believed that the entire industrialized world could be brought to recognize the advantages of assisting rather than exploiting China. In trying to convince the Kuharas and Morgans to take this long-range view, and in assuming that, if necessary, he could outsmart them, Sun was of course naive. Yet, during the first twenty years of his career he had had few alternatives. The conditions for building indigenous power had been absent.

However, the continued modernization of Chinese society began widening avenues for political mobilization. New currents of thought, stimulating awareness of social responsibilities, permeated student and intellectual ranks. Without Yuan's repressive dictatorship these ideas flowed more freely. Industrialization, stepped up by the European war, enlarged the native entrepreneurial and working classes. Change came more slowly to the countryside. The masses, as Sun Yat-sen had recently declared, took "no active part in politics." Yet, rural exploitation, unchecked, grew more vicious, and intensified traditional peasant outbursts. Here was a gigantic reservoir of discontent, waiting to be channeled into positive political action. Chu Chih-hsin, the independent-minded revolutionary who had contributed the most original articles on socialism to *People's Report* during the previous decade, began tapping this reservoir in the campaigns against Yuan. The trouble was that the ripening of these new conditions coincided with the entrenchment of regional militarists, whose "treachery" Sun had predicted during the waning days of Yuan's rule.

For about a year after Yuan's death the well-meaning but powerless Li Yüan-hung — successor to the presidency — tried to maintain a facade of republicanism in Peking.

Sun stayed in the background while giving moral support to Li's effort to restore the provisional constitution of 1912 and the parliament that Yuan had dissolved. For Sun this was a period of reflection, writing and speaking. Again, as in 1912–13, he accepted failure with outward equanimity and took refuge in the astonishing claim that constitutional government was in working order. Assuming once more the mantle of elder statesman, he wrote a primer on parliamentary procedure. The purpose was to teach the people how to use still-nonexistent democratic rights. (*First Steps in Democracy,* later incorporated in a larger work, *Plans for National Reconstruction,* was finished in February 1917.) With his party in shambles he shelved the idea of tutelage and looked toward the establishment of a "pure republic" within ten years. Taking Cleveland, Ohio, and Switzerland as his models, he advocated a system of local government based upon the rights of suffrage, recall, initiative and referendum. Then the fight over entering the World War thrust him back into the real world of Chinese politics.

With Yuan Shih-k'ai out of the way, and more pliable militarists in the ascendancy, Japan changed course and urged China to declare war on Germany. Underwriting and supervising a Chinese war effort seemed easy ways of augmenting influence on the continent. But first, in early 1917, Japan made sure that China's participation would not endanger Japan's postwar claims on Shantung. Secret agreements with the European entente powers assured Japan of their support. On the Chinese side the premier, Tuan Ch'i-jui, welcomed the prospect of a 段祺瑞 Japanese-backed arms buildup and loans. The president, Li Yüan-hung, and many others denied that this was China's fight and that she had anything to gain by joining. Though his not-so-secret dealings with Japan had tarnished his credibility, Sun rushed into the fray championing the cause of neutrality.

In March he sent a telegram to Lloyd George and

asked that Britain, for her own sake as well as China's, stop pressing for a declaration of war. He also wired members of the Chinese parliament. Claiming that most Chinese could not differentiate between Germans and other Europeans, he warned that war against Germany could fan latent anti-Westernism. He also warned that Chinese Muslims were liable to cause trouble if they had to fight Turkey. But Sun and the old Kuomintang parliamentary bloc had a more practical reason for opposing entry into the war. They suspected that Tuan Ch'i-jui's military clique would use extraordinary war powers to throttle what was left of constitutional government.

Sun's antiwar arguments were spelled out in a lengthy treatise, *The Question of China's Survival,* later translated into English under the title *The Vital Problem of China.* Completed in the summer of 1917, the booklet was actually written by the gifted Chu Chih-hsin, who is said to have been briefed by Sun. But whatever Sun's share in the writing, the fact that he endorsed it is highly important. Never before had he openly subscribed to views so harshly critical of imperialism, especially the British variety. Though Britain and the other entente powers wanted China in the war — Chinese laborers were already performing valuable service in Europe — Japan was the main war lobbyist in Peking. Nonetheless, Sun and Chu built the antiwar case almost entirely on antagonism to Britain. That Britain, as the leading imperialist power, had done nothing to deserve China's help was of course uncontestable. Much less tenable was the prediction that if victorious Britain would sell out China to divert Russia from India, or if forced into a stalemate, would sacrifice China to Germany. The attempt to whitewash Japan fell flat. Japan, the authors insisted, really did not want China in the war, but they could not divulge "the diplomatic secrets . . . obtained from absolutely reliable sources" that could confirm this.

Yet the main message that Sun and Chu tried to get

across was sound enough: China could expect no favors by performing coolie service for warring imperialists. The treaty revisions that prowar circles hoped to get were nothing less than China deserved. She was not, the authors contended, a "prisoner before the bar" who needed to show evidence of "meritorious conduct" before applying for a "pardon." China's duty, they said, was to stay neutral, put her own house in order, and work for better relations between the United States and Japan, the two countries they considered China's true friends. (U.S.– Japanese relations had soured since 1915. Despite her own entry into the war, America was not anxious for China's involvement if it would cause internal turmoil. These were the feelings of President Wilson, who in June received Sun's telegram asking that America use her influence to keep China out.)

In singling out Britain for condemnation Sun was also trying to settle a personal score. He could never forget that the British had backed Yuan Shih-k'ai. Yet, as always with Sun, pursuit of a particular tactical course did not foreclose other options. In March the London Foreign Office recorded Sun's purported fear that Japan would take advantage of China's participation in the war. And when he learned of the March revolution Sun also thought of the possibility of getting a loan from the new Russian government. According to Sun, China's republican revolution had inspired the Russians to overthrow the tsar! It was Germany, however, that supplied his major windfall from the war issue. The Germans were prepared to subsidize any group committed to Chinese neutrality.

The Chinese government, pressured by Tuan Ch'i-jui, broke relations with Germany on March 14. Before leaving, however, German diplomats got in touch with Sun, whose anti-British stand attracted their notice. According to German records they paid Sun 2 million dollars (US$1 million), which he requested in order to unseat Tuan.

Despite Sun's subsequent denial to the Americans, the payoff probably took place. In the summer he had sufficient cash to finance a reentry into politics.

In June the war issue precipitated a showdown between the militarists and parliament. Parliament lost and was dissolved. A general of the old school marched into Peking with a band of pigtailed soldiers and for two weeks in July celebrated the restoration of the Manchu dynasty. Tuan, leading the Peiyang coterie, then "restored" the republic and reorganized parliament. This was the government that declared war on Germany on August 14. But the only war that was fought was at home. Fighting began in the fall, when the Peiyang generals tried to extend their authority to the south but were obstructed by several independent military governors. The Peiyang combination, which controlled the Peking government and thereby gained international recognition, was the strongest warlord group. Yet rivalry between its two factions — Anfu and Chihli, each commanding a force of several hundred thousand soldiers — prevented it from making a clean sweep of the country. The subsequent fracturing and realigning of combinations would plunge China into the turmoil that Sun Yat-sen had predicted. For a while, Tuan Ch'i-jui's Anfu clique had the upper hand. Aided by Japanese loans, Tuan made the most of China's participation in the European war. China's main contribution was to send laborers to France, Russia and the Middle East. (The first batch of coolies had been sent the previous year; by the end of the war there would be close to two hundred thousand of them.)

In the beginning of July 1917 Sun Yat-sen had made his move. He persuaded or bribed naval commanders to remove several vessels — the better part of the Chinese fleet — to Canton. One hundred members of parliament — later the number rose to 250 — were similarly induced. In Canton Sun formed a military government whose ostensible aim was to "protect the constitution." On September 1 this "extraordinary session" of parliament elected him grand marshal. But real power was in the hands of the provincial militarists who had no more concern for constitutionalism than their northern counterparts. Sun had some influence with the parliament and the small navy, a shaky claim to legitimacy, and nothing else.

Again, weakness at home sent him scurrying for outside help. Since the Peking warlords were monopolizing the benefits of China's "war effort," Sun did a quick about-face on this issue. Convinced that Europeans were fighting for aggrandizement, not principles, he had no qualms about offering his services to all combatants. The only thing wrong with this strategy was that he had little to sell.

In August and September, when the ink on his antiwar essay was barely dry, Sun notified the American consul in Canton that he was ready to join the war under American auspices and offered investment opportunities in return for loans. He also tried to plant the idea that Japan was bidding for a deal, but professed preference for making it with the United States. On September 26 his Canton government did acknowledge a state of war with Germany. However, the Americans, who had heard rumors of Sun's German connections, considered him too unreliable. They neither recognized his government nor granted loans. No foreign government, in fact, recognized Canton. The Japanese, whom he never stopped soliciting, turned him down. And in 1918 he apparently courted the Germans. Despite his government's declaration of war he sent an agent to Germany with a proposal that, in return for Chinese raw materials, Germany, combined with Russia, help him against the northern warlords, and against Britain and Japan. The war ended before Berlin could consider this proposition. By that time, moreover, the southern warlords were no longer hospitable.

Rejecting Sun's scheme for a northward drive to re-store constitutional government, the militarists took steps to curb his influence. In January and February 1918 a number of Sun's bodyguards and his chief ally, the naval minister, were murdered. In April Sun's opponents can-celed the post of grand marshal and relegated him to mere membership in a seven-man directorate. Fed up, but still contending that the Canton parliament, having been elected in 1913, represented the only legitimate government, Sun left Canton in May. In June he spent several weeks on an unsuccessful hunt for support in Japan. The Japanese, who at this time were buying con-cessions from the Peking warlords and gaining influence in the northern military setup, kept Sun at a distance. He was not even allowed to enter Tokyo. (In 1917–18 Tuan Ch'i-jui's Anfu clique, then in control of the Peking gov-ernment, received Japanese loans or bribes amounting to about US$100 million.) At the end of the month Sun retired to the French concession of Shanghai, where he resumed writing. For over two years he would remain in the shadows. While dissecting past failures and polishing his program, he would still be on the lookout for foreign allies.

The first fruit of his labors, *The Doctrine of Sun Wen* (also called *Psychological Reconstruction,* and translated into English under the title *Memoirs of a Chinese Revo-lutionary*), was probably completed in May 1919. Sun's purpose was to teach his comrades how to correct the erroneous thinking that had led to the failure of the rev-olution and to the increased misery of the people. If they had not considered his ideals "too elevated and unattain-able," he argued, he could "very easily" have put into effect his program of nationalism, democracy, socialism and the five-fold constitution. Why, he asked, had they not followed him? While acknowledging that as the leader part of the responsibility may have been his, the root trouble, he insisted, was in his comrades' "mode of thought." Sun then claimed to have made another theoretical breakthrough.

He attributed his comrades' lack of conviction and, indeed, China's weakness over the centuries, to the ancient dictum that "knowledge is easy, but action is difficult." He himself, he wrote, had once believed this, but several years of study had led to the discovery that the opposite was true: "To understand is difficult, but to achieve is easy." He then set out to prove this by citing examples — not always clearly relevant — from Chinese and world history, and especially from the Japanese experience.

In other words, Sun tried to stir his comrades into action by convincing them that the real obstacle to China's salvation — knowledge — had already been surmounted by himself. If they had faith in him the "work of reconstruction" would "be just as easy as the turning of a hand or the breaking of a twig." He continued: "Mind is the beginning of everything. . . . While we believe in our minds in the practicability of any plan, be it to move mountains or to fill up the sea, it can be easily accomplished."

People, according to Sun, are divided into three categories: the leaders or innovators, the transmitters or disciples, and the performers — "those who carry out what they receive from the . . . first two groups without doubting and without hesitating." He obviously saw himself in the first category, the party in the second, and the masses in the third.

In speaking to the Tokyo students Sun had struck these same voluntarist, elitist tones. Now, by tackling the knowledge-action dualism, which had exercised more subtle Chinese minds than his, Sun tried to give philosophical trappings to the concept of single-party tutelage under a prescient leader. His attitude toward the masses, furthermore, meshed with traditional Confucian elitism.

For the Master himself had said: "The people may be made to follow it [the Way], but may not be made to understand it." Yet Confucianism also conceded an infinite potential to education: anyone, if properly trained, could rise to the status of a sage. In positing republicanism as a feasible goal, Sun displayed a similar faith in education: "If an ox can be trained to plow, and a horse to carry a rider, then what about man? Can we tell a father that his child cannot be admitted to school because he does not know written characters? It is precisely because he does not know characters that he must immediately start learning them." He also acclaimed American rule of the Philippines as a successful example of tutelage — though twenty years earlier he had plotted with Aguinaldo's insurrectionists.

This didactic essay was directed toward a party that had ceased to exist as a unified body. Sun did not rush to revive it. Too impatient to engage in routine organizational affairs, he was also still resentful of the shabby treatment his comrades had showed him. He preferred waiting for opportunities to work through the power holders both at home and abroad. The end of the war seemed to offer such opportunities. Nor did the Bolshevik victory in Russia escape his attention. In the summer of 1918, just after leaving Canton, he cabled Lenin in the name of the south China parliament and the Chinese Revolutionary Party. Expressing "profound admiration of the relentless struggle" waged by the Russian revolutionaries, he hoped that revolutionaries of both countries could "join forces for a common struggle." The existence of a socialist republic in Russia for eight months, he said, gave hope to the peoples of the East that they might establish similar new social orders. In August, Chicherin, the Soviet commissar for foreign affairs, replied to the "leader of the Chinese revolution" and agreed that "the great proletariat of Russia and China" had common interests. Yet it was not Soviet ideology that attracted Sun.

In that department he felt completely self-sufficient. What he had in mind was military assistance. However, he saw this as only one of his foreign options, and by far not the most promising.

In late November, on the chance that a newly formed cabinet would be more receptive, and playing on Japanese fears of postwar Anglo-American "arrogance," he again called for East Asian solidarity. In 1913 he was reputed to have offered Manchuria in return for Japanese aid against Yuan Shih-k'ai. This time, according to a Japanese industrialist, he was ready to throw in Mongolia as well in return for help against Yuan's successors, who already had their own deal going with Japan. In December Sun's request, relayed through the Japanese consul-general in Shanghai, was turned down. At the same time, the end of the war, and the hope, inspired by Woodrow Wilson, that a new era of world peace and cooperation was in the offing, prompted Sun to draw up one of the most ambitious modernization schemes ever put on paper. While opening lines to the newly established socialist homeland, and while still cherishing the dream of anti-Western pan-Asianism, he made his greatest bid so far to Western capitalists.

Soon after the armistice of November 1918 Sun began writing his book *The International Development of China*. Originally written in English since it was intended for Westerners, this work expanded upon his earlier scheme for railway building. He drew up plans for improving communications — railways (one hundred thousand miles), paved roads (one million miles), canals, telephone and telegraph systems, river conservancy; for building three new harbors, each matching the capacity of New York's; for developing cities, water power, iron, steel and cement works, mineral extraction, agriculture, irrigation, reforestation; and for colonizing Manchuria, Mongolia, Sinkiang and Tibet. He envisaged a Chinese automobile industry producing enough cars

cheaply "so that everybody who wishes it may have one."
Fuel, he predicted, would be no problem, for "China is
known to be a very rich oil-bearing country."

This was a program for rapidly recapitulating the industrial revolution and overtaking the West and Japan.
Foreigners would supply the management and training,
and the Chinese masses the labor. (On road building, for
example, he divided the projected million miles into 400
million and came out with one mile for every four hundred people: "For four hundred people to build one mile
of road is not a very difficult task.") But what about
capital?

Unless goodwill and cooperation replaced cutthroat
competition and the "scrambling for territories," the
world, Sun contended, was headed for another war. Assuming that common sense would prevail — and the
words of Wilson encouraged him to believe so — he saw
no reason why the major powers could not jointly invest
in China a fraction of what they had expended upon war
supplies. Half that sum — US$60 million daily or close to
$22 billion annually — would, in his estimation, be suffi-
cient to carry out his program. It would provide profits
for foreign capital, high wages for labor, the expansion of
production, and the benefits of nationalized industry. "In
a nutshell," he concluded, "it is my idea to make capitalism create socialism in China."

Sun's ideas about China's modernization had not really changed since the turn of the century. He still saw
advantages in Chinese backwardness: "Unlike the West,
China was not troubled by a class struggle between capital and labor," he now wrote. "However, China must
develop her industries by all means. Shall we follow the
old path of western civilization? The old path resembles
the sea route of Columbus' first trip to America. . . . But
nowadays navigators take a different direction to America
and find that the destination can be reached by a distance
many times shorter. The path of Western civilization was

an unknown one and those who went before groped in the dark as Columbus did on his first voyage. . . . As a latecomer China can greatly profit in covering the space by following the direction already charted by Western pioneers." As before, Sun believed that the real interests of the industrialized world — and he was impressed by Kropotkin's answer to the Social Darwinists — lay in mutual aid rather than struggle. "The goal of material civilization," he wrote, "is not private profit but public profit." China, he felt, would be the testing ground for postwar morality.

Friends helped Sun write his book, and in early 1919 he began sending outlines to various foreign officials and governments. (Parts were also published in a Shanghai English-language journal. The first edition of the book appeared in 1920, the second in 1921, and in the following year it was also published in England and the United States by G. P. Putnam.) Though all his projects — some of which he borrowed from other sources — could not be faulted in principle, the idea of taking on the package as a whole staggered the imagination. Sun's respondents, including the American minister to Peking and the U.S. secretary of commerce, made polite noises. They expressed sympathy with his sentiments but pointed out that it would take years just to work out the details of the plan. Even under normal circumstances — and this was when a ravaged Europe was struggling to its feet — it would be nearly impossible to raise the billions of dollars required for only some of the projects. Sun was reminded that China's revenues were already "too heavily burdened with the interest charges on existing government loans to warrant further charges." More modest proposals concerning specific projects, he was told, might be "sufficiently remunerative to attract private capital." The U.S. minister, Dr. Paul S. Reinsch, who showed the most interest, gave the best advice: scale down everything and concentrate on the development of agriculture, which engaged eighty percent of the Chinese people. But Sun was not in a position to develop anything. Without a political foothold, and encouraged only by his young wife and a handful of personal followers who paid homage at the rue Molière in Shanghai's French concession, he cut a sorry figure as he bombarded Western statesmen with his colossal scheme for developing China and preventing another pointless war.

Presumably, Sun thought that his plan would induce the powers to look favorably upon its author. But besides its unfeasibility, Sun's reputation worked against him. In November 1918, when he appealed directly to President Wilson to support the southern parliament against the Peking warlords, Wilson, though admitting some sympathy for Sun's ideals, refused to reply. His secretary of state told him that "there are some very ugly stories" about Sun "in regard to his acceptance of bribes and his readiness to serve the highest bidder." (The overture to Wilson coincided with Sun's latest plea to Japan and his warning against Anglo-American dominance.) Sun's pronouncements on socialism also aroused suspicion.

And yet, like so many of his ideas, there was a prophetic quality about Sun's modernization scheme. International aid in development would not always remain a farfetched notion. Nor, sixty years later, would it seem laughable to speak of making foreign "capitalism create socialism in China." The cars he envisaged for every Chinese family are still far off, but he was apparently right about the oil. The trouble of course was that Sun always tried to make everything seem so easy. It was as if he were completely detached from reality and had no idea of the time and conditions required for realizing his program. He expected that after ten years China would be well on the way to industrialization, could dispense with foreign experts, and start paying back loans.

He was also out of touch with the mood of his countrymen. Resentment of Japan and power politics had been building up since 1915. Then, in the spring of 1919, betrayal at the Versailles Peace Conference produced the psychological turning point of Chinese nationalism. It now became a tremendous energizing force, stimulating popular action and intensifying intellectual and social ferment. During the next and final phase of his career Sun Yat-sen would try to adapt the old strategy and slogans to this new political climate.

SEVEN

Riding the New Wave

THE DECISION of the Paris peacemakers to endorse Japan's takeover of Shantung precipitated the greatest nationalist protest that China had ever known. It began with a student demonstration in Peking on May 4, 1919. But what is commonly known as the May Fourth Movement refers to a much broader phenomenon. It takes in the intellectual excitement that from around 1915 to the early 1920s evoked a critical appraisal of traditional culture. Disappointment in the 1911 Revolution and the realization that the Manchus alone had not been responsible for China's troubles directed attention to deeper causes that the revolution had left untouched. Inspired by foreign ideas, a handful of writers and academics boldly proposed creating a new culture to replace the old one that still fashioned the behavior of most Chinese. This revolutionary notion, especially after the patriotic outburst of 1919, gained ground in student-intellectual circles. Though it soon split on ideological issues, the movement had the ultimate effect of bringing nationalist and socially conscious intellectuals into the service of mass political action.

To be sure, traditional attitudes had begun breaking down much earlier. The Opium War, China's first clash with industrialized civilization, had awakened interest in foreign technology, especially in the military sphere. By the end of the century pioneer reformers like Yen Fu and Liang Ch'i-ch'ao introduced foreign political and social philosophy. Picking up momentum during the post-Boxer reform period, intellectual modernization also nourished antidynasticism. Yet the revolutionaries, and notably Sun Yat-sen, emphasized changing the form of government rather than modes of thought and social institutions. Thus Yen and Liang, rather than Sun, whose simplistic notion of political change they ridiculed, had pointed the way for the new generation. In its intensity and impact, the May Fourth Movement was unprecedented. Never before had traditional institutions, including that hitherto inviolable bastion of Confucianism, the family system, been so devastatingly attacked. In less than twenty years the intellectual mood had shifted from reformism to iconoclasm.

Ch'en Tu-hsiu, a thirty-six-year-old former classical scholar who had studied in Japan and France, fired the opening shots in 1915, when he launched his magazine, *New Youth,* in Shanghai. His lead article, "Call to Youth," contrasted the sterility of the East with the dynamic vitality of the West. Shackled by outmoded customs, laws, ethics and social obligations, Chinese thought, he contended, was a thousand years behind that of the West. Unless animated by a new individualistic spirit China would suffer the fate of ancient Babylon. Darwinian natural selection showed no mercy. As he developed this theme in subsequent articles, Ch'en would argue that democracy and science epitomized the modern, creative spirit of the West, and that Confucian morality, including filial piety, and the entire structure of traditional culture and beliefs, were antithetical to these life-giving values.

Individual writers began echoing Ch'en's call for a transformation of values. In 1917 a reorganized Peking University opened its doors to the new thought and gave it a thriving home. Previously, because of the lifestyles of students and teachers, this government institution had been popularly known as the Brothel Brigade and the Gambling Den. It had been a stronghold of conservative learning and careerism. Under a new chancellor, Ts'ai Yüan-p'ei, who had studied in Germany and France, it became a center for the free pursuit of knowledge. Once an outstanding classical scholar and an anti-Manchu revolutionary, Ts'ai disregarded political considerations and looked only for scholarly excellence in his faculty. Student organizations for mutual help and cultural improvement were encouraged. This was an atmosphere that bred nonconformism, initiative and civic spirit. (In 1918 Mao Tse-tung, then almost twenty-five years old, audited classes and worked in the library. The previous year he had written an article for *New Youth*.)

In 1917 Ts'ai appointed Ch'en Tu-hsiu dean of the School of Letters. Ch'en continued to edit *New Youth*, and the magazine's circle of contributors and readers, and its emulators, grew. That year Hu Shih, another giant of the cultural revolution — and Ch'en's future ideological opponent — also joined the faculty. Fresh from earning a doctorate under John Dewey at Columbia University, the twenty-six-year-old Hu stressed the need for applying the critical methods of science to the study of history, philosophy and literature. His promotion of the use of the spoken language (*pai-hua*) as the written medium made him famous.

The elliptical literary language, replete with classical quotations, could be fully mastered only by the tiny elite that had used it as an instrument for ruling traditional society. Its replacement by *pai-hua*, like that of Latin by the national vernaculars of Europe, was an essential step toward the spread of literacy and greater popular involvement in the political and cultural life of the country. This was not the first time that the change had been proposed, and some political writers had already been using the vernacular. But Hu's persuasive arguments came at the right time. By 1920, only three years after his original proposal, most periodicals were written in the vernacular.

China had had great hopes for the Paris Peace Conference. For the first time in modern history she was on the winning side of a war. Moreover, according to Woodrow Wilson this had not been just another war, but one to end power politics. The Chinese tended to believe him. Despite the October Revolution in Russia, Wilson, not Lenin, seemed to be the prophet of the new age — at least until 1919. China expected a new deal from her allies. Her delegation to the conference — representing both the northern and southern governments — proposed changing the unequal treaties. A minimum and more urgent demand was for the return of the former German concessions in Shantung. This at least would have wiped out the stain of the Twenty-one Demands. The conference rejected both proposals at the end of April. Woodrow Wilson, upon whom the Chinese had counted so much, bowed down to the Japanese, who flashed their secret, wartime agreements with Britain and France. Adding to the fury and frustration of Chinese patriots was the disclosure that their own government in Peking had in September 1918 also given Japan a secret assurance on Shantung.

On May 4 over three thousand students from various schools in Peking, led by a group from the university, gathered at the famous T'ien-an Gate, and then marched to protest the Shantung decision and to condemn their government's collaboration with Japan. What began as a peaceful demonstration soon turned violent. The students burned the house of one "traitorous" official, beat up another, and clashed with the police. One student died of injuries and thirty-two were arrested. Within a few weeks students in over two hundred cities responded and launched a multiclass protest movement.

The centerpiece of their campaign was an anti-Japanese boycott that benefited from rising economic nationalism. (While Europe exported less, imports from Japan had tripled during the war years.) Students formed ten-man teams to enforce the boycott and lead street meetings and demonstrations. A Shanghai mass meeting drew one hundred thousand people. Students went on strike in the major cities, and sometimes were followed by merchants and workers. A general strike paralyzed the largest city, Shanghai, and its International Settlement, for a week. Even the notorious Shanghai underworld declared a patriotic recess! In various cities, including foreign concessions, police and troops wounded demonstrators and killed a few. Though intermittent boycotting continued for over a year, the main campaign subsided at the end of June, when the students achieved their immediate objective: the Chinese delegation in Paris did not sign the peace treaty. The students scored other successes — the cabinet resigned, and the government dismissed three pro-Japanese officials and released over a thousand students who had been arrested.

One of the most remarkable features of the May–June protest is that no political party or established organization set it off. Students proved their mettle as organizers and propagandists. Also revealing was the broad appeal of nationalist slogans. Businessmen and beggars, secret-society gangs, and coolies as well as skilled workers responded. The peasants were still not directly involved: this was an entirely urban phenomenon. What happened in the cities, however, underscored the effects of modern education as well as the rapid industrialization of the war period, and the worsening crisis of the traditional agricultural economy.

By 1919 the number of people who had gotten a taste

of modern education — if only in elementary schools —
since the reforms of the preceding decade, may have been
as large as ten million. Even this, probably inflated figure
covered less than three percent of the population. Still,
the high concentration of educated youth in the cities
produced a large reserve of potential nationalist agitators.
Many of these young men and women came from the new
commercial class: family connections hastened the involvement of merchants in patriotic activities.

During the war indigenous capital had been diverted
from agriculture into urban light industry. New industrial centers sprouted in the hinterland; older ones on the
coast expanded. Landless peasants, streaming into these
cities, formed a volatile *lumpenproletariat*. And by 1919
there were close to one and a half million industrial
workers, almost triple the number of 1914. Both this
working class and the native capitalist class emerged from
the May Fourth incident with rich organizational experience. Though nationalism gave them a common cause —
over forty percent of industrial workers were employed in
foreign enterprises — it could not muffle the rising sound
of class conflict. In 1919 workers returning from Europe
invigorated trade-union activity.

The new culture movement gathered force. Active
promoters were still a relatively small group — Peking
University, for example, had less than twenty-five hundred students — but their influence on the literate community was enormous. Their indictment of tradition — of
the family and clan systems, ancestor worship, foot-bind-
ing, female subjugation, Taoist magic, and the whole
gamut of old beliefs and customs — became more audacious. Thousands read their publications. During the six
months following the May Fourth incident some four
hundred new vernacular-language periodicals appeared.
A craving for Western literature engendered a flood of
translations. At the same time the cultural movement acquired a more practical bent.

Students formed dozens of new organizations and engaged in public-oriented activities and projects such as night schools, free schools for poor children, public libraries and lectures, work and study groups, and wall newspapers. Behind all this was the growing feeling of the need to reach the masses. Though their main effort was still confined to the cities, students began going out to the villages. But there were limits to what could be accomplished under warlordism. What was the sense of preaching the virtues of education when feuding satraps wasted sixty to eighty percent of the national revenue on armies that did not defend the country but ripped it apart? Appropriations for education were probably less than what they had been during the waning years of the dynasty. Yet the demands of nationalist modernizers were much greater, and more freely expressed.

Under divided and unstable warlord rule public opinion could not be stifled with the cruel efficiency of a centralized police or a totalitarian state. During the May–June disturbances, for example, Shanghai was beyond the reach of the Peking authorities. Paradoxically, the entire period of warlordism — 1916–1928 — coincided with the flowering of modern Chinese intellectual life. Yet if warlordism was too weak to apply effective restraints to thought — warlords fought with guns and money, not ideas — its wanton brutality and waste of life and resources obstructed the larger aims of nationalist modernizers. Ordinary people were worse off than under the Manchu dynasty. Hunger produced hundreds of thousands of peasant recruits — including boys less than fifteen years old — for warlord armies, which were maintained by extortionate taxation, the cultivation of opium, and collaboration with foreign powers. Despite the nationalist sentiments of individual warlords, the system prolonged the influence of imperialism. These were the conditions which, within a few years after the May Fourth incident, brought frustrated young intellectuals into a sustained political struggle against both warlord-ism and imperialism.

Already in the summer of 1919 the argument over the need for a new monolithic ideology to replace the Confucianism they rejected began dividing the cultural revolutionaries. Marxism–Leninism, with its triple appeal — as the most modern Western ideology, as a strategy for seizing power, and as the antithesis of imperialism — attracted more attention. The contrast between the capitalist democracies, which stuck to the old imperialism, and the socialist homeland that renounced it, was to have a profound effect on student attitudes. In March 1920 they would learn that in the previous July, a Soviet spokesman, Leo Karakhan, had declared his government's willingness to abrogate the unequal treaties which the tsarist government had imposed upon China. Marxism did not capture the May Fourth Movement, but its appeal to influential leaders, including Ch'en Tu-hsiu, whose yearning for dramatic change clouded his earlier vision of democracy and individualism, foreshadowed a shift away from cultural-educational endeavors toward revolutionary political action. In 1919 Ch'en spent several months in jail because of his support of student demonstrators. Two years later he would be one of the founders of the Chinese Communist Party. The new trend in the student movement, however, would first benefit Sun Yat-sen and the Kuomintang.

Sun was not an early enthusiast of the May Fourth Movement. Though Shanghai was the center of the 1919 disturbances Sun, still busy with his grandiose development scheme, was only an observer, not a participant, and certainly not a leader. It has been said that the French allowed him to remain in their concession on the condition that he stay inactive politically. But there are other explanations for his ambivalent attitude toward the new-thought movement as well as the nationalist protest.

Sun had little patience with intellectuals, who had always given him trouble. And since he seemed to claim exclusive possession of transcendent knowledge, he was not impressed when academics and students displayed an infatuation with Western ideas. Their wholesale indictment of tradition bothered him. Despite his Western background and habits, including an enthusiasm for croquet which he played on his lawn in Shanghai, Sun had a sentimental attachment to the teachings of the sages except when, as in the case of "knowledge and action," he claimed to have corrected them. Only products of mainstream gentry education could have treated tradition as cavalierly as the new-thought radicals did. For an outsider like Sun the classics probably held a mystifying attraction. This may also explain his objections to the abandonment of the literary style, though he was less accomplished in it than the champions of the vernacular language were. As an elitist, Sun did not attach that much importance to the spread of literacy, or to its implications for politicizing the masses. Also, predicating China's revival upon a cultural revolution upset his schedule for a sudden leap to great-power status. As he had once complained to Yen Fu, for how long was China doomed to lag behind others?

Sun was of course a nationalist. Who at this time was not? But he had his own way of showing it, and it did not include militant responses to imperialism, such as the students provoked in 1919. He had never had confidence in what he called "mob action" — demonstrations, strikes and boycotts. Imperialism, moreover, was not his immediate concern. He first wanted to supplant the warlords of Peking and realize the ambition that had driven him for the past quarter of a century. Yet the Japanese, from whom he expected active support, were sustaining his enemies. And the Americans, from whom he expected political or moral support, dealt only with warlord appointees in Peking. Then he saw student power erupt in the streets of Shanghai, and found that even militarists had to bend before the wave of anti-imperialism.

Sun did not suddenly scrap the old strategy, and would never do so entirely, even during the last year of his life, when he led a popular nationalist movement. Despite the May Fourth incident he still doubted the effectiveness of mass movements, and kept hoping to achieve power faster by exploiting foreign or warlord rivalries. What happened in the summer of 1919, though, showed him the possibility of an additional course: with the help of students and intellectuals he could revitalize his party and create an autonomous political force. This meant, first of all, that he would have to stop equivocating on the most inflammatory nationalist issue. This came easily, since he had just about exhausted his patience with Japan.

On June 13, when the Shanghai general strike had just ended, Sun told a Japanese reporter that Japan's policies since 1915 had irreparably damaged Sino-Japanese relations. The reporter wanted to know why the Chinese had singled out Japan as an object of hatred. In his reply — printed in the Tokyo and Osaka editions of *Asahi* on June 22 — Sun charged Japan with worse behavior than the Europeans. He compared Japan to a younger brother who joins a gang of thieves in robbing his elder brother's house, and who then complains that, despite their relationship, his brother hates him more than the rest of the gang. "This," Sun wrote, "resembles Japanese arguments about the same racial stock and identical language." And in October, speaking to students in Shanghai, he made his first public attack on the Twenty-one Demands.

Sun now gave more attention to the propaganda weapon. *The Weekly Review,* founded in Shanghai by his followers in June 1919, joined the anti-imperialist chorus. The monthly magazine *Reconstruction,* established in August, printed his own recent writings and enabled more theoretically inclined comrades to take part in the raging intellectual discussions. Articles by Tai Chi-t'ao, a twenty-nine-year-old journalist who had been close to Sun since 1912, and by the veteran disciple Hu Hanmin, helped spread interest in Marxism. While applying Marxist analysis to explain the economic origins of imperialism, both soft-pedaled the class-struggle concept. Both were later fierce opponents of the Communist Party.

As part of his overture to the intellectuals, Sun also made his peace with the new culture movement. In January 1920 he announced: "The success of the revolution . . . must depend on a change of thought . . . the new culture movement is really a most valuable thing." And in order to capitalize on this intellectual ferment Sun created a new party format.

He had made a beginning in October 1919, when he reconstituted the Kuomintang in place of the Chinese Revolutionary Party abroad. The following year he began reorganizing the domestic Kuomintang. A new constitution, presented in Shanghai on November 9, 1920, incorporated the Three Principles, the five-power constitution and his plan for single-party tutelage. Though he discarded the more objectionable authoritarian features of the ineffective Revolutionary Party, he still claimed supreme power for his role as *tsung-li*. It was common practice, he pointed out, to identify individuals with the religions, theories or doctrines they originated. Buddha, Confucius, Jesus, Darwin and Monroe were well-known examples. Thus, obeying Sun Yat-sen, he said, simply meant pledging allegiance to his Three Principles and five-power constitution: personal and ideological obedience were inseparable.

Nationalism was restored as one of the Three Principles. No longer claiming that its aims had been fully realized with the overthrow of the Manchus, Sun now touched on the heart of the problem: China's lowly international status. He warned that extraterritoriality gave foreigners coercive powers, as in Shanghai, where he was

living. Even Siam, he lamented, enjoyed a better standing in the world. He urged resistance to foreign attempts
at domination, and called for integration of the five
ethnic communities — Han, Mongol, Tibetan, Manchu
and Moslem — into one great Chinese nation. (What he
was advocating, as he later explained, was the assimilation
of the minorities by the Han Chinese along the American
melting-pot model.) Thus, by 1920 Sun had finally
begun speaking the real language of nationalism. Yet his
plan for building an open political party was immediately sidetracked. A supposedly friendly warlord captured
Canton, and on November 29 Sun was back, with renewed hope of conquering the country from a regional
base.

Sun's host in Canton was Ch'en Chiung-ming, a forty-
two-year-old, independent-minded member of the Kuomintang who had often given trouble to Sun and his entourage. Since 1918 Ch'en had been running a reformist
government in the Fukien–Kwangtung border region
where he had his own army. Though he could not completely break out of the warlord mold, he cultivated some
of the May Fourth intellectuals, advanced education, and
tried working with labor and peasant movements. Besides
personal rivalry, the big difference between him and Sun
was that he wanted to rehabilitate his native province of
Kwangtung rather than waste resources on Sun's dubious
military scheme.

Concentrating on a northern military expedition instead of on building a revolutionary political base was a
mistake. Kwangtung was too poor to support such a
campaign, and Sun's government, not unlike typical warlord establishments, would have to impose vicious taxation. Sun enjoyed considerable popularity — especially
among students and workers — in his home province, but
his war policy aroused opposition, and not just among
gentry taxpayers. The local Communist leader supported

Ch'en. Sun paid no attention to the agrarian problem, and would even begrudge assistance to the Hong Kong seamen, whose strike (January–March 1922) marked the beginning of intensified labor action. From every aspect Sun's plan was reckless. He had no army of his own, and overestimated his ability to sway Ch'en. Though nominally his subordinate, Ch'en had more direct control over provincial military and financial resources than Sun did. Waging a national campaign, moreover, would draw Sun into the dangerous game of warlord politics. He would have to form alliances with the same northern militarists whom he and the student nationalists had condemned. He also neglected the party.

Interest in party affairs and so-called "reorganization" usually flared up when his big plans miscarried and died down at the first sight of a chance for a power maneuver. Now, especially, his obsession with assuming national leadership drove everything else from his mind. In April 1921 he had himself elected "Extraordinary President of the Chinese Republic" and formed a national government in Canton. Though he disputed the legitimacy of the Peking government, the legality of his own was highly questionable. A little over two hundred members — not enough for a quorum — of the parliament that had been dissolved in 1917 elected him. Ch'en Chiung-ming was unhappy, and even an admirer like Chiang Kai-shek felt that Sun's move was premature. At his inauguration on May 5 Sun spoke approvingly of provincial autonomy and of national unification through peaceful means. This was only a few weeks before he embarked upon his military ventures. Forming a national government, however, was not just, or even primarily, for domestic purposes. Sun saw it as a bid for foreign, particularly American, support. He wanted recognition badly, especially since it would have given him a share of the surplus customs revenue, now being remitted to Peking, though the military coterie there controlled only a small part of the country.

In a declaration to foreigners Sun promised to respect treaty rights and to encourage foreign investments. Though he had become more assertive on the nationalist issue during the past year or so, there was still nothing militant or threatening in his attitude. If anything he leaned over backward to placate Western fears. The previous year, in addressing a delegation of American congressmen in Shanghai, he had limited his attacks to Japan and the Twenty-one Demands, and to the Chinese warlords who, he charged, were instruments of Japanese expansionism. He recalled with approval John Hay's Open Door notes, and asked for a renewal of intervention to protect China. He took this same moderate approach at a party meeting in Canton in June 1921. He spoke of nationalism in Wilsonian terms of self-determination, and again emphasized the positive aim of amalgamating China's ethnic communities. But moderation did not pay off. The Americans did not just turn him down, but humiliated him.

In March, Washington had refused to acknowledge his congratulatory message to the newly inaugurated president, Warren Harding. Nor would the State Department acknowledge receipt of his *International Development of China*. A letter sent to Harding in May was returned. In another letter, submitted to the State Department by his representative, Sun pleaded for recognition by the "Mother of Democracy." In September still another letter to Harding never reached the president but was filed away in the State Department. In it Sun predicted that unless the United States supported Canton and withdrew recognition from Peking, Japan would conquer Manchuria by 1925. His government, he claimed, stood for a *"Chinese* China"; Peking was a plaything of Japan. At this time plans for the forthcoming Washington Conference, scheduled to deal with the China problem, were under way. Canton wanted representation. America recognized only Peking. The State Department even stopped American investors from dealing with the Canton government. The British forbade the Hong Kong Chinese to celebrate Sun's inauguration.

Now, given Sun's capriciousness, posturing and impracticality, it is understandable that Western diplomats were quick to dismiss him. Militarily, Sun and the Kuomintang counted for practically nothing in a China that was divided into armed camps, filled with over a million men. And yet . . .

Sun's personal appeal was growing. No one matched his magic on a platform. At a time when Chinese patriots, especially the young, had few heroes to applaud, Sun's long struggle for democracy, some form of socialism, and great-power status took on heroic dimensions. Unlike most political figures he also had a record for personal honesty: he had made no money out of politics. He was not the ideal statesman or political leader. But who else was there? The Western powers were still looking for the "strong man" who could unite China and satisfy their so-called interests. But the rise of nationalism spelled doom for nineteenth-century treaty arrangements. New forces were surfacing in China; it would have been realistic to try to accommodate them. And who was more accommodating than Sun Yat-sen, the author of the *International Development of China?* The few voices suggesting that the United States stop ostracizing Sun's Canton regime, and stop antagonizing him personally, went unheeded.

When Sun took office a U.S. vice-consul in Canton suggested that America should "extend real sympathy" to a government that represented China's best chance for democracy. The consul-general considered Sun "the one honest and patriotic administrator in China," and tried to persuade the Peking legation and Washington not to insult him. In June the visiting educator-philosopher John Dewey, while more enthusiastic over Ch'en Chiungming than Sun, advised a policy of "benevolent neutrality" toward Sun's "national" government. Bertrand Russell, who also visited China at this time, spoke favorably of Sun and the Canton government, which he considered the best in the country. And in September a New York *Times* editorial claimed that there were two governments in China and that both should be represented at the Washington Conference. The paper even contended that Canton had a better right to de jure status than "the creatures of the warlords in the North."

Then, by plunging into the northern expedition, Sun dismayed many of the people who admired his ultimate aims. In the summer of 1921 Ch'en supported him against the Kwangsi generals, who threatened Kwangtung, but he balked when Sun, elated by the conquest of Kwangsi, decided to press on. Developments in the north seemed to fit Sun's plans. At the end of the year relations between Wu P'ei-fu, the mainstay of the ruling Chihli faction, and Chang Tso-lin, the Manchurian satrap, worsened. This was the combination that had ousted the Anfu government in 1920. Sun tried to deal with each, and was successful with Chang and Tuan Ch'i-jui, the Anfu leader. He had earlier denounced both as tools of Japan. Now he sent agents north to negotiate with them, and entertained their representatives in Canton in February 1922. According to the terms of the agreement, if the Chihli clique were ousted, Sun would become president in Peking, and Tuan, vice-president. Depending on warlords was risky, but Sun had rarely passed up a chance to negotiate his way to power. The agreement was never put to the test.

In May Wu P'ei-fu defeated Chang Tso-lin and got a firm hold on Peking. And while Sun was leading an army in northern Kwangtung, forces loyal to Ch'en Chiungming, whom Sun had recently dismissed from his civil and military posts, took over in Canton. Sun rushed back there on June 1. Attempts to placate the opposition, and to bluff them with the threat of a poison-gas barrage, failed. Ch'en, now allied with Wu P'ei-fu, demanded Sun's resignation, and on June 16 Sun barely escaped from an impending attack upon his presidential palace. He took refuge in a gunboat, ordered a bombardment of the city, and waited for loyal forces to come to his rescue. He waited for about six weeks before being convinced that the situation was hopeless. After the failure of a face-saving attempt to get the Canton consular corps to mediate with the "rebels," Sun asked the American consulate to arrange safe passage to Shanghai. The consulate was under orders to stay out of internal Chinese affairs and turned him down. The British, anxious to have him out of the area, transported him to Hong Kong on August 9. The next day he boarded a ship bound for Shanghai.

In a life studded with disappointments Sun had rarely suffered the humiliation of the past two months. While he had been trying to save his position in Canton, Wu P'ei-fu's victorious clique, backed by considerable public opinion, restored the constitution of 1912 and the remnants of the old parliament. On June 11 Li Yüan-hung — Yuan Shih-k'ai's original successor — was installed as president. Though warlords still held the reins, the unity and constitutionalism that Sun had been advocating now finally seemed possible — but without him. He had lost his claim to legitimacy, and even people like Ts'ai Yüan-p'ei, an old and respected comrade, advised him to resign and not to upset the nation's hopes. In 1912 Sun had accepted a similar argument. This time he refused, and continued to issue "presidential" proclamations even while Ch'en Chiung-ming's soldiers were threatening him. Then came his offshore ordeal, shared by none of the Kuomintang's other leaders. But Chiang Kai-shek answered Sun's call for help. He joined Sun on June 29 and stayed for the return to Shanghai. Impressed with Chiang's loyalty, Sun would now mark him for great responsibilities.

During the night trip to Hong Kong on a British gunboat Sun, again displaying amazing resilience, outlined strategy for foreign policy. China's immediate interests, he said, required close cooperation with Soviet Russia and Germany. In terms of geographical contiguity and "intimate relations," Russia was uniquely important. Lenin's government, he said, was being unjustly accused of excessive radicalism, when actually its New Economic Policy reflected a shift from communism to state capitalism. And Germany, though beaten in the war, possessed human talent and learning that could be of help in China's industrialization. Germany had no aggressive designs on China; relations would be mutually beneficial. However, he still contended that the new China should implant particular French, British and American values, and that foreign policy should not ignore these maritime nations. But instead of "blindly following other countries," China should look after her own interests and give special attention to the continental powers — Russia and Germany. This was exactly what he had been doing during his year and a half in Canton.

Treated like an outcast by the major powers, Sun had begun seeking links to the international outcasts. Russia and Germany, both dissatisfied with the postwar settlement and isolated, were now building the cordial relationship that was formalized at Rapallo in April 1922. Neither belonged to the imperialist establishment in China. Though negotiations with Peking had not yet been concluded, the Russians since July 1919 were committed to the abrogation of the unequal treaties. And Germany, by virtue of the peace treaty signed at Peking in May 1921, had become the first European power to treat China according to principles of equality and reciprocity: no more extraterritoriality or other privileges except those normally prescribed by international law.

At first Sun was more interested in the Germans. They

had helped him in 1917, and he had tried to get more help in 1918. At that time, while the war was still in progress, he had first thought of a triple alliance that would include Soviet Russia. After his return to Canton he negotiated with the German consul who arrived in September 1921. Official contacts with the Soviet Union, which still had no diplomatic relations with China, were more difficult. Besides this practical problem of communication, Sun was more impressed with Germany's armament industry and her overall capacity for giving economic assistance. Russia, in any case a less developed country, had yet to recover from the effects of civil war and intervention, and was still fighting off economic collapse.

In Canton Sun pressed the consul for diplomatic recognition and economic aid. He also had a secret agent in Berlin in the person of Chu Ho-chung, a former overseas student who had joined Sun's movement there in 1905. Chu's current mission was to submit proposals for economic cooperation to foreign ministry officials and industrialists. Discussion of the tripartite alliance was reserved for Admiral Paul von Hintze, a former foreign minister who shared Sun's taste for conspiracy. During the war he had served as minister to Mexico and then to China, and had been one of the originators of the scheme to set Mexico and Japan against the United States. (This had been the substance of the notorious Zimmermann telegram of January 1917.) It was also Hintze who, before leaving China in 1917, had issued the order to subsidize Sun Yat-sen. In January 1922 Chu reported that the like-minded Hintze had on his own already thought of a Sino–German–Russian alliance. Subject to the approval of the German prime minister, he was ready to go to Canton and take charge of an assistance program that would include German advisers and materials.

Nothing came of the scheme. German diplomats hesitated to play a lone hand in China, and also had doubts about Sun's position in Canton, which were confirmed when Ch'en Chiung-ming expelled him. Berlin, like other foreign capitals, would hear from Sun again. In the meantime, the proposed triple alliance was not kept secret. In September a Hong Kong paper published translations of correspondence left behind in Sun's Canton headquarters, and gave sensational treatment to the reputed Bolshevik connection. Sun replied that he was merely seeking normal, reciprocal relations with the two countries. Denying an ideological affinity with communism, Sun called attention to his *International Development of China* and to the still-standing offer to Western capitalists. But the imputation of Bolshevik leanings gave the British and Americans an additional reason for welcoming his latest defeat. The Germans denied having had any official contacts with him. Sun's other candidate for partnership was much less inhibited.

Soviet Russia, still an international pariah, was not fastidious in choosing allies. Moscow, moreover, was not bound by conventional methods of diplomacy. It was also the nerve center of international communism. More than any other country Russia was temperamentally and organizationally primed for direct involvement in Chinese politics. Other powers saw the May Fourth Movement as a threat; to the Russians it was an opportunity. And Lenin's strategy, a fluid mix of *realpolitik* and ideology, enabled the Soviets to exploit it. At the Washington Conference of November 1921–February 1922 the Western powers and Japan still hesitated to immediately restore Chinese sovereignty, but Karakhan's repudiation of the unequal treaties, announced in 1919, and repeated, with some qualifications, in 1920, had put Russia on record as the defender of Chinese nationalism.

The belief that Chinese nationalism, and Asian nationalism in general, served the interests of world communism grew out of Lenin's probing for the weak spots of capitalism. Since 1900 he had been casting sympathetic glances at anti-imperialist movements in the exploited countries. In *Imperialism: The Highest Stage of Capitalism,* written in 1916, he concluded that imperialism and imperialist wars were inevitable results of monopoly capitalism. He also quoted with approval from Rudolf Hilferding's *Finanzkapital,* published in 1910. Hilferding, an Austrian socialist, had pointed out that the intrusion of European capitalism into the dependent countries was gradually endowing "the vanquished" with the means and resources for their liberation. What they were striving for was the "same goal which once seemed highest to the European nations: the creation of a united national state as a means to economic and cultural freedom. This movement for national independence threatens European capital just in its most valuable and most promising fields of exploitation." Thus, nationalism in the colonial and semicolonial areas was seen as an auxiliary force in the struggle against capitalism.

Lenin also noted that the huge profits reaped by imperialism enabled capitalists to "corrupt certain sections of the working class" in the industrialized countries and to "detach them from the main proletarian masses." In 1920 he further emphasized the danger of "labor leaders and the upper stratum of the labor aristocracy" being bribed with the "superprofits" of imperialism. In other words, imperialism, while in the long run digging its own grave by arousing resistance in the backward countries, was in the meantime blunting the class struggle and impeding proletarian revolutions in the advanced ones. By 1920 Lenin had decided that Asian nationalist movements were not only helpful but necessary for expediting the overthrow of capitalism.

Sheer size alone made Asian masses a formidable ally. As a Comintern spokesman put it, "The Communist International is convinced that there will hasten under its banner not only the European proletariat but the heavy mass of our reserve, our foot-soldiers — the hundreds of millions of peasants inhabiting Asia, our Near and Far East." Lenin's last words on the subject, delivered in 1923 when the prospects for immediate socialist revolutions in the West were dimming, also stressed this advantage in numbers: "In the last analysis, the outcome of the struggle will be determined by the fact that Russia, India, China, etc., account for the overwhelming majority of the population of the globe . . . so that in this respect there cannot be the slightest doubt what the final outcome of the world struggle will be. . . . The complete victory of socialism is fully and absolutely assured." Illness had incapacitated Lenin by 1923. For several years before that, however, Russian and Comintern agents had been trying to apply Leninist strategy in China.

In 1920 the Second Congress of the Comintern accepted his formula for "temporary" alliances with "national-revolutionary" movements in the exploited countries. These movements, according to Lenin, were bourgeois-democratic. Because they fought native "feudalism" and foreign imperialism, they deserved support. But because their goal was the establishment of capitalism, such support could only be temporary. The victory of indigenous capitalism, while serving the national interests of the dependent countries, and the class interests of the Western proletariat, would pave the way for Asia's socialist revolutions. Lenin thus imposed a dual role upon Asian Communists: to help the bourgeoisie fight the common enemy and to prepare to fight the bourgeoisie itself. While pursuing the first goal they were not to neglect their second, "special" task. Lenin ordered Asian Communists to agitate among workers and peasants, and to preserve their independence and proletarian purity. With help from Russia and other socialist states, if they arose in the West, even uninterrupted socialist revolutions were conceivable. Alliances with the bourgeoisie, a class destined, according to the scriptures, for the dustbin of history, would last only as long as necessary.

What was known about Sun Yat-sen placed him in the suitable petit-bourgeois, nationalist category. In 1920 Foreign Commissar Chicherin, who had responded to Sun's initiative in 1918, sent him another friendly letter, and Lenin invited him to visit Russia, but Sun was unable to accept. Interest at this time was mutual but neither side pressed for an alliance. The Comintern was not sure of the Kuomintang's potential and Sun still preferred wealthier and more accessible allies. He also feared that a link with the Bolsheviks might provoke British intervention. In the fall of 1920 he had an inconclusive talk with Gregory Voitinsky, the Comintern's first agent in China, who had helped form the Chinese Socialist Youth Corps in August. The following year, when Sun headed a government in Canton, the Russians paid him more attention, and because of the insults being heaped upon him by the West, he was in a more receptive mood.

In early December 1921 Sun's remarks about the Russian revolution combined skepticism with sympathy. The Russians, he said, had abolished capitalism, but the people were suffering immensely and the future was uncertain. He cited these difficulties in order to show the advantage of carrying out a social revolution before capitalism became entrenched. Later in the month another Comintern emissary, J. F. M. Sneevliet, came to see him and cleared the way for closer relations.

Sneevliet was a Dutch Communist who had previously introduced united-front strategy in Indonesia, where he may have heard about Sun from the *hua-ch'iao*. In China, using the alias Maring, he followed the two-pronged approach ordered at the Second Comintern Congress, which he had attended. He participated in the founding congress of the Chinese Communist Party in July 1921 and also scouted the field for bourgeois-nationalist allies. This led him first of all to Wu P'ei-fu. The northern warlord had solid nationalist credentials. He had supported the students during the May Fourth excitement, had defeated the pro-Japanese Anfu clique and was at this time at odds with Japan's latest favorite, Chang Tso-lin. As a result of Maring's negotiations the Communists organized the Peking–Hankow railway workers and would protect the line during Wu's war with Chang Tso-lin.

Maring visited Sun at Kweilin, in Kwangsi, the headquarters for the northern expedition, and stayed for several days during the last week of December. During their long talks Sun learned more about Soviet policies, including the New Economic Policy, which, to his mind, bridged considerably the ideological gap between Lenin and himself. When Maring wanted to know what inspired Sun's revolution, he received the disconcerting reply that Sun was merely expanding upon the unbroken tradition handed down by China's ancient sages. Not overly impressed with Sun's political thinking nor with his military prospects, Maring nevertheless felt that the Kuomintang might fit into the Comintern's plans. He is said to have broached the subject of an alliance. Sun, according to this report, was not ready to risk it. He was hoping to invade the Yangtze Valley, which was Wu P'ei-fu territory and also the British sphere of influence. Were he to combine with the Russians, Sun feared that the British would back Wu. He suggested instead a "moral" affiliation with Russia. Shortly after seeing Maring, Sun acclaimed the social achievements of the Bolshevik revolution and also took a tougher line on imperialism.

In a speech in January 1922 Sun declared that while France and the United States represented old models of republicanism, Russia had produced a new model, and China would have the newest, based upon his Three Principles. Nationalism, he said, meant equality among the world's races; democracy, political equality within the nation; and people's livelihood, economic equality. This last principle, he said, had been practiced in Hung Hsiu-ch'üan's Taiping kingdom, and most recently in Russia.

Speaking to soldiers that month Sun made it clear that,

despite admiration for Soviet aims, he preferred his own methods for China — land value taxation and nationalization of key industries. And he still favored borrowing development capital from abroad. But he used the Russian example to show the inevitability of social upheavals and the feasibility of a multipurpose revolution. The Russian combination of political and social revolutions was only one step short of his own three-in-one formula. "We live in a foul world," he said. The new one would be that which Confucius had idealized: " 'when the Great Way was practiced, the world was shared by all alike.' . . . At the present time, only the newly formed Russian government seems to resemble this." Though the Russian revolution had come after China's, it had accomplished more, Sun said, because the Russians had paid attention to public welfare. Nevertheless, he felt that China would ultimately get the better results because "Russia is in the Arctic Circle and China is in the temperate zone, and Russia had capitalists while China has none."

Sun also noted the panicky response of the capitalist nations to the victory of Russian socialism. Afraid that their own countries would become infected by the idea of social revolution, they had been waging war against Russia for four years, but were unsuccessful because of "Russia's ideological superiority." This example fitted the theme of his lecture "The Spiritual Education of the Soldier."

Earlier, Sun had suspected that foreign capitalists did not like the idea of a modernized China. Given the Russian precedent he could anticipate their attitude toward a socialist China. Though in theory and practice his socialism, he claimed, was inspired by Confucius, Mencius, Hung Hsiu-ch'üan, Henry George, and even Abraham Lincoln — but not Marx — Sun had reason to feel affinity with Lenin. Both advocated socialism, and both aroused enmity in the West.

Actually, the West had been rejecting Sun mainly because he threatened its hopes for stability in China; single-tax socialism was considered just another of his impractical schemes. Yet by continuing to reject him Britain and America pushed him closer to the Soviets and caused him to stiffen his position on nationalist issues. In this same speech to soldiers in January 1922 he made his strongest attack as yet on the entire imperialist treaty system. He declared that extraterritoriality, foreign enclaves, and foreign control of the maritime customs had turned China into a "semi-independent" country, and that the next goal of nationalism was to restore full sovereignty. Otherwise, he warned, China might end up like Burma.

From April to mid-June Sun had talks with another Comintern representative, the young Serge Dalin, who had come to attend the congress of the Socialist Youth Corps. While Dalin described the advantages of a united front, Sun spoke wistfully of having Soviet cadres in Canton and of getting Russian help in building railways — including a line connecting Canton with Moscow; yet he merely promised to recognize Russia after the expected capture of Hankow. Again, he argued that a premature move could provoke British intervention: Canton, he said, was vulnerable to attack from Hong Kong. In other words, at this time the risks involved in a Russian connection still outweighed the need.

Sun apparently felt that he could succeed with the northern expedition on his own. This would establish him as a front-rank contender and perhaps force the Western powers to come to terms, which they were more likely to do if he were not stigmatized by the Bolshevik label. If they still rejected him he could always turn to the Russians. Then, a few days after Sun's last talk with Dalin, Ch'en Chiung-ming's rebellion shattered his hopes for the northern expedition. The time for taking risks was drawing near. As already described, while fleeing Canton Sun disclosed his decision to give the highest priority to Russia and Germany.

On his return to Shanghai on August 14, 1922, he was ready to deal with anyone. And despite his recent setback and poor prospects, Sun's personal popularity was growing. Thousands turned out to greet him. He was a national figure who, with apparently little chance of achieving power on his own, had sufficient public appeal to warrant the attention of the power holders. Warlords of all factions were willing to make use of him. And so were the Chinese Communists.

Earlier (May–July 1922), the Communists held their Second Party Congress. At this meeting, which was not attended by Maring, the party declared its formal affiliation to the Comintern and its acceptance of Comintern discipline. In line with Moscow's strategy, the Congress called for a "united front of democratic revolution" with the Kuomintang. But neither the Comintern nor the Chinese Communists were at this time proposing anything more than a loose alignment that would not subordinate the Communists to the bourgeoisie. The Communists had little respect for Sun and his party, and some even doubted whether cooperation was worthwhile. A united front, however, held the promise of a wider field of operations and the benefit of the Kuomintang's reputation and greater respectability. (The Communist Party, founded the previous year with fifty-seven members, still had less than three hundred enrolled. The Kuomintang, though never as large as Sun claimed, had several thousand registered members in China, and many more sympathizers among students and in the Canton labor unions.) The Kuomintang, the Communists decided, was the only party with some "democratic and revolutionary spirit." Its organizational weakness suited Comintern strategy, which called for manipulating bourgeois allies within a united front and discarding them when the time was ripe. Sun Yat-sen, whose prominence was the Kuomintang's main asset, was expected to be a pliable ally. Had not Lenin in 1912 remarked on his "in-

imitable, one might say, virginal naiveté?" Sun's bound-
less confidence did prove convenient for Comintern nego-
tiators. Yet he did not behave exactly like a political
virgin.

He was not afraid of being swallowed up by the puny
Communist Party, and saw advantages in a coalition.
These "youngsters," as he called them, could give the
Kuomintang much needed enthusiasm and organizing
talent. What was more important, if left on their own the
Communists could become rivals for Soviet aid. He also
knew that if he did not cooperate with the Communists,
the Russians could choose another candidate, such as
Ch'en Chiung-ming. Sun wanted a monopoly of Russian
arms, money and advisers, just as he wanted his own party
to be the supreme revolutionary vehicle and the nation's
sole caretaker during the projected period of political
tutelage. The more he learned about the Bolsheviks' success, the more determined he was to carry out his plan for
a single-party dictatorship.

Thus in August, when Maring showed up in Shanghai
to press for a united front, Sun agreed, but only if the
Communists joined the Kuomintang as individuals and
submitted to its discipline. This was a "bloc within," not
the "bloc without" that the Chinese Communists and
presumably Lenin himself had had in mind. Maring,
later backed by Moscow, overcame local Communist
objections, and in September party leaders began joining
the Kuomintang. Maring's rationale was that the Kuomintang represented all classes opposed to imperialism,
and not just the bourgeoisie. Ch'en Tu-hsiu, the top
Communist, received an organizational assignment from
Sun, who, as usual, contemplated party reorganization
when other enterprises failed.

However, the Communists insisted upon maintaining
their separate party organization. Sun agreed. Permitting
the anomaly of dual membership was part of the price for
Russian support. In February he had received another

flattering letter from Chicherin, commissar for foreign affairs, and in August he began corresponding with a Soviet diplomat, Adolph Joffe.

Joffe was in Peking trying to conclude a treaty with the government backed by Sun's archenemy, Wu P'ei-fu. While Comintern agents fanned the flames of anti-imperialism and revolution, Joffe and others who had preceded him since 1920 defended Russia's national interests. Communists, or a least some of them, believed that what was good for Russia could not be bad for world revolution. But Peking's professional diplomats found it hard to distinguish between Soviet and tsarist policies. For when it came to negotiations the Soviets qualified their original blanket renunciation of imperialist privileges. They were still ready to give up extraterritoriality and various other rights, but claimed title to the juiciest fruits of tsarist imperialism — control of the Chinese Eastern Railway in Manchuria and dominance of Outer Mongolia. Peking had been refusing to recognize Soviet Russia on these terms, and the Russians hoped that their flirtation with Sun Yat-sen would soften resistance, just as their courtship of Peking made Sun more anxious to deal with them. Moreover, when Joffe arrived in August the Kremlin had high hopes for Wu P'ei-fu, winner of the latest warlord contest. Wu, now cooperating with the local Communists, was expected to make negotiations easier. Some Comintern strategists and Chinese Communists also considered him an ideal partner for Sun Yat-sen. With Wu's military power and resources, including those of the rich Yangtze Valley, and the Kuomintang's political potential, the "bourgeois nationalist" front could become the formidable force that the Comintern had been seeking.

Wu's ascendancy was in fact hailed in many quarters. British and American observers, while still discounting Sun and the Kuomintang, had only praise for Wu. A typical comment tabbed him as "the best man that has forged his way to the top . . . since the establishment of the Republic." His anti-Japanese record and steps toward restoring parliamentary government also impressed many educated Chinese, including Kuomintang sympathizers. It was natural, then, that Sun Yat-sen, who was trying everything else, should not overlook the chance of a rapprochement with his erstwhile enemy.

Discussions through go-betweens began in August, and in September, according to press reports, Wu helped ease Sun's difficult financial situation. (Sun, who as usual depended mainly upon *hua-ch'iao* donations and loans, was also said to have received a contribution from Wu's enemy, Chang Tso-lin, who was still entrenched in Manchuria.) At the end of the month the proposed entente seemed to be jelling: a new cabinet in Peking — the so-called Able Men Cabinet — included four Kuomintang members or sympathizers. Within a few months, however, Sun gave up on the Wu P'ei-fu option, and it would not be long before many of Wu's admirers changed their minds.

Wu, though interested in Sun's proposals for national unification and disbandment of troops, balked at his demand for the presidency. And even if he had agreed, other militarists in the Chihli clique, which was not a solid bloc, would not have surrendered power. Though deservedly credited with patriotism and personal honesty, Wu was inextricably tied to the warlord system and its ultimate reliance upon coercive power. Like other super-militarists, he headed a loose, clanlike cluster of generals who were never more restless than when the time came to divide the spoils. In November he could not stop them from wrecking the Able Men Cabinet, the best that China had had during this period. The following month Sun's last attempt to reach an agreement failed when Wu dismissed his emissary with the pronouncement that Sun was "an idle dreamer." Before that, in October, Wu's brutal suppression of a strike in a British-run mining establishment had dismayed Communist labor organizers. (The Chinese Communists would be further disillusioned in February 1923, when Wu's troops massacred striking workers of the Peking–Hankow Railway, his most valuable strategic and economic asset.) Less sensitive to the fate of Chinese workers, the Russians still considered Wu a potential ally. However, when the Peking Foreign Ministry remained stubborn on the Manchurian and Mongolian issues, Joffe stepped up negotiations with Sun Yat-sen.

In November Sun informed Chiang Kai-shek that these negotiations, while "difficult," were progressing satisfactorily. The "difficulties" presumably concerned his request for military aid and efforts to stop Russia from establishing relations with Peking. The recapture of Kwangtung, he felt, would enhance his bargaining position. Yet he was confident that the Russians rated him highly: had they not ordered the Chinese Communists to join the Kuomintang? What the Communists expected to gain by joining was now being explained at the Fourth Comintern Congress in Moscow (November 1922). "We can rally the masses around us," boasted a Chinese delegate, "and split the Kuomintang."

Hoping to reassure the Russians and perhaps to jolt the West into a change of heart, Sun began publicizing pro-Soviet sympathies and even raised the threat of a broad anti-Western coalition. The Anglo-Japanese Alliance had expired earlier in the year. Japan now seemed an easier target. In an interview with a Japanese correspondent in November, Sun urged Japan to join hands with Russia "in opposing the aggression of the Anglo-Saxons." If Japan, he claimed, had followed his advice and backed Germany instead of the Allies, Annam, Singapore and India would have revolted. Because Japan had not "understood high politics . . . realization of the pan-Asiatic plan has been delayed indefinitely," and "it will be China that will be called upon to make Asia a place for

Asiatics in the future." Japan, he said, could still undo her error by promoting relations with Russia: "Russians are Asiatics. There runs in their veins Asiatic blood."

On January 2, 1923, the Kuomintang, meeting in Shanghai, adopted the new constitution and manifesto which the committee appointed by Sun several months earlier had drafted. The Three Principles and the five-power constitution remained the basis of party doctrine: nothing would ever change that, which "the leader . . . had selected out of the experience of the entire world." But the principle of nationalism now included a demand for "national self-determination" and international equality. The unequal treaties, it was charged, had reduced China to the status of a colony. Among the new organs established were the Central Cadre Council — analogous to the Communists' Central Committee — and the Peasant-Labor Committee. In addressing his comrades Sun emphasized the crucial role of the party and its propaganda function. The party, and not military operations, he claimed, would guarantee the success of the revolution. Clearly, aspects of the Bolshevik model, which he had learned about from Comintern visitors and which had succeeded so well in Russia, appealed to him.

Moscow in the meantime was more satisfied with the anti-imperialist and "anti-feudal" potential of the Kuomintang. On January 12, the Comintern's Executive Committee decided that it was "expedient for members of the Chinese Communist Party to remain within the Kuomintang." But the party was again cautioned to preserve its "specific political aspect." Joffe, still stymied in Peking, now responded to Sun's invitation for discussions in Shanghai. He arrived on January 17, just two days after Sun's mercenaries had driven Ch'en Chiung-ming from Canton. Sun now had his base which, however tenuous, strengthened his hand. On the twenty-sixth he and Joffe issued a statement that was published in the Chinese and world press.

First, Joffe endorsed Sun's view that neither communism nor the Soviet system could be introduced into China "because there do not exist here the conditions for the successful establishment of either." He also pledged Russia's support for China's "national unification" and "full national independence." Next, he confirmed Soviet intentions to renounce tsarist treaties with China. Sun, for his part, backed Russian demands for sharing in the management of the Chinese Eastern Railway, but asked that his ally, Chang Tso-lin, be consulted. Finally, he accepted Joffe's denial of Soviet imperialist aims in Outer Mongolia and recognized the inadvisability of an immediate withdrawal of Soviet troops.

The statement was a milestone in Sun's career. For the first time a foreign power acknowledged his claim to speak for China and, by implication, promised support. The price paid — recognition of Russian interests in Manchuria and Mongolia — was no more than he had previously offered Japan. And the part about communism being unsuited for China — conveniently omitted in Russian newspapers — gave Sun further assurance of being able to handle local Communists. This too was a signal to the West.

While negotiating with Joffe, Sun had his foreign affairs secretary, the West Indian–born barrister Eugene Chen, assure the British consul-general that he wanted to improve relations. Chen also hinted that if Britain and other powers "with whom Dr. Sun had really more in common" continued to oppose him, he might join with Japan, Russia and Germany. And the day after the Sun–Joffe statement was issued, Chen let it be known that Western policies would determine how far Sun would go with the Russians. "Continued hostility to Russia," he wrote in a Shanghai paper on January 27, "and what appears like hostility to Sun Yat-sen on the part of certain great powers might force an alliance between Russia and China."

Nothing, of course, was more characteristic of Sun's style than its fluidity: any alliance was possible and none was exclusive. However alluring the prospect of Russian aid and the sharing of revolutionary experience, he respected the superior power of Britain and America. They also had the capital Sun wanted for China's rapid development. Who else could possibly help realize his dream of covering the country with thousands of miles of railways? Then there was the question of ideology. Seeing Lenin as a Confucian humanist did not make Sun a Marxist. Despite his exasperation with the Anglo-American strong-man fixation and his strictures against their "arrogance," Sun did have "more in common" with the cultural and political traditions of Britain and America than with those of Soviet Russia. The Comintern leader, Gregory Zinoviev, suspected as much when he warned that some of Sun's followers believed that the "blessings of democracy and progress" would flow from America. From time to time — and he would have only two more years to live — Sun would give the Kremlin cause for concern. Only America and Britain, by playing their imperialist roles to the hilt, would keep him from backsliding.

Accustomed to seeing Sun swivel in all directions, the British and Americans were not alarmed by the Sun–Joffe communiqué. Without an army Sun seemed unimportant. The New York *Times* was derisive: how could Sun, reputed to have been a tool of Japanese expansionists, and now working with Chang Tso-lin, contribute to Chinese unity? "If Mr. Joffe is genuinely enthusiastic for the reunion and independence of China," the *Times* editorialized, "he is in strange company." (Many educated Chinese thought differently. Only a few weeks earlier an American-owned weekly published the results of a poll to determine who was "the greatest living Chinese." Sun Yat-sen was first, followed closely by the "Christian General," Feng Yü-hsiang. The respondents were Chinese students and businessmen.) Joffe in the meantime went off to Japan accompanied by one of Sun's closest associates, and two months later Moscow would decide to allocate a million dollars (US) to Sun's government in Canton.

Before tangible aid arrived, however, Sun intensified his efforts toward the Western powers. He even invited them to use their hold over Chinese revenues to bring about the peaceful unification of the country and the disbandment of troops. Sun's reasoning was that since they were already intervening in Chinese affairs by allocating surplus revenue to the warlord government of Peking, they might as well intervene for positive purposes: they could hold back payments until a popular-based government was installed. His proposal, conveyed to the State Department in February, included a suggestion that Secretary of State Charles Evans Hughes be sent to mediate among Chinese leaders. Sun was apparently willing to gamble on winning a contest based upon popularity and not military strength. Washington dismissed the idea as another of his fanciful schemes. Sun left Shanghai on February 15 with an entourage that included three bodyguards, among them a colorful Canadian, Colonel Morris "Two-gun" Cohen.

On his way back to Canton, Sun stopped in Hong Kong. Aware of his influence with the Hong Kong labor movement and in their Southeast Asian colonies, the British were much less antagonistic than previously, even friendly. The manager of the Hong Kong and Shanghai Banking Corporation, one of the pillars of the British imperialist establishment, had tea with him. The governor invited Sun to lunch and was impressed by his declarations of goodwill. Sun's people let it be known that he was in the market for all kinds of assistance and advice. The climax to this fence-mending mission took place at his alma mater, the University of Hong Kong. Introduced as a man "whose name was synonymous with that of China," Sun was greeted enthusiastically by the stu-

dents. Foreigners were pleasantly surprised to hear him
disavow extremism; all he wanted, he insisted, was orderly and good government. Hong Kong, he declared,
had been the birthplace of his revolutionary ideas. He
told the students that "England should be our model and
we must spread the English example of good government
throughout China." On the twenty-first he returned to
Canton for his third attempt to build a base from which
to unify the country. He was still not sure whether the
anti-imperialist Russians or the Western imperialists
would be his allies. He held the door wide open to both.
Nor, in the most frantic search for outside support that
he had ever undertaken would Sun forget about Germany or the dream of a pan-Asian alliance with Japan.

Without such support it seemed unlikely that he could
keep his precarious hold on Canton. On March 2 he became generalissimo of a military government that was at
the mercy of "guest armies" — outside forces that had entered Kwangtung in search of loot and were milking the
province dry. Only in Canton itself, where his son Sun Fo
was mayor, did the Kuomintang have direct control. But
the city was under constant threat from warlord armies,
including that of Ch'en Chiung-ming. Sun shelved plans
for the party's reorganization and concentrated on military operations. Squeezed by his mercenaries he tried to
squeeze extra taxes from the Cantonese. After a few
months he began dipping into salt revenues that had
been mortgaged to foreigners. Simultaneously he tried
to cash in on the goodwill he had spread in Hong Kong.

In March and during the next few months Sun and his
associates offered various inducements to British capital.
He invited British experts to overhaul his government's
financial administration and requested a massive loan.
Though British officials were now on talking terms with
Sun, London agreed with its minister to Peking that any
sign of intervention on his behalf would hurt British interests. The minister also pointed out that, despite Sun's

"friendly remonstrances," he had "tampered" with the British-managed salt administration — which various warlords had also been doing — and had "probably reached some understanding with Bolsheviks."

However, there were signs that Sun still hoped that his "understanding" with Moscow would have the opposite effect on Britain, America and Japan. In an interview with a YMCA official that appeared in the New York *Times* in July — but which probably was held a few months earlier — Sun delivered a bitter, impassioned attack on America and other imperialist powers. China's tragedy, he charged, was that she had not only lost her independence but that she had many masters while ordinary colonies had only one. The revenue issue incensed him. Foreigners collected customs and salt taxes in the south but refused to remit a penny to Canton. The Peking government, he claimed, could not exist for a day without payments from foreign tax administrators, and was using southern tax receipts to wage war against the south. (Sun falsely claimed that six southern provinces were loyal to him, though he did not even control most of Kwangtung.) "We have lost hope of help from America, England, France or any other of the great powers," he said. "The only country that shows any sign of helping us . . . is the Soviet Government of Russia."

Yet, Sun also renewed his compromise offer: the foreign powers could keep collecting taxes in the south as well as the north, but should "hold them until we Chinese . . . can straighten out our internal affairs" and establish a representative government. In other words, all he wanted was real neutrality.

In May a message to Japan similarly blended censure with an offer of a new beginning. In an interview with a Japanese writer Sun declared that "Soviet Russia is a country upon which China could rely," and if the two were to conclude an offensive-defensive alliance, the rest of the world would have nothing to fear. He included

Turkey, Persia, Afghanistan and Germany — countries where the Soviets had scored diplomatic successes — among China's allies. But while blaming Japan for having sabotaged the 1911 Revolution, he expressed love for Japan and eternal gratitude for having granted him political asylum in the past. And he still had hopes for the future. Japan, he said, was essential for the defense of the Orient. Moreover, "we place more hope in the revival of the Oriental people under the leadership of Japan than in any Soviet alliance." Japan, in other words, was potentially more important than Russia. But Japan "had to abandon Western-style aggression, stop helping the Peking government, and get out of Manchuria." Concurrently, Sun let the Russians know that their alliance, still not consummated, would not be unconditional.

He warned Maring, now lecturing him on how to reshape the Kuomintang: "If the Communists do not obey the Kuomintang, I shall expel them; if Soviet Russia stands on the side of the Chinese Communists, I shall oppose Soviet Russia." This did not faze the Russians. In June the Third Congress of the Chinese Communist Party, echoing recent Comintern resolutions, confirmed the strategy of building Communist power while transforming the Kuomintang. But the Communists were disturbed by the Kuomintang's expectations of help from capitalist powers and its preoccupation with military action. Neither of these "erroneous notions" proved curable.

On August 18 — just two days after he sent Chiang Kai-shek on a three-month study tour to Russia — Sun wrote to an emissary in Berlin giving guidelines for a renewed approach to Germany. As in 1921 he argued that Chinese resources and manpower plus German machinery and science would make a formidable combination. He wanted German experts in all fields — military, industrial and administrative — and suggested that the German government and private firms, like the Hugo Stinnes Company, draw up a master plan. Transformed into a major power, China, he promised, would help Germany throw off the shackles of the Versailles Treaty. At a time when he had already declared his faith in Russia, Sun wrote: "If the German government would consider China its only lifeline, China would consider Germany its sole mentor." Interested, but cautious, the Germans made no commitments as Sun kept plying them with offers of economic benefits.

In September 1923 Sun began corresponding with Leo Karakhan, Russia's new negotiator in Peking. Still fighting for his life in the south, Sun proposed that the Soviets help him attack Peking from the northwest. But there was no place for military adventurism in Moscow's plans for the Kuomintang. And even now, while assuring Karakhan that Canton would help foil anti-Soviet, capitalist intrigues in Peking, Sun could not resist a sideglance at the United States. In September renewed appeals for American sponsorship of a Chinese peace settlement fell flat.

Nothing else, then, was in the pipeline when the Sun–Joffe accord began bearing fruit nine months after it was signed. On October 6 Michael Borodin arrived in Canton with two Russian officers and a letter from Karakhan. "With the arrival of Comrade B.," Karakhan had written, "things will be pushed ahead much more speedily."

The thirty-nine-year-old Borodin was no ordinary Comintern functionary but a veteran Bolshevik with close links to Lenin and other leaders. Despite public denials he was an official representative of the Soviet government. Born in Russia, he had been an early member of the Bolshevik faction, active in the 1905 Revolution, and a party recruiter. Arrested, he had been allowed to leave and in 1907 settled in the United States, where he studied in a university and taught school. He returned to Russia in 1918 and subsequently took on Comintern assignments in Spain, Mexico and the United States. His last post had been in Britain, where, as "George Brown," he served a short prison term before being deported. A dynamic organizer and a dedicated but pragmatic Marxist with rich international experience, Borodin was as well qualified as anyone could be for steering the tricky course Moscow had charted in China. He was a tall, powerfully built man with a commanding presence. His real name was Gruzenberg. But Sun Yat-sen would tell inquisitive Americans, "His name is Lafayette."

Borodin impressed him from the beginning. Finding Sun in bad health and hemmed in by warlords, though still talking recklessly of a northward march, he urged him to concentrate on building political strength. In January Sun had exhorted the party to win mass support; Borodin showed him how to do it. Unlike Homer Lea, who had fed Sun's fantasies, Borodin stressed practical revolutionary agitation. Within a few weeks Sun appointed the Provisional Central Executive Committee to plan still another reorganization of the Kuomintang. As the Committee's adviser, Borodin became its guiding spirit. His formula combined militant nationalism with specific policies designed to appeal to peasants and workers. Only a month passed before he shocked Kuomintang veterans by proposing that the party come out in favor of confiscating and distributing landlord holdings. Sun, as the final arbiter, agreed to a program calling for a twenty-five percent reduction of land rent, and for benefits to labor, such as a minimum wage and an eight-hour day. Borodin's advice carried weight, but not as much as he would have wanted.

Realizing that Sun was the key to the Kuomintang, Borodin flattered him, though he considered him nothing more than an "enlightened little satrap" with poor political sense. Sun, he once wrote, sees himself as another Confucius, "the hero and the others the mob." Nevertheless, he worked hard at building up Sun and the Kuomintang. Obeying instructions, the Communists would do the same. Their connection with Borodin was kept unobtrusive. At an early briefing, however, he reminded them that the ultimate aim was to strengthen their own party.

Sun, who felt that the Chinese — in contrast to Europeans — had always enjoyed too much individual liberty, admired Russia's success in realizing his dream of ruling a country through a party. He envied the discipline of the Russian Communists. Above all, he envied their party army. While his own revolution was the hostage of "guest armies," he found that a large party army, purged of disloyal elements, had made the Russian revolution secure. Why, he asked his comrades at the end of November, had their party failed? "It was because we lacked a model and precedent. . . . Now we have a good friend, Mr. Borodin, who has come from Russia. . . . He is to train our comrades. . . . If we wish our revolution to succeed, we must learn the methods, organization and training of the Russians."

He wanted to emulate the Bolsheviks' use of propaganda. But it was his own gospel he still insisted on spreading. Only now — and assuming, perhaps, that this would make it easier to sell the alliance to his comrades — he claimed to have discovered a complete identity between the Three Principles and Russian ideology. Originally, he said, the Russian revolution had stressed only democracy and people's livelihood. But Borodin had explained that as a result of foreign intervention nationalism had become its main driving force.

Sun himself continued to express nationalist feelings more freely. He spoke about recovering territory and sovereignty, and promised that when the revolution was complete, all concessions made by the Manchus would come under review. He reminded young people that Chinese were discriminated against in America, and of the sign forbidding entrance to "Dogs and Chinese" in a foreign park in Shanghai.

Yet, in October he told students that boycotting Japan was ineffective and demeaning. Why should a "great country" like China, with its "400 million people — one quarter of the world's population — and 4,000-year-old civilization," advertise the fact that little Japan was bullying her? To be oppressed by Japan was like an adult being harassed "by a four- or five-year-old grandson." The way to gain respect abroad, he said, was to restore order at home. With good internal government, there would be no foreign problems. But a country in disorder could not conduct foreign relations. Fears of foreign domination or partition, he said, were as baseless as when Liang Ch'i-ch'ao had sounded them twenty years earlier. Lamenting that the Chinese had "lost the style of a great country," he urged giving precedence to completing the internal revolution.

That international prestige would automatically follow the restoration of internal order was a traditional Confucian argument. And Sun never doubted its validity. However, he could not avoid concluding that, except for Russia, the foreign powers were intent upon stopping him from unifying China. He had been making this point with increasing frequency, and on November 16 gave it full treatment in a letter to his former benefactor, Inukai Ki. Through Inukai, a member of a newly formed Japanese cabinet, Sun hoped to harness Japan to a pan-Asian–Soviet front against Western imperialism.

The next war, Sun predicted, would not be between the white and yellow races, nor between Europe and Asia, but between "oppressors" and "oppressed." England and France were the main oppressors, both in Europe and Asia. "The United States either joins them or remains neutral, but is never a friend of the oppressed." Russia, on the other hand, is the "center" of Europe's oppressed nations. India and China play the same role in Asia. Russia is their only friend. And what about Japan? In order to prepare for war, her first duty was to help complete the Chinese revolution. The Meiji Restoration, he said, had been the origin of the Chinese revolution. Both had the same goal — the revival of Asia. With Japan's help China could easily throw off imperialist shackles. The war-weakened Western powers were unable by themselves to carry out their imperialist design in East Asia. But they still had a firm economic base in China. Since the Chinese revolution threatened this base, the imperialists required Japanese cooperation. Japan's mistake was in not recognizing her common interest with China in opposing Western imperialism.

The Chinese revolution, he went on, is what the European powers fear the most. For it would be immediately followed by the independence of Annam, Burma, Nepal, Bhutan, India, Afghanistan, Arabia, Malaya and other nations, and bring about the defeat of European imperialism and economic aggression. This was inevitable, for "the Chinese revolution is actually the preliminary announcement of the death-sentence for European imperialism." Japan would be "committing suicide" if she continued to go along with the imperialists in opposing the Chinese revolution. Instead, just as "England had helped Spain 100 years ago, and America had recently helped Panama," Japan should help China.

Sun also urged a Russo-Japanese rapprochement. Soviet ideology, he claimed, was no different from the Great Harmony of Confucius, and since Japan was a nation that revered Confucius, she should be the first to recognize Russia. If Japan waited for the other powers to act, they would have the inside track and use Russia against Japan: "Russia has the strongest army in the world." England and America each had stronger navies than Japan, and what was the purpose, he asked, of their preparations in Honolulu and Singapore? He warned that Japan would face an unbeatable land-sea attack and share the fate of Germany.

Sun's letter, which was never answered, combined pan-

Asian sentiments with Leninist arguments. But he did not need the Russians to show him who his enemies were. When he wrote to Inukai the surplus customs issue was bringing him to the brink of a confrontation with the capitalist powers.

In September the Canton Foreign Ministry had sent a well-argued request for its share of customs receipts. This and subsequent memoranda were ignored by the foreign diplomats. Sun, who needed money badly to defend Canton, started talking tough in November. He threatened to seize the Canton customhouse and warned that he might listen to "Bolshevik and Indian agitators" who wanted help in driving Britain out of Asia — which was exactly what he was already proposing to Japan. The diplomatic body — three months after the initial request — replied that Peking alone could receive and allocate surplus revenue. Considering interference at Canton a threat to the entire customs service, if not to the treaty system itself, the powers decided to send a naval force to Canton. Gunboats began arriving on December 5 and Sun backtracked. He announced he would wait two weeks before taking action. When the ultimatum expired, sixteen warships confronted him. Six, the largest contingent, were American, and the rest from four other countries, including Japan. In the Anglo-French concession on Shameen Island marines put up barbed wire and sandbag defenses opposite the Canton shore. Sun's bluff was called. He did not lay a hand on the customhouse but fired a propaganda barrage at Western public opinion.

Their forefathers, he reminded Americans, had also resisted unjust taxation: he had only been planning another Boston Tea Party. America, he said, has inspired the Chinese revolution, but instead of a Lafayette had sent a hostile fleet. He also appealed to Ramsay MacDonald, leader of the British Labour Party. Brushing aside Sun's protests, the powers congratulated themselves on having put him in his place and preserved the integrity of the customs service. Toward the end of December they began reducing forces, though several months would pass before the last warship left.

Sun, who had been talking as if he knew what imperialism was all about, should not have been shocked. But he was, especially by the United States. How could a people whose history and way of life he admired so much contemplate fighting him on this issue? Britain's support of Yuan Shih-k'ai had produced a similar emotional crisis. Only now he was not isolated: he had Russia to fall back on.

Speaking at an American missionary college in December, Sun paid homage to American civilization: he wished for hundreds of such schools. (In October he had also praised the character-building contribution of the YMCA.) Then, before a smaller group of faculty and students he poured out all his bitterness in a frenzied indictment of Britain and America. He repeated what he had written to Inukai about the coming struggle between "oppressors" and "oppressed," and included American Negroes in the latter category. Hearing Sun threaten to send a Chinese fleet to San Francisco in ten years time, some of the Westerners feared for his sanity.

Among Chinese his prestige soared. In Canton, newspapers and mass meetings denounced gunboat diplomacy. Even some officials of the Peking government could not help admiring Sun's stand against foreign interference. More than at any previous time in his life, he spoke for China, and in particular for the students of the May Fourth Movement.

At a ceremony in December marking the twenty-fifth anniversary of the founding of Peking University, about a thousand people — mostly intellectuals — were asked whom they considered the greatest Chinese of the time. Sun took first place with 473 votes, more than twice the number given to the Communist leader, Ch'en Tu-hsiu. Yet when polled on their ideological preference, more voted for socialism than the Three Principles, which confirms the impression that Sun's appeal to intellectuals was largely personal and emotional. In addition, his rivals in Peking now simply inspired disgust. In October, Wu P'eifu's nominal superior, Ts'ao K'un, had bribed the parliament and bought the presidency of the republic in what was the rawest case of corruption during the notorious warlord period. This was the government that Britain and America backed during the customs dispute.

Russia, of course, capitalized on Western myopia. (At that same gathering at Peking University, 497 respondents picked Soviet Russia, and only 107, the United States, as "China's friend.") The Soviets, moreover, were able to cater to Chinese nationalism without giving up the imperialist legacy inherited from the tsars. Northern Manchuria and Mongolia, the objects of Russian national interests, were peripheral to the Chinese heartland. Infringement upon sovereignty in these areas was less offensive to nationalist feelings. But the omnipresent and, to the Chinese, most painful symbols of imperialism — like extraterritoriality — meant much less to Russia than to the maritime nations with their more extensive trade and investments in China proper. The irony of it all was that Western capitalists could probably have done more business if their governments had not insisted upon retaining obsolescent rights. The Russians, on the other hand, gladly gave back to China what China wanted most, and kept what they, the Russians, wanted to keep. The Soviets' all-purpose strategy would pay off handsomely in 1924. While implementing their alliance with Canton, they would sign a treaty, on their terms, with Peking (May 31) and a favorable agreement with Chang Tso-lin's Manchurian government (September 24).

Though he kept trying, Sun Yat-sen was much less successful in spreading his bets. Despite Borodin's influence, and despite the rankling customs issue, he made another play for American support, which he still considered the biggest prize, on January 6, 1924, when the U.S. minister to Peking, Jacob Gould Schurman, visited Canton. After going through the now familiar routine of attacking the capitalist powers — including the United States — Sun suddenly shifted course and told Schurman that the United States was the only nation China could trust. He again requested American mediation to end China's civil strife and, according to a New York *Times* correspondent, went much further. He is said to have suggested that America and other Western powers undertake joint intervention and tutelary rule in China for a period of five years!

Though unconfirmed, the story rings true. Sun had been broaching similar ideas since the Boxer crisis of 1900, and in February 1923 had invited British administrative assistance. Nor was it difficult for him to reconcile temporary foreign tutelage with nationalist goals. As recently as October he had told a student audience to take Japan as an example of a country which, despite extensive use of foreign advisers, had quickly regained complete sovereignty. One further point concerning Sun's reluctance to give up on the United States: he knew that despite the show of force at Canton, in terms of trade and investments America played a minor imperialist role in China. He wanted to believe that the United States was mistakenly following Britain's lead.

If Sun did propose Western tutelage at this time, the American minister did not see fit to report it to Washington. He did not even mention Sun's declaration of trust in the United States. What got back to the State Department was Sun's anti-imperialist harangue and Schurman's impression of a deranged mind. A week later, in an interview with a Chicago correspondent, Sun again cited the United States as the country that had the confidence of the Chinese people. And the week after that, on January 20, he presided over the First National Congress of the reorganized Kuomintang and, listening to Borodin, committed the party to a more radical stand, both on domestic and foreign issues, than it had ever taken before.

Boycotted by foreign diplomats, except Karakhan, Russia's representative in Peking who sent a congratulatory message, the Congress heard Sun sing the praises of the Soviet model. Its party organization was superior, and its principles were similar to his own. When the news of Lenin's death on January 22 reached Canton, the congress adjourned for three days of mourning and sent a telegram of condolence. Western diplomats began paying more attention to Russian influence in the Kuomintang. Previously they had dismissed Sun as a nonentity, but now he was becoming a threat.

Yet Sun resisted Borodin's efforts to tie the Kuomintang firmly to the Soviets' worldwide, anti-imperialist front. Disturbed by Sun's talk with Schurman, Borodin wanted an unequivocal statement on this score, but Sun refused to antagonize Britain and France any more than he had to. What finally emerged was strong enough: a denunciation of foreign imperialists, the warlords who "conspire" with them, and the Chinese capitalists who "share the profits." The first plank in the party's foreign policy platform called for the abolition of unequal treaties and an end to leased concessions, extraterritoriality, and foreign control of the maritime customs. Again, Sun rejected Borodin's plea for radical land redistribution. The party's manifesto, however, did attack monopolistic landownership, and promised land to the landless and support of workers. It also called for state management of natural monopolies and large-scale enterprises — banks, railways and shipping lines — regardless of whether natives or foreigners owned them. The keynote of the manifesto was its direct appeal to the masses. Peasants and workers were told that the nationalist revolution would liberate them because the Kuomintang opposed "imperialists, warlords and privileged classes."

Now draped with the revolutionary, anti-imperialist

banners Moscow preferred, the Kuomintang also adopted a Bolshevik type of organizational form. The new party constitution, drafted by Borodin, incorporated the principle of democratic centralism. All in all, then, Borodin could claim to have achieved a notable success during his first three months. And three years later, after Chiang Kai-shek had purged them, the Communists and their sympathizers could start claiming that in 1924 Sun Yatsen had infused his "old Three Principles" with the "Three Great Policies" — alignment with Soviet Russia, collaboration with the Communists, and support of workers and peasants. But the 1924 reorganization, while definitely a watershed in the party's and China's history, was not nearly so unqualified a Russian success as was assumed. Sun, who never used the term "Three Great Policies," had taken a new tactical course without changing his basic outlook and style.

Only with difficulty had Borodin gotten him to accept the radical party manifesto. The Russian alliance had not been Sun's first choice, and his attitude toward the capitalist powers still owed more to their rejection of him than to Borodin's tutorials. True, he now blamed foreign imperialists for all China's misfortunes, including the misery of peasants and workers. But he had previously put the blame on the Manchus, out of the same unrevolutionary reluctance to incite class conflict. Sun would not live to see the violent split between the Kuomintang and the Communists, and in the Kuomintang itself, that would come in 1927. But the coalition engendered friction at the very outset. Nor were signs of class conflict absent.

Less than two months before the Congress convened, some Kuomintang veterans, now forming the party's right wing, had criticized Borodin's handiwork and charged that the party's program and structure were designed to facilitate a Communist takeover. Sun assured them that Moscow backed him and not the Communists, and that he himself had gone over Borodin's draft constitution. It was probably at the urging of these apprehensive comrades that Sun changed Borodin's draft so that he would be guaranteed lifetime tenure as the party's leader. In its final version the constitution stated: "This party acknowledges Mr. Sun, creator of the Three Principles and Five-power constitution, as its *tsung-li*." In addition the leader enjoyed veto power over decisions taken by the highest elective organs. This major deviation from the Leninist model formalized the personal leadership Sun had been claiming since 1914.

Once the coalition went into effect, right-wing leaders had greater cause for concern. In the summer of 1924 the discovery of an internal Communist directive, which unfolded Lenin's original strategy of helping the Kuomintang for the purpose of controlling it, prompted a demand for the Communists' expulsion. Sun needed all the prestige and authority he could muster in order to maintain the coalition. Borodin undoubtedly reminded him that working with the Communists was part of the package deal he had made with Moscow. And rather than face overt competition, Sun still preferred having the Communists in his camp, at least as a temporary expedient. On the surface, in fact, the Communists seemed to be strengthening and not weakening the Kuomintang. They started recruiting the masses in the name of the senior party. By the end of 1924, when the Communist Party would have less than a thousand hand-picked members, the Kuomintang would have tens of thousands. With his usual self-assurance, Sun believed that Moscow would be convinced of the greater potential of his own party and would keep its protégés in line. But to many of his comrades, the Kuomintang's gains, spearheaded by the Communists, spelled danger.

Nationalism could not permanently cement conflicting social interests within Sun's party. While anti-imperialist and antiwarlord slogans drew wide support, the implied threats to wealth and property frightened the Kuomintang's important middle-class component. Meanwhile, the Communists and the Kuomintang's non-Communist left wing pursued the new orientation with enthusiasm. The Communists did not dominate the Kuomintang, but with Sun's endorsement they exerted more influence at all levels of the party hierarchy than their numbers warranted. Having both the training and motivation, they specialized in labor and peasant affairs. Students, awakened to their social responsibilities by the May Fourth Movement, helped forge links to the masses.

Benefiting from direct confrontation with imperialism, labor agitation produced fast results. But, though warlordism had intensified both natural and man-made causes of rural poverty, traditional loyalties and prejudices, and fear, hindered peasant mobilization. (As Sun admitted, many peasants still waited for a new "Son of Heaven" to establish a righteous dynasty.) Communists trained students, and students undertook the slow and often frustrating task of organizing peasant associations for resisting excessive rent and taxation. In 1924 these beginnings of what in a few years would lead to China's greatest mass movement since the Taiping Rebellion were most marked in Kwangtung, still the Kuomintang's only stronghold. Trying hard not to alarm their Kuomintang comrades, the Communists steered peasant and labor organizations toward relatively moderate economic objectives. Nevertheless, class violence surfaced as rural landlords and Cantonese merchants used armed force to defend the status quo. While Sun was alive, however, the struggle was just beginning and did not yet rip open the class fissures of the Kuomintang. All factions, moreover, claimed allegiance to Sun's principles. But his final attempt at clarification failed to resolve the conflicting claims.

The famous lectures on the Three Principles of the People (*San-min chu-i*) did not add up to a systematic guide for policy. What was intended as the definitive version of Sun's political philosophy, and what subsequently became the party bible and compulsory text for Chinese schoolchildren, was a series of hastily prepared speeches containing tedious digressions and homilies, and inconsistencies and errors of fact. Sun apparently never stopped reading Western literature, and made extensive but not always discriminating use of contemporary works. But a large part of the lectures simply repeated his earlier speeches and writings. Except for the substitution of anti-imperialism for anti-Manchuism, the Three Principles had not changed appreciably in twenty years.

Spread out over the period from January to August 1924, the lecture series was interrupted by Sun's illness and preoccupation with political and military crises. He did not complete the talks or carefully revise those he had given. His successors, therefore, did not do his memory service by treating them as a coherent treatise deserving reverent obedience. Sun was not a political philosopher and the lectures simply incorporated the shifting moods and incongruities that characterized his normal style.

The importance of the *San-min chu-i* lectures was not a matter of intellectual coherence or of particular policies, but of exhortative effect. Making the most of his seniority and knowledge of the outside world, and his rhetorical skill, Sun succeeded in driving home his central message: China was in mortal danger but there were no objective reasons why she could not quickly recover and serve as a beacon for all mankind.

Several thousand party officials and members, and students, packed the auditorium of the Canton Higher Normal School to hear Sun's talks. The first six, devoted to nationalism, were held weekly beginning on January 27, 1924. Designed to alarm young Chinese as well as awaken their pride, the talks were also highly assuring to Borodin. As Sun now explained it, the main role of nationalism was to save the Chinese race from being crushed by the imperialist powers. Still indignant over the surplus customs issue, he intensified the anti-Western tones sounded in recent talks with foreigners and in his letter to Inukai. He totally condemned the West for its past behavior and warned that the worst was yet to come. Besides cataloguing China's economic and territorial losses — and defining traditional Chinese territory in the widest possible sense — he raised the specter of the white peril: the Chinese were liable to share the fate of the American Indians! China's population, he warned, was in danger of being engulfed by the more rapidly expanding populations of Europe and America. "When I compare their increase with China's, I tremble. . . . If the United States, a hundred years hence, should try to subjugate China, there would be ten Americans to four Chinese and the Chinese would be absorbed by the Americans." (Sun arrived at this absurd conclusion by assuming that China's population, which he estimated at either 310 or 400 million, would remain static, while populations in the industrialized countries would increase at the same rate as they had in the nineteenth century.)

The world, he said, was divided into two camps, girding for a Darwinian struggle for survival. But Russia had split off from the white race and had joined the oppressed races of Asia. Though now helpless, China's cultural achievements and moral doctrines proved her innate superiority. "One generation has succeeded another and we are still the world's most cultured people." (Sun also claimed that the Chinese had advanced furthest on the evolutionary ladder because their bodies were less hairy than those of Europeans.) Europe excelled only in material civilization. "The Chinese are really the greatest lovers of peace in the world. 1 have constantly urged the people of the world to follow China's example; now the Slavic people of Russia are keeping pace with us and espousing the cause of peace with us, and their one hundred millions want to cooperate with us." All China had to do was restore her national spirit and adopt the latest achievements of Western technology; the Japanese had proved how fast Asia could catch up with the West. In resisting imperialism China should use the boycott weapon and adopt the Indian technique of noncooperation. But national rejuvenation should start with personal behavior. (Though he boasted of the cultural superiority of the Chinese as a collective, Sun condemned the morals and "bad habits" of individual Chinese, and justified social discrimination by Europeans.) And once rejuvenated, China should not forget her obligations to the smaller states of Asia, formerly protected by China's "noble policy" of "rescuing the weak and lifting up the fallen." Sun concluded: "When we become strong and look back upon our own sufferings . . . and see weaker and smaller peoples undergoing similar treatment, we will rise and smite that imperialism."

In the six lectures on democracy, given in March and April, Sun amplified his earlier formulations, which combined elitism with specific Western political devices. Unlike Europeans, the Chinese, he felt, enjoyed too much personal liberty and, as he had also remarked previously, were like "a sheet of sand." Nor did China, which had gotten rid of feudalism much earlier than the West, suffer as much from inequality. He was not impressed by the record of Western parliamentary democracy: "Democratic states have progressed less rapidly than autocratic states like Germany and Japan." Sovereignty, he claimed, belonged to all the people, but government should be run by specialists — "men of ability and skill." His solution was to guarantee power to the people by granting them the rights of suffrage, recall, initiative and referendum — as in Switzerland and some American cities — and to organize the government on the basis of the five-power constitution.

After a lapse of several months Sun resumed lecturing in August, but gave only four lectures on his third principle — people's livelihood, which he usually equated with socialism — before being distracted by military affairs. He had intended devoting seven or eight lectures to this topic. What he said, however, removed much of the sting from the series on nationalism, and angered Borodin. Sun not only argued that Marxism was inapplicable to China but, with the help of an obscure book by Maurice William, a New York dentist, and the example of Henry Ford, he undertook a thoroughgoing refutation of Marxist theory. In repudiating the concepts of surplus value and class struggle Sun relied heavily on Dr. William's work, *The Social Interpretation of History*. Sun apparently read it in 1924, three years after publication. Contrasting these lectures with those on nationalism delivered six months earlier, the dentist later claimed that he had converted Sun from communism. But Sun had not needed saving from an ideology he never believed in.

Marxism, however, was influencing Chinese students, and Sun wanted ammunition for mounting a counterattack. He thought he found it in William's thesis that social and not economic forces supplied the mainspring of history. This meshed with his own ideas on social progress, which emphasized reconciliation, not struggle, and voluntarism, not determinism. Though he now expressed greater concern over the problem of rural tenancy, and hoped that in the future "each tiller of the soil will possess his own field," he still saw the ideal solution in terms of Henry George's method. "Equalization of land rights" was still a taxation device to prevent future speculation in land, particularly in cities, and to give the government the option of buying back land from large owners. But as previously, Sun assured landowners that they could "set their hearts at rest." Neither they nor Chinese capitalists had reason to fear that the principle of people's livelihood involved drastic redistribution of wealth. "There are no great rich among us," he said, "only differences between the fairly poor and the ex-

tremely poor." He still advocated regulation of capital
and state ownership of large-scale industry; despite his
recent attacks on economic imperialism, he planned on
borrowing development capital from abroad. He also expected to use "foreign brains and experience to manage"
new industries. The goal, the same as that announced in
his *International Development of China*, was to "use existing foreign capital to build up a future communist
society in China." (Communism in this context owed
more to Confucius' vision of the Great Commonwealth,
or Great Harmony, than to Marxism–Leninism.)

Still, how does one explain the strident anticapitalist,
pro-Bolshevik tones of the lectures on nationalism? Besides wanting to start off on a good footing with the Russians, Sun at that time was still wrought up over the
customs crisis. Foreign warships were still prowling Canton waters. Understandably, his patience with the West
had been wearing thin and had frequently snapped during the previous year. By August he had cooled off.

That Sun was still his own man and owed little in the
way of ideology to Borodin can also be seen in his *Fundamentals of National Reconstruction for the National
Government of China*. Drawn up earlier, and presented
in April, soon after the lectures on nationalism, Sun considered this document a distillation of his ideas for China's future. On his deathbed a year later he would include it among the basic instructions bequeathed to his
followers. In twenty-five concise paragraphs he summarized all the familiar programs, including political
tutelage, land-value taxation, and Western-adapted pro-
cedures for popular democracy. Even nationalist objectives were stated in muted tones: self-determination for
minorities, resistance to foreign aggression, and revision
of the unequal treaties. Had he never heard of the Bolshevik revolution Sun could have written this summary
in exactly the same way. Nor had Borodin's presence

stopped Sun from seeking other patrons while waiting for the full flow of Russian cash and arms.

His talk with the U.S. minister in January had failed to budge the Americans. In February, when Canton was badly pinched for funds, and while he was blasting imperialism in his lectures, Sun tried to borrow US$15 million from Mitsui, the giant Japanese firm. He offered a Canton cement factory as security. Even extra inducements, such as provincial mining and coastal fishing rights, failed to move the Japanese (Sun also tried to bring Japan into a Soviet–East Asian front against the British). Germany, too, was still on Sun's list.

In the beginning of 1924 he had tried to push to a successful conclusion the negotiations he had started several years earlier. Told by the German consul in Canton that the Versailles Treaty strangled the German armament industry, Sun suggested that they might circumvent restrictions by operating abroad, for example, in China. (The Reichswehr was already operating abroad — in Soviet Russia. But in the 1930s Chiang Kai-shek and General von Seeckt, the architect of Russo-German military collaboration in the 1920s, would realize Sun's idea of Sino-German military cooperation. The Germans helped Chiang fight the Communists.) Sun told the consul that if Germany armed China's masses, the two countries could attack Anglo-French holdings in East Asia. He also offered valuable concessions for exploiting China's natural resources, but mostly in territory he did not control. All he actually held was a small part of the single province of Kwangtung. Convinced that Sun was trying to trick them into parting with money, the consul filed a negative report in June, and the negotiations fizzled out. Again, Sun was left with the Russians, who were more willing than ever to gamble on him.

Just how much money the Soviets poured into Canton is not known. At least one million dollars (US), it will be recalled, had been budgeted for the Kuomintang the previous year. Borodin started off with a small staff that included two officers. More followed, so that by 1925 the Soviet military mission would comprise about one thousand advisers and instructors. Though he welcomed Borodin's advice on how to reorganize the party, what Sun wanted most was military aid. The Russians eventually came through with a program the like of which would not be seen until World War II. June 16, 1924, was a landmark in Sun's career. He presided at ceremonies formally opening the Kuomintang's military academy at Whampoa Island, near Canton. Long dependent on mercenary armies, Sun looked to Whampoa to supply skilled and indoctrinated officers to form the nucleus of a party army. He wanted a replica of the Red Army; the Russians did their best to build it for the Kuomintang.

They supplied the money — probably more than one million dollars (US) — for establishing the academy, and sent instructors who introduced organizational and training methods that had a lasting effect upon Kuomintang armies. It was at Whampoa, for example, that the Russian system of attaching party representatives — political commissars — to all army units was first adopted. Long after he had parted company with the Communists, Chiang Kai-shek retained faith in this Russian innovation. In fact, he would later claim that, because American advisers persuaded him to abolish the system of political commissars in 1947, "we lost the mainland of China."

In May the first class of five hundred cadets was admitted to Whampoa's six-month course; a second class entered in August, and a third in January 1925. In October 1924 a Russian ship, coming from Odessa via the Indian Ocean, brought the first load of Soviet arms — thousands of rifles, and ammunition, machine guns and artillery. In October, too, a distinguished Soviet officer, General Vasily Blücher — using the pseudonym Galen — arrived to head the Soviet military mission. Since this tangible Russian aid started flowing only in late 1924, Sun did not live long enough to reap its full benefit. But Chiang Kai-shek did.

Chiang, now thirty-seven years old, was becoming the Kuomintang's indispensable military man. As one of the few professional soldiers of proven loyalty to Sun, he was a natural choice to head Whampoa. Borodin had no doubts about his suitability. Chiang had made the pilgrimage to Moscow and appropriate revolutionary noises after his return in December 1923. As commandant of Whampoa and mentor of the party's future officer corps, Chiang would build an impregnable position in the party army, which, thanks to Soviet help, would become China's strongest military force and his springboard to power. Trusting Chiang, the so-called "Red General," was Borodin's biggest mistake. He simply assumed that a Chinese who accepted their money and arms, adopted their techniques, and mouthed their slogans would necessarily be a faithful servant of Soviet policy. Significantly, Whampoa, a major beneficiary of the Soviet aid program, was least susceptible to Communist influence. Though the young Chou En-lai, recently back from France, was appointed deputy director of its political department, he and other Communists in the academy were overshadowed by Sun's people, headed by Chiang. And Sun himself, as has already been emphasized, had not surrendered his independence to the Russians. In fact, his last most important decisions clashed with Borodin's strategy and overrode Communist objections.

In terms of organization, size, popular appeal and military potential, the Kuomintang had made remarkable gains since January. Yet Sun would not wait for further growth and consolidation of mass political support. He had been impatient all his life. Now, exhausted by emotional strain and illness, he sensed that time was running out fast. Besides the Communist issue, which continued to cause friction within the party, he faced troubles on all sides. His extraprovincial mercenaries, never dependable, were less so while watching the Kuomintang start building its own military arm; Ch'en Chiung-ming still threatened Canton from eastern Kwangtung; and, despite Sun's conviction — repeated at a giant May Day rally — that only foreign and not Chinese capitalists oppressed Chinese workers, in August merchants challenged his government with a powerful private militia. Sun would also find class oppressors cooperating with national oppressors.

Led by a comprador of the Hong Kong and Shanghai Banking Corporation, Cantonese merchants organized a corps of fighters to defend them against rampaging soldiers as well as to resist higher taxes and the growing power of organized labor. The manager of the bank and a customs official — both Britishers, acting without the knowledge of their government — connived with the merchants in an attempt to smuggle in a large shipment of arms. Sun had the arms confiscated and stored in Whampoa academy. At the end of August the merchants retaliated by declaring a general strike. Infuriated, Sun threatened to bombard a business section of his own city, Canton! The foreign consular body protested, and the British warned that their navy would take action if the threat materialized. Sun of course had to back down, just as he had done during the customs crisis. This time, too, he had spoken impulsively and without serious intent to follow through. But the British threat to intervene in Chinese internal affairs produced an explosive verbal reaction. Sun's Russian advisers could not have been more pleased as he denounced British hypocrisy and the atrocities of British imperialism in India, Ireland, Singapore and Egypt. Intensifying its anti-imperialist propaganda, the Kuomintang won acclaim from nationalists throughout the country. The merchants ended their strike but the arms issue was not yet settled.

The incident confirmed Sun's fears that Canton was too close to Hong Kong, the stronghold of British imperialism, and gave him an additional reason to shift his attention elsewhere. The opportunity arose in early September, when the northern warlords resumed fighting. Still allied to Chang Tso-lin's anti–Wu P'ei-fu combination, Sun was asked to help. Despite objections from some of his own people as well as the Communists, and despite the lack of enthusiasm on the part of his mercenary army, Sun called for a northern expedition. On September 12 he left Canton to take charge at an advance base in northern Kwangtung. True to form, he wanted to give up Canton and the hard-earned gains of the past year and gamble for higher stakes in a game in which warlords held stronger hands. Chiang Kai-shek disagreed and was right. Sun did not accomplish anything with the northern expedition, but Canton held firm. In mid-October Chiang, leading a mixed force that included some Whampoa cadets in their baptismal battle and units sent back from the north, crushed the merchants' corps during two days of destructive street fighting. Looting and burning by his troops caused millions of dollars of damage in the business quarter and hardened merchant hostility to Sun and the Kuomintang.

Until now, Wu P'ei-fu's Chihli clique had the upper hand in the northern warlord contest. Then, on October 23, Wu's "adopted son," Feng Yü-hsiang, switched sides, seized Peking, and shifted the balance against Chihli. When the dust settled in early November, Wu was no longer China's "strong man" and Ts'ao K'un no longer president. Feng and Chang Tso-lin formed a new but unstable combination that included Tuan Ch'i-jui, who had only his seniority going for him. Sun Yat-sen, who had contributed little to the defeat of Wu, nevertheless ended up in what was for him a rare position: theoretically, he belonged to the winning side. Out of deference to the Kuomintang, now indisputably the nation's most popular political force and enjoying considerable support from students and intellectuals in the north, the ruling trio invited Sun to Peking to talk about the formation of a new government. But nothing had really changed: the warlords had no intention of giving him authority or allowing the public to express its will. Though the Communists and some of his close colleagues realized this, Sun, who had returned to Canton on October 30, accepted the invitation with alacrity.

Also undertaken independently was Sun's renewed courtship of Japan. In October he sent an emissary to Tokyo along with a Japanese reserve officer who was his military adviser. The special envoy spent over a month plugging a pan-Asian alliance. He saw high officials, including the prime minister. The Japanese were evasive: their idea of Sino-Japanese friendship did not square with the Kuomintang's position on the unequal treaties. Ultrarightists, including Sun's old cronies in the Black Dragon Society, welcomed his agent, but only because Chang Tso-lin's victory — to which the Japanese army had contributed — seemed to reassure them regarding Japanese interests in Manchuria and Mongolia.

On November 13 Sun left Canton with his young wife and a large entourage. (Borodin, whose attitude toward the northern trip is not clear, also left, but may have traveled separately.) Before leaving, Sun met his recently returned emissary, who apparently convinced him that a visit to Japan was worthwhile. Sun reached Shanghai on the seventeenth and stayed in his home in the French settlement for four days. An editorial in a British-owned paper urging that he not be allowed to live in the city prompted a sharp rebuke: Sun reminded foreigners that they were guests and had better behave accordingly. He called for the abolition of foreign settlements. Claiming that this was "probably the most defiant public message ever uttered by a Chinese," the American consul-general also favored Sun's expulsion from foreign concessions.

Westerners now blamed Sun for inciting antiforeignism, and saw the evil influence of Bolshevism behind his hostility. But the rise of Chinese nationalism was not the handiwork of a few agitators. Anti-imperialism was now trumps, and Sun its most eloquent tribune. Crowds welcomed him in Shanghai; others would do so in the next stages of his journey.

Sun sailed for Japan on the twenty-first, planning on only a short stay. Apparently he hoped that Inukai, who had not acknowledged his letter of the previous year, would meet him. His larger purpose was to win public support for Japanese help to rid China of the unequal treaties. Sun left just as news from the north hinted that the warlords would not wait for him. Tuan Ch'i-jui announced that he was to become "provisional chief executive" and organize a temporary government before convening a national assembly. Sun's formula, which he had publicized on November 10, was to convene representatives of various organizations and professions for a preliminary conference, and then have these bodies elect members to the national assembly. If public opinion would be exercised freely, he could expect to be elected president.

Sun arrived in Kobe on the twenty-fourth and stayed for almost a week. Inukai did not come but sent a representative with whom Sun had an inconsequential talk. The government ignored him and did not extend the invitation to Tokyo that he wanted. But the public, still feeling emotional ties to this veteran apostle of Sino-Japanese friendship, received him warmly. His anti-British statements went over big, less so his appeal to Japan to abolish unequal treaties with China — now probably more important for Japanese imperialism than for European. Sun promised that by forgoing short-range benefits Japan would earn "far greater privileges in the future" from economic and military cooperation. (But he did not offer any territory, such as Manchuria, which was paramount in Japanese considerations.)

The highlight of Sun's visit was his famous pan-Asian speech, delivered on the twenty-eighth before a large audience in a Kobe school. Appealing for racial solidarity against a predatory West, Sun called on Japan to fulfill the mission that history had assigned her. "Japan," he said, "is the first nation in Asia to completely master the military civilization of Europe." Her victory over Russia in 1905 gave all Asians the hope of eventual freedom. Japan should now return allegiance to her Oriental heritage, based upon "benevolence and justice," and lead a united front against the Occidentals. The issue, he said, would be decided by force, and Asians not only had the advantage of greater numbers, but could also count upon Russia, which "is attempting to separate from the White peoples of Europe. Why? Because she insists on the rule of Right and denounces the rule of Might." The audience responded with shouts of "Banzai" as Sun ended what was to be his last major speech: "Now the question remains whether Japan will be the hawk of the Western civilization of the rule of Might, or the tower of strength of the Orient. This is the choice which lies before the people of Japan."

Reverberating with the bitter anti-Western tones of the lectures on nationalism earlier in the year, the speech would be used by Sun's disciple and immediate successor, Wang Ching-wei, to justify collaboration with Japan in the 1940s. As Sun had hoped, Japanese military might did drive the white man out of Asia. But he had not anticipated an even cruder form of imperialism under the name of pan-Asianism.

Sun was in pain when he sailed for Tientsin on the thirtieth. After his arrival there, the condition grew worse and he was confined to bed. The foreigners insulted him to the end, as the French denied him entry to their concession. His political hopes also faded rapidly. Egged on by foreign diplomats, the ruling triumvirate went ahead without him. Tuan Ch'i-jui was told that his government would be recognized by the powers only if it acknowledged China's treaty obligations. He agreed, despite Sun's objections. Nor did the warlords accept Sun's plan for including labor, peasant and other occupational organizations in a preparatory conference.

Sun's spokesman, Eugene Chen, tried to convince Western diplomats that Sun's bark was worse than his bite. He told them that Sun was not a Bolshevik, which was certainly true, and that he did not demand immediate repudiation of treaty rights, which was probably also true. Sun is reported to have admitted in private that the demand was simply a propaganda ploy. But publicly he now held an unequivocally anti-Western position. This of course made him popular with student nationalists but unacceptable to the diplomats whom the warlords and, indeed, any Chinese government had to placate. But the question of Sun's participation in a new government soon became academic. German and Japanese doctors examined him and suspected cancer of the liver.

At the end of December he was taken to Peking for treatment. A crowd of one hundred thousand welcomed him at the station. Surgeons at the Peking Union Medical College Hospital — a project of the Rockefeller Foundation and a former missionary institution — operated on January 26 and confirmed the earlier diagnosis: cancer of the liver, and incurable. Sun was told a few days later, and on February 18 was moved to a private home. There he spent his remaining days. His young wife, his thirty-year-old son Sun Fo, and numerous friends and followers attended him. Among the highest party officials, only Wang Ching-wei was present. Hu Han-min and Chiang Kai-shek remained in Canton, where the situation was still critical. But Borodin visited the dying man.

On the twenty-fourth Sun was requested to leave final instructions for his followers. On March 11, with his wife guiding his hand, Sun signed a testament that had been drafted by Wang Ching-wei and approved by an emergency political council. The Leader's Will, which millions of Chinese still consider a sacred injunction, stated that he had devoted "forty years" to the national revolution, "the object of which is to raise China to a position of independence and equality." To attain that goal, 'the people must be aroused and . . . we must associate ourselves in a common struggle with the peoples of the world who treat us as equals." The revolution was not yet complete. His comrades should follow his writings — the Plans of National Reconstruction, the Three Principles of the People, and the Manifesto of the First Congress. "Above all," the testament ended, "my recent declaration in favor of holding a National Convention of the People of China and abolishing the unequal treaties should be carried into effect as soon as possible."

That same day Sun signed another document, which some members of the Kuomintang later claimed he had not studied thoroughly. This was a farewell message to the Soviet Union, which Eugene Chen, in consultation with Borodin, had drafted in English. Addressed to the Central Committee of the U.S.S.R., it was explicitly anti-imperialist and admiring of the "heritage of the immortal Lenin." The letter closed: "In bidding farewell to you, dear comrades, I wish to express the fervent hope that the day may soon dawn when the U.S.S.R. will greet, as a friend and ally, a strong and independent China, and the two allies may together advance to victory in the great struggle for the liberation of the oppressed peoples of the world."

Sun died the next day, March 12, 1925, at the age of fifty-eight. Various final words have been attributed to him. Borodin reported to Moscow that Sun kept repeating, "Only if the Russians continue to help . . ." Others claim that with his last breath he murmured the name of Chiang Kai-shek. He is also said to have reverted to the faith of his youth, and to have commanded a left-wing follower, "Don't make trouble for the Christians!" Remembered too are the words, "Peace, struggle, save China."

After a private, Christian funeral service — insisted

upon by his widow and son despite his party's strained relationship with the missionary community — the Kuomintang and its Russian allies presided over a large public ceremony, with Karakhan, the Russian ambassador, a conspicuous mourner. Memorial services were held throughout the country and abroad. Weeks passed before emotions subsided. Soon the mythmakers would go to work, all of them exaggerating Sun's achievements but pointing in different directions for "completing the revolution." Under Chiang Kai-shek the nationalist government would canonize Sun as the "father of the revolution," while the successor Communist government honors him as the "pioneer of the revolution." The dispute over Sun's legacy helped perpetuate his memory. The marble mausoleum near Nanking, to which his coffin was removed from Peking in 1929, is still a national shrine.

Epilogue: The Reluctant Revolutionary

IF SUN YAT-SEN had one consistent talent, it was for failure. Yet he remains a national hero because the more than quarter of a century in which he was active was the darkest period of modern Chinese history, and without his memory it would seem even darker. Recalling the humiliations inflicted by foreigners and the ineptness or venality of their own leaders, the Chinese can still point to one man who insisted that this was an unnatural state of affairs, and that by an act of will the nation could quickly assume her rightful place in the world. No one had more confidence in China's potential than Sun, nor tried harder and more selflessly to realize it. Many of his ideas were impractical, but the slogan with which he is identified — nationalism, democracy, socialism — is as good as any for representing the goals of modernization.

His style was puzzling because he was in fact a reluctant revolutionary. While dedicated to the aims of revolution, Sun preferred the least forceful measures for achieving them. This was a result of circumstances and temperament. The fear inspired by foreigners inhibited a direct confrontation with imperialism; only at the very end did Sun back into such a confrontation. He was even more reluctant to sanction class warfare, and would never admit that indigenous causes of injustice might require violent means of solution. For all his audacity, Sun lacked the ruthlessness that marks the true revolutionary. Put simply, he preferred negotiating to killing, and compromise to prolonged struggle. These were qualities that made him seem quixotic and strangely unrevolutionary, but more genuinely human.

But if Sun failed, so did the foreigners whose friendship he sought. The West, especially, failed to come to terms with Chinese nationalism and made an enemy of the most accommodating of nationalist leaders. Ironically, Western insults added luster to his image: Sun was never so popular as when he lost control of his emotions, shook his fist at Britain and America, and dramatized the frustration and defiance of a whole generation of Chinese nationalists.

No Chinese political figure has ever been as open to outside influences as he was. Japan supplied the precedent for Sun's dream of rapid modernization; America and England, the institutional models for modernization; and Russia, methods of organization, which he absorbed only incompletely. Enough has been said to show that he did not become a Soviet pawn. While it is unlikely that Sun would have purged the Communists and their working-class supporters as viciously as Chiang Kai-shek did in 1927, it is certain that he would not have continued to tolerate a coalition with a foreign-controlled party bent upon undermining his own.

Sun's capacity for national leadership was never really tested; this, of course, made it easier for him to become a legend after his death. Had he lived longer he would have found that the problems of social revolution and modernization could not be solved as easily as he had promised. The records of his successors, both on the left and the right, have revealed how difficult these problems are. Yet recent developments are substantiating some of his most firmly held beliefs. The Western world and Japan — especially Japan — are discovering the advantages of cooperating with a strong and modernizing China. And post-Mao China *is* trying to use foreign capitalism to build socialism.

The bungling conspirator has been forgotten but the symbolic Sun Yat-sen endures and may even serve China again in the future. If the demystification of Mao Tse-tung continues, the People's Republic may have greater need for glorifying Sun as the prophet of Chinese nationalism. He is now the only modern hero shared by the Mainland and Taiwan. Their common celebration of Sun's memory could prove a useful psychological bridge if they are ever to be reunited peacefully.

Bibliographical Notes

❧

The literature on Sun in all languages, but especially Chinese, is enormous. What follows is a selection, including the works that I have found most helpful. Lyon Sharman's *Sun Yat-sen: His Life and Its Meaning* (New York, 1934; reissued, Stanford, 1968) was for many years the best biography and is still valuable, especially for debunking the Kuomintang's cult of Sun Yat-sen. It has been superseded by C. Martin Wilbur's monumental work, *Sun Yat-sen: Frustrated Patriot* (New York, 1976), now the most thorough and objective study of Sun's career, particularly the final four years. *Kuo-fu nien-p'u tseng ting pen* [A chronological biography of the father of the country, enlarged and collated], compiled by Lo Chia-lun and Huang Chi-lu (2 vols.; Taipei, 1969), gives a day-to-day account of Sun's entire life. The entry on Sun Yat-sen in vol. 3 of Howard L. Boorman and Richard C. Howard, eds., *Biographical Dictionary of Republican China* (5 vols.; New York and London, 1967–79), is an authoritative and balanced summary of Sun's life and work. Harold Z. Schiffrin's *Sun Yat-sen and the Origins of the Chinese Revolution* (Berkeley and Los Angeles, 1968) covers Sun's career until 1905. The Kuomintang's reverence for Sun' teachings is expressed in John C. H. Wu's *Sun Yat-sen: The Man and His Ideas* (Taipei, 1971). Mao Tse-tung, Soong Ching-ling, et al., *Dr. Sun Yat-sen: Commemorative Articles and Speeches* (Peking, 1957), gives the Communist interpretation. S. L. Tikhvinsky's *Sun Yat-sen: On the Occasion of the Centenary of His Birth (1866–1966)* (n.p., 1966) is a recent Russian tribute. For Sun's speeches and writings I have relied mainly on *Kuo-fu ch'üan-chi* [Collected works of Sun Yat-sen] (6 vols.; rev. ed., Taipei, 1957). Documents in the Public Record Office, London (FO 17, FO 371, CO 129, CO 273), provide rich material on British policy. I have used the following works for historical background: John K. Fairbank, Edwin O. Reischauer, and Albert M. Craig, *East Asia: The Modern Transformation* (Boston, 1965); Marius B. Jansen, *Japan and China: From War to Peace, 1894–1972* (Chicago, 1975); and Li Chien-nung, *The Political History of China, 1840–1928*, trans. by Ssu-yu Teng and Jeremy Ingalls (Princeton, 1956).

CHAPTER ONE

For the Opium War, and its background and impact, see John K. Fairbank, *Trade and Diplomacy on the China Coast: The Opening of the Treaty Ports, 1842–1854* (2 vols.; Cambridge, Mass., 1953); Michael Greenberg, *British Trade and the Opening of China, 1800–42* (Cambridge, Eng., 1951; reprinted 1969); and Tsung-yu Sze, *China and the Most-Favored-Nation Clause* (New York and Chicago, 1925; reprinted Taipei, 1971). Edward J. M. Rhoads, in *China's Republican Revolution: The Case of Kwangtung, 1895–1913* (Cambridge, Mass., 1975), analyzes the political and social climate in Sun's home province; the statement about Kwangtung's traditionalism is from p. 7. On the compradors, see Hao Yen-p'ing's *The Comprador in Nineteenth Century China: Bridge between East and West* (Cambridge, Mass., 1970). G. William Skinner, in *Chinese Society in Thailand* (Ithaca, 1957), provides a sociological analysis of a *hua-ch'iao* community. Franz Michael, in *The Origin of Manchu Rule in China: Frontier and Bureaucracy as Interacting Forces in the Chinese Empire* (Baltimore, 1942), explains the Manchu conquest as an example of the cyclic pattern of Chinese history. Mark Elvin, in *The Pattern of the Chinese Past: A Social and Economic Interpretation* (Stanford, 1973), p. 312, is quoted on the "input-output relationships" of the nineteenth-century economy. Kung-chuan Hsiao, in *Rural China: Imperial Control in the Nineteenth Century* (Seattle, 1960), studies secret-society and other dissident activities. The observation on the situation in 1835 and the remarks of Karl Marx are from pp. 500 and 503. The Taiping Rebellion is treated thoroughly in Franz Michael, *The Taiping Rebellion* (vol. 1, history; Seattle, 1966). The official report on how a heretical sect developed into a rebel movement is from C. K. Yang, *Religion in Chinese Society* (Berkeley and Los Angeles, 1961), p. 220. On the post-Taiping recovery, see Mary C. Wright, *The Last Stand of Chinese Conservatism: The T'ung-Chih Restoration, 1862–1874* (Stanford, 1957). For the Taiping influence on Sun and anecdotes of Sun's early life, see Jen Yu-wen, "The Youth of Dr. Sun Yat-sen," in Jen Yu-wen and Lindsay Ride, *Sun Yat-sen: Two Commemorative Essays* (Hong Kong, 1970). Sun's proposal to Li Hung-chang is in *Ch'üan-chi* 5:1–12.

CHAPTER TWO

The remarks of the British vice-consul are in FO 17/1234, Bourne to O'Conor, in O'Conor's no. 141, April 16, 1895. The view attributed to Count Cassini is from G. F. Hudson, *The Far East in World Politics*

(Oxford, 1937), p. 98. Wu T'ing-fang is quoted by Rhoads, *China's Republican Revolution*, p. 39. For the Canton plot and the London kidnapping, see Schiffrin, *Sun Yat-sen*, chs. 4 and 5. Cantlie's role is described in James Cantlie and Sheridan C. Jones, *Sun Yat-sen and the Awakening of China* (New York, 1912). Sun's not-too-accurate version is in Sun Yat-sen, *Kidnapped in London* (Bristol, 1897; reprinted, London, 1969). Chün-tu Hsüeh, "Sun Yat-sen, Yang Ch'ü-yün, and the Early Revolutionary Movement in China," in Hsüeh, ed., *Revolutionary Leaders of Modern China* (New York, 1971), discusses the activities of the Hsing Chung Hui through 1900. On K'ang Yu-wei and the 1898 reform movement, see Jung-pang Lo, ed., *K'ang Yu-wei: A Biography and a Symposium* (Tucson, 1967). For the role of the Japanese I have relied mainly on Marius B. Jansen, *The Japanese and Sun Yat-sen* (Cambridge, Mass., 1954) and Fujii Shōzō, *Son Bun no Kenkyū* [A study of Sun Yat-sen] (Tokyo, 1966).

CHAPTER THREE

For the Boxer episode, I have used Victor Purcell, *The Boxer Uprising: A Background Study* (Cambridge, Eng., 1963), and Chester C. Tan, *The Boxer Catastrophe* (New York, 1955). Purcell quotes Kaiser Wilhelm on pp. 91–92 and 258, and the Russian war minister, Kuropatkin, on p. 258. Ho Kai's statement to the foreign powers is in Hsüeh, "Sun Yat-sen," pp. 117–118. The British consul-general in Hankow is quoted by Schiffrin, *Sun Yat-sen*, p. 223. Sir Robert Hart's account is in his *These from the Land of Sinim: Essays on the Chinese Question* (London, 1901). The quotations from the *Daily Mail* and *Times* on the purported Peking massacre are from Lo Hui-min, ed., *The Correspondence of G. E. Morrison* (vol. 1, 1895–1912; Cambridge, Eng., 1976), pp. 139–140. Schiffrin, *Sun Yat-sen*, chs. 7 and 8, and Rhoads, *China's Republican Revolution*, deal with Sun's activities, including the Waichow uprising, during this period.

CHAPTER FOUR

The post-Boxer reforms are described in Meribeth E. Cameron, *The Reform Movement in China, 1898–1912* (Palo Alto, 1931; reissued, New York, 1963); Rhoads, *China's Republican Revolution*, ch. 4; and Joseph W. Esherick, *Reform and Revolution in China: The 1911 Revolution in Hunan and Hubei* (Berkeley and Los Angeles, 1976), chs. 2–4. On Yen Fu, see Benjamin Schwartz, *In Search of Wealth and Power: Yen Fu and the West* (Cambridge, Mass., 1964). The Yen-Sun conversation is described on pp. 146–147. Sun and the French are the subject of J. Kim Mulholland, "The French Connection That Failed: France and Sun Yat-sen, 1900–1908," *Journal of Asian Studies* 32 (1972): 77–95. On the student nationalists and the formation of the Alliance, see Shelley Hsien Cheng, *The T'ung-Meng-Hui: Its Organization, Leadership and Finances, 1905–1912* (Ann Arbor, University Microfilms, 1962), chs. 2–3; this is the most informative work on the Alliance, and I have used it extensively. See also Chün-tu Hsüeh, *Huang Hsing and the Chinese Revolution* (Stanford,

1961), chs. 1–4; K. S. Liew, *Struggle for Democracy: Sung Chiao-jen and the 1911 Chinese Revolution* (Berkeley and Los Angeles, 1971), chs. 3–4; Schiffrin, *Sun Yat-sen*, chs. 9–11; Robert A. Scalapino, "Prelude to Marxism: The Chinese Student Movement in Japan, 1900–1910," in Albert Feuerwerker, Rhoads Murphey and Mary C. Wright, eds., *Approaches to Modern Chinese History* (Berkeley and Los Angeles, 1967); Mary Backus Rankin, *Early Chinese Revolutionaries: Radical Intellectuals in Shanghai and Chekiang, 1902–1911* (Cambridge, Mass., 1971), chs. 1–8; and Don C. Price, *Russia and the Roots of the Chinese Revolution, 1896–1911* (Cambridge, Mass., 1974), chs. 4–6. Martin Bernal, *Chinese Socialism to 1907* (Ithaca and London, 1976), ch. 3, discusses Sun and socialism. The report on Sun's visit to the secretariat of the Second International is on pp. 65–66. See also Harold Z. Schiffrin, "Sun Yat-sen's Early Land Policy: The Origin and Meaning of 'Equalization of Land Rights,'" *Journal of Asian Studies* 16 (1957):549–564. *The True Solution of the Chinese Question* is reprinted in the latest edition of Sun's collected works, *Kuo-fu ch'üan-chi* (Taipei, 1973), 5:111–121. Sun mentioned the impact of the Russo-Japanese War in his speech in Kobe on November 28, 1924. See *The Vital Problem of China* (Taipei, 1953), p. 164. His speech to the Tokyo students on August 13, 1905, is in *Ch'üan-chi* 3:5–6.

CHAPTER FIVE

The uneven social effects of modernization on the eve of the revolution are analyzed in Rhoads, *China's Republican Revolution;* Esherick, *Reform and Revolution;* and Ernest P. Young, *The Presidency of Yuan Shih-k'ai: Liberalism and Dictatorship in Early Republican China* (Ann Arbor, 1977), ch. 1. Jean Chesneaux, *The Chinese Labor Movement, 1919–1927,* trans. by H. M. Wright (Stanford, 1968), gives a detailed and vivid picture of early-twentieth-century labor conditions. Mary Clabaugh Wright, ed., *China in Revolution: The First Phase, 1900–1913* (New Haven and London, 1968), is the best single volume on the revolution; the editor's introduction is especially good for evoking the new nationalist mood. The Shanghai merchant's remarks on the boycott are in Margaret Field, "The Chinese Boycott of 1905," (Harvard) *Papers on China* 11 (1957):68. Sun's introduction to the first issue of *People's Report* is translated in *Fundamentals of National Reconstruction* (Taipei, 1953), pp. 194–198. The "Six Great Principles" are summarized and partly translated in W. T. de Bary, Wing-tsit Chan, and Burton Watson, comps., *Sources of the Chinese Tradition* (New York, 1960), pp. 762–765. The Program of the Revolution is partly translated in Ssu-yü Teng and John K. Fairbank, *China's Response to the West: A Documentary Survey, 1839–1923* (Cambridge, Mass., 1961), pp. 227–229. See also Ta-ling Lee, *Foundations of the Chinese Revolution, 1905–1912* (New York, 1970), pp. 43–46. Sun's speech of December 1906 is in *Ch'üan-chi* 3:8–16. On the debate between reformers and revolutionaries, see Michael Gasster, *Chinese Intellectuals and the Revolution of 1911: The Birth of Modern Chinese Radicalism* (Seattle and London, 1969); see also Bernal, *Chinese Socialism;* Robert A. Scalapino and Harold Z. Schiffrin, "Early Socialist

Currents in the Chinese Revolutionary Movement," *Journal of Asian Studies* 18 (1959):321–42; Harold Z. Schiffrin, "The 'Great Leap' Image in Early Chinese Nationalism," *African and Asian Studies* 3 (1967):101–119. For understanding Liang's position, I have benefited greatly from Hao Chang's *Liang Ch'i-ch'ao and Intellectual Transition in China, 1890–1907* (Cambridge, Mass., 1971). See also Joseph R. Levenson, *Liang Ch'i-ch'ao and the Mind of Modern China* (Cambridge, Mass., 1953). Esherick, *Reform and Revolution*, pp. 58–65, gives a graphic description of the Ping-Liu-Li uprising. Cheng, *The T'ung-Meng-Hui*, is my main source for the military and financial activities of the Alliance. On Sun and Russel, see Price, *Russia and the Chinese Revolution*, p. 160. Sun's letter to Russel is quoted in Harold Z. Schiffrin, "The Enigma of Sun Yat-sen," in M. C. Wright, ed., *China in Revolution*, p. 472. Hsüeh, *Huang Hsing*, and Liew, *Struggle for Democracy*, are essential for correcting official accounts that magnify Sun's role in the Alliance. For a view of an Alliance uprising from the government side, see Roger V. Des Forges, *Hsi-Liang and the Chinese National Revolution* (New Haven and London, 1973), pt. III. Fujii, *Son Bun*, pp. 52–54, and Rhoads, *China's Republican Revolution*, pp. 135–141, deal with the *Tatsu Maru* incident and the boycott. The main source for "Red Dragon" is the Charles Beach Boothe Papers, deposited with the Hoover Institution of Stanford University. See also Key Ray Chong, "The Abortive American-Chinese Project for Chinese Revolution, 1908–1911," *Pacific Historical Review* 41 (1972):54–70; Los Angeles *Times*, October 13, 1966. On Lea and Social Darwinism, see Richard Hofstadter, *Social Darwinism in American Thought* (rev. ed., Boston, 1955), pp. 190–91. Wilbur, *Sun Yat-sen*, p. 70, quotes from Sun's letter to Lea offering to sell Japanese military plans. A translated extract of Sun's Penang speech was filed with the British Foreign Office (FO 371/1086, no. 4028, February 3, 1911). See also Wang Gungwu, "A Letter to Kuala Pilah, 1908," *Malaya in History* 6 (1961): 22–26. On the railway and other issues that incited antidynastic sentiment, see Frederic Wakeman, Jr., *The Fall of Imperial China* (New York, 1975), ch. 11; Cameron, *The Reform Movement*, ch. 9; Esherick, *Reform and Revolution*, ch. 5. In ch. 6, Esherick has an exciting account of the Wuchang rising. The reprimand to the British consul at Chengtu is in FO 371/1080, no. 34247, August 31, 1911. Liew, *Struggle for Democracy*, p. 113, quotes the revolutionaries' cautious prognosis on the eve of the Wuchang rising. M. C. Wright, "Introduction," in *China in Revolution*, p. 56, quotes the British consul on the inhibitions of the revolutionaries. In this same volume, Schiffrin, "The Enigma of Sun Yat-sen," covers Sun's activities during the revolution, including his overture to Sir Edward Grey; and Ernest P. Young, "Yuan Shih-k'ai's Rise to the Presidency," gives an objective evaluation of Yuan's role. A British opinion of Sun as an "armchair politician" is cited by Anthony B. Chan, "Yuan Shih-k'ai's Barbarian Diplomacy," *Asian Profile* 5 (1977): 13, n. 22. Sun's conversation with Hu Han-min and other comrades in Hong Kong is quoted in *Kuo-fu nien-p'u*, 1:404–405. Morrison's warning is in Lo, ed., *Morrison Correspondence*, 1:685. In *Memoirs of a Chinese Revolutionary: A Programme of National Reconstruction for China* (1918; reprinted, New

York, 1970), pp. 223–224, Sun recalls his announcement upon arriving in Shanghai.

CHAPTER SIX

Sun's complaint against his comrades, made in 1914, is quoted by Hsüeh, *Huang Hsing*, pp. 165–166. For the Nanking and early republican periods I have used mainly the following: Liew, *Struggle for Democracy;* George T. Yu, *Party Politics in Republican China: The Kuomintang, 1912–1924* (Berkeley and Los Angeles, 1966); and Lo, ed., *Morrison Correspondence.* Yen Fu's opinion of Sun is in 1:656; and Yuan's opinion is in 1:740. Missionary views of Sun during this period are in Michael V. Metallo, "American Missionaries, Sun Yat-sen, and the Chinese Revolution," *Pacific Historical Review* 47 (1978):261–282. Metallo's *The United States and Sun Yat-sen, 1911–1925* (Ann Arbor, University Microfilms, 1974) has been my main source for the American position. Coolidge's early impression of Sun is mentioned on p. 255, n.73. Sun's ideas on the "mob" were reported by the British consul at Nanking in FO 371/1314, no. 9538, January 11, 1912. Sun's optimistic speeches in April–May 1912 are in *Ch'üan-chi* 3:21–41. For his speeches on socialism, see Schiffrin, "Early Land Policy," pp. 556–557. Sun's lectures to the Socialist Party in October are in *Ch'üan-chi* 6:12–31. The lectures are discussed in Edward Friedman, *Backward Toward Revolution: The Chinese Revolutionary Party* (Berkeley and Los Angeles, 1974), pp. 23–27. Sun's explanation of his railway plan, on July 22, 1912, is in *Ch'üan-chi* 3:49–50. Donald's reaction is in Lo, ed., *Morrison Correspondence*, 1:811–814. Sun's talk with Katsura is summarized in Albert A. Altman and Harold Z. Schiffrin, "Sun Yat-sen and the Japanese, 1914–1916," *Modern Asian Studies* 6 (1972):386–387. Sun's press interview in Shanghai is reported in Jansen, *The Japanese and Sun Yat-sen*, p. 162. In discussing Yuan, I have followed closely Young, *The Presidency of Yuan Shih-k'ai.* See also Jerome Ch'en, *Yuan Shih-k'ai* (2nd rev. ed., Stanford, 1972). For the reorganization loan, see K. C. Chan, "British Policy in the Reorganization Loan to China 1912–1913," *Modern Asian Studies* 5 (1971):355–372. B. L. Putnam Weale, *The Fight for the Republic in China* (New York, 1917), describes the financial straits of the republic. Metallo, "Missionaries," p. 279, quotes Rev. Arthur H. Smith on Sun's purported mental disturbance. Sun's letter to his American supporter, James Deitrick, on August 14, 1914, is in *Ch'üan-chi (1973)*, 5:392–396. Friedman, *The Chinese Revolutionary Party*, is an important source for the anti-Yuan effort. Sun's comments on Michels's book is from Schiffrin, "The Enigma of Sun Yat-sen," pp. 473–474. The British concern over the "China for Chinese" idea is expressed in FO 371/1318, no. 22592. Sun's letter to Ōkuma is in *The Vital Problem of China* (Taipei, 1953), pp. 135–142. Ian Nish, *Japanese Foreign Policy 1869–1942: Kasumigaseki to Miyakezaka* (London, 1977), p. 97, quotes Katō Kōmei (January 1913) on Japan's waiting for the "psychological moment." For the Twenty-one Demands and the diplomatic activities of the war period, I have used Madeleine Chi, *China Diplomacy, 1914–18* (Cambridge, Mass., 1970); the British minister's remark on an "Oriental fencing match" is on p. 41. Huang Hsing's warning to Sun is in Hsüeh, *Huang Hsing*, p. 177. H. H. Kung's letter (April 3, 1915), expressing concern over Sun's mental state, is quoted in Altman and Schiffrin, "Sun Yat-sen and the Japanese," pp. 388–389. In his speech of September 30, 1916, Sun claimed that the republican system had been restored (*Ch'üan-chi* 3:158). The quotations from *Vital Problem* are on pp. 57 and 21. In his speech of July 17, 1917, Sun attributed Chinese influence to the Russian revolution (*Ch'üan-chi*, 3:161). On the German connection see Josef Fass, "Sun Yat-sen and the World War I," *Archiv Orientalni* 35 (1967):111–120. The quotations from *Memoirs of a Chinese Revolutionary* are on pp. 5–6, 10, 112, 133. On "knowledge and action," see David S. Nivison, "The Problem of 'Knowledge' and 'Action' in Chinese Thought Since Wang Yang-ming," in Arthur F. Wright, ed., *Studies in Chinese Thought* (Chicago, 1953). Sun's earliest contacts with the Russians are in Wilbur, *Sun Yat-sen*, ch. 5. Part of Sun's telegram to Lenin is quoted in Tikhvinsky, *Sun Yat-sen*, p. 23. Sun's overture to the Japanese in December 1918 is described in Fujii, *Son Bun*, p. 141. I have used the 2nd edition of *The International Development of China* (reprinted, London, 1928). The quotations are from pp. 151, 155, 158, 161, 172. Metallo, *The United States and Sun Yat-sen*, p. 152, quotes Secretary of State Lansing on the "ugly stories" about Sun.

CHAPTER SEVEN

Wilbur, *Sun Yat-sen*, has been my chief guide for following Sun during these final years. The definitive work on the May Fourth Movement is Chow Tse-tsung, *The May Fourth Movement: Intellectual Revolution in Modern China* (Cambridge, Mass., 1960). See also Joseph T. Chen, *The May Fourth Movement in Shanghai: The Making of a Social Movement in Modern China* (Leiden, 1971), and Herman Mast III, "Tai Chi-t'ao, Sunism and Marxism During the May Fourth Movement in Shanghai," *Modern Asian Studies* 5 (1971):227–249, for Sun's attitude toward the movement. On Ch'en Tu-hsiu's conversion to Marxism, see Benjamin Schwartz, "Ch'en Tu-hsiu and the Acceptance of the Modern West," *Journal of the History of Ideas* 12 (1951):61–72. Mast, p. 248, n.47, cites Sun's doubts about "mob action." Sun's article in *Asahi* of June 22, 1919, is reprinted in *Vital Problem*, pp. 143–147. In his speech of October 8, 1919 (*Ch'üan-chi* 3:172) Sun criticized the Twenty-one Demands. His praise of the new culture movement is quoted by Chow, *May Fourth Movement*, p. 195. Yu, *Party Politics*, pp. 156–157, discusses Sun's concept of personal obedience. In his speech of November 4, 1920 (*Ch'üan-chi* 3:184) Sun bemoaned China's low international status. On the 1922 seamen's strike, see Ming Kou Chan, "Labor and Empire: The Chinese Labor Movement in the Canton Delta, 1895–1927" (Ph.D. diss., Stanford University, 1975), ch. 10. Pichon P. Y. Loh, *The Early Chiang Kai-shek: A Study of His Personality and Politics, 1887–1924* (New York and London, 1971), p. 139, n.111, cites Chiang's reservations about Sun's assumption of the presidency in Canton. Sun's talk to the congressmen of August 1920 is in *Ch'üan-chi* 3:174–179. His speech at the party meeting in Canton on June 6, 1921, is in *Ch'üan-chi* 3:187–200. Metallo, *The United States and Sun Yat-sen*, pp. 178–207, is the source for American views of Sun. The Canton consul-general is quoted on p. 184; John Dewey, on pp. 188–189; the New York *Times*, on p. 196. For an excellent characterization of the warlord style, see James E. Sheridan, *China in Disintegration: The Republican Era in Chinese History, 1912–1949* (New York, 1975), ch. 3. On Wu P'ei-fu and Sun's relations with him and other warlords, see Odoric Y. K. Wou, *Militarism in Modern China: The Career of Wu P'ei-fu, 1916–1939* (Canberra, 1978). Sun's views on future strategy, as disclosed on his trip to Hong Kong, are in *Ch'üan-chi* 4:518–519. Josef Fass, "Sun Yat-sen and Germany in 1921–24," *Archiv Orientalni* 36 (1968): 135–148, covers the later phase of the German connection. Barbara W. Tuchman, *The Zimmermann Telegram* (New York, 1958; Bantam Book ed., 1971), pp. 52–54, describes von Hintze's background. Among the numerous books on Soviet policies and activities in China, I have found most useful Allen S. Whiting, *Soviet Policies in China, 1917–1924* (New York, 1954; reissued, Stanford, 1968); Conrad Brandt, *Stalin's Failure in China, 1924–1927* (Cambridge, Mass., 1958); and C. Martin Wilbur and Julie Lien-ying How, eds., *Documents on Communism, Nationalism, and Soviet Advisers in China, 1918–1927: Papers Seized in the 1927 Peking Raid* (New York, 1956; reprinted 1972). I have used the translation of the 1920 edition of Lenin's *Imperialism* (New York, 1939). The quotations are from pp. 121, 126, 106, 13. See also George Lichtheim, *Imperialism* (New York, 1976), ch. 7. O. Edmund Clubb, *Twentieth Century China* (New York and London, 1964; paperback edition, 1965), p. 113, quotes Gregory Zinoviev on the formidable size of the Asian masses. Whiting, *Soviet Policies*, pp. 104–105, quotes Lenin's remarks in 1923, and on pp. 49–51 summarizes Lenin's theses at the 1920 Comintern Congress. Wilbur, *Sun Yat-sen*, p. 117, describes Sun's meeting with Voitinsky. Sun's remarks about the Russians' problems, from his speech of December 7, 1921, are in *Ch'üan-chi* 3:218. Sun's lecture to the soldiers of January 1922 is in *Ch'üan-chi* 6:109–143. Wilbur, *Sun Yat-sen*, pp. 121–123, describes Sun's talks with Dalin in April–June, 1922. The text of the manifesto of the Second Congress of the Chinese Communist Party is in Conrad Brandt, Benjamin Schwartz and John K. Fairbank, *A Documentary History of Chinese Communism* (Cambridge, Mass., 1959), pp. 54–63. See also Wilbur and How, eds., *Documents on Communism*, p. 83. Lenin's remarks on Sun's "naiveté" are from Whiting, *Soviet Policies*, p. 22. Shao Chuan Leng and Norman D. Palmer, *Sun Yat-sen and Communism* (New York, 1960), describe Sun's motives in allying with Moscow, and show how little he was influenced by Marxism. Wou, *Militarism in Modern China*, p. 188, quotes favorable comments on Wu P'ei-fu. Sun's letter to Chiang of November 21, 1922, is in *Ch'üan-chi* 5:495–496. Whiting, *Soviet Policies*, p. 95, quotes the boast of a Chinese delegate to the Fourth Comintern Congress in 1922. Sun's interview with the Japanese correspondent was published in the *Japan Advertiser*, November 25, 1922. For the Kuomintang reorganization, I have used Yu, *Party Politics*, and James Robert Shirley, "Political Conflict in the Kuomintang: The Career of Wang Ching-wei to 1932" (Ph.D. diss., University of California, Berkeley, 1962). Translations of the Kuomintang manifestos of 1923 and 1924 are in Li Chien-nung, *Political History*, pp. 446–458. Sun's speech at the 1923 Congress is in *Ch'üan-chi* 3:235–238. Whiting, *Soviet Policies*, pp. 240–241, quotes the resolution of the Comintern Executive Committee on January 12, 1923. Wilbur, *Sun Yat-sen*, pp. 137–138, gives the text of the Sun-Joffe communiqué, and on pp. 140–141, quotes Eugene Chen. Zinoviev's suspicions of pro-American sympathies in the Kuomintang, which were voiced at the First Congress of the Toilers of the Far East (January 1922), are quoted in Brandt, *Stalin's Failure*, p. 28. Leng and Palmer, *Sun Yatsen and Communism*, p. 65, quote the New York *Times* editorial of January 29, 1923, which ridiculed the Sun-Joffe statement. The poll taken by the *Weekly Review of the Far East*, and published on January 6, 1923, is referred to in Lucien W. Pye, *Warlord Politics: Conflict and Coalition in the Modernization of Republican China* (New York, 1971), p. 123. Wilbur, *Sun Yat-sen*, p. 140, cites Moscow's decision to subsidize Sun. The summary of Sun's speech at Hong Kong University is in Jen and Ride, *Sun Yat-sen*, pp. 21–22. This is reprinted from the *China Mail* of February 20, 1923. Sun's talk with the YMCA official Fletcher S. Brockman is quoted by Wilbur, *Sun Yat-sen*, pp. 144–146. Sun's interview with a Japanese reporter, Tsurumi Yosuke, in May 1923, is quoted by Fujii, *Son Bun*, pp. 176–177. Wilbur, *Sun Yat-sen*, p. 150, quotes Sun's warning to Maring. Sun's letter to his emissary in Germany, Teng Chia-yen, is in *Ch'üan-chi* 5:558. Karakhan's letter to Sun is in Wilbur, *Sun Yat-sen*, p. 158; Borodin's background is described on pp. 171–172. On Borodin, see also Louis Fischer, *Men and Politics* (New York, 1941), and *The Soviets in World Affairs* (abridged ed., New York, n.d.), ch. 22. Borodin's opinion of Sun is quoted in Wilbur, *Sun Yat-sen*, p. 363, n.62. Sun's speech of November 25, 1923, in which he praised the Russian model is in *Ch'üan-chi* 3:281–290. His strident nationalist speeches of October are in *Ch'üan-chi* 3:252–281. The letter to Inukai is in *Sun Chung-shan hsüan-chi* [Selected works of Sun Yat-sen] (2 vols., Peking, 1957), 2:467–471. Metallo, *The United States and Sun Yat-sen*, pp. 234–253; and Wilbur, pp. 183–186, discuss the customs dispute. Sun's speech at Canton Christian College (Lingnan) on December 21, 1923, is in *Ch'üan-chi* 3:308–318. References to the Peking University poll are Tatsuo Yamada, "Son Bun dokusaika ni okeru Ō Sei-ei no yakuwari [The role of Wang Ching-wei under the dictatorship of Sun Yat-sen]," *Hōgaku Kenkyū* 41 (1968):42, n.4; and M. I. Sladkovskii, *History of Economic Relations Between Russia and China* (trans. by M. Roublev; Jerusalem, 1966), p. 151, n.22. Hallet Abend, in *Tortured China* (New York, 1932), pp. 12–15, describes Sun's reputed offer to Schurman, but mistakenly dates it a year earlier. See Wilbur, *Sun Yat-sen*, pp. 188–189. The quotations from the 1924 Kuomintang declarations are from Li Chien-nung, *Political History*, pp. 453–456. On the "three great policies," see Leng and Palmer, *Sun Yat-sen and Communism*, p. 197, n.50. Shirley, "Political Conflict," p. 261, n.41, describes how Borodin's draft of the party constitution was changed. For the Chinese text of the article in the constitution dealing with the *tsung-li*, see Lo Chia-lun, comp., *Ko-ming wen-hsien* [Documents of the revolution] (61 vols., Taipei, 1953–) 8:130. Roy Hofheinz, Jr., *The Broken*

Wave: The Chinese Communist Peasant Movement, 1922–1928 (Cambridge, Mass., 1977), is indispensable for understanding the problems of rural political organization. Writings on the Three Principles are voluminous. I have usually followed the translation of Frank W. Price, *San Min Chu I: The Three Principles of the People* (Chungking, 1943). The quotations, in their order of appearance, are from pp. 22–23; 30; 96–97; 138; 146; 147; 191; 312; 314; 456; 431; 417–18; 443; and 442. For an excellent summary and critical evaluation of the lectures, see Victor Purcell, *Problems of Chinese Education* (London, 1936), ch. 5. The Fundamentals, in English and Chinese, are in *Fundamentals of National Reconstruction*, pp. 9–16. Sun's offer to Mitsui in February 1924 is described in Fujii, *Son Bun*, p. 187. On Whampoa, see Roderick L. MacFarquhar, "The Whampoa Military Academy," (Harvard) *Papers on China* 9 (1955):146–172. David D. Barrett, *Dixie Mission: The United States Army Observer Group in Yenan, 1944* (Berkeley, 1970), p. 87, quotes Chiang on the abolition of the commissar system. Sun's remarks about the foreign oppressors of Chinese workers, from his May 1, 1924, speech, are in *Ch'üan-chi* 3:420. Wilbur, *Sun Yat-sen*, pp. 249–252, describes the merchant corps crisis. On Chiang's role, see S. I. Hsiung, *The Life of Chiang Kai-shek* (London, 1948), pp. 200–205. Fujii, *Son Bun*, pp. 203–210, describes Sun's last visit to Japan. The consternation of the American consul-general in Shanghai is noted in Metallo, *The United States and Sun Yat-sen*, p. 262. Translations of the pan-Asian speech and other statements in Japan in November 1924 are in *The Vital Problem of China*. Sun's testament, and message to the Soviet Union, and the circumstances under which they were written, are in Wilbur, *Sun Yat-sen*, pp. 277–280. The various versions of Sun's last words are in Wilbur, *Sun Yat-sen*, p. 279; "Draft Chronology of President Chiang Kai-shek's Life: 1887–1975," *China Forum* 3 (1976):012; Sharman, *Sun Yat-sen*, p. 310; and *Kuo-fu nien-p'u* 2:1197.

Index